DURCHSTARTEN
ENGLISCH
GYMNASIUM

ÜBUNGSBUCH

9

Verfasserinnen: Sonja Häusler und Katrin Pürer

Diesem Buch ist ein Lösungsheft zu den Übungen beigelegt.

Entspricht der Rechtschreibreform 2006

Bibliografische Information der Deutschen Bibliothek:
Die Deutsche Bibliothek verzeichnet diese Publikation in der Deutschen Nationalbibliografie; detaillierte bibliografische Daten sind im Internet über http://dnb.ddb.de abrufbar.

VERITAS-VERLAG, Linz
www.durchstarten.at
Alle Rechte vorbehalten, insbesondere das Recht der Verbreitung (*auch durch Film, Fernsehen, Internet, fotomechanische Wiedergabe, Bild-, Ton- und Datenträger jeder Art*) oder der auszugsweise Nachdruck

Lektorat: Klaus Kopinitsch
Grafische Gestaltung: Gottfried Moritz
Illustrationen: Helmut »Dino« Breneis
Satz: Anton Froschauer
Herstellung: Julia Dresch

Gedruckt in Österreich auf umweltfreundlich hergestelltem Papier

5. Auflage 2016   ISBN 978-3-7058-8288-1

Gemeinsam besser lernen

INHALTSVERZEICHNIS

ALLGEMEINES 4
   Vorwort 4

LISTENING COMPREHENSION 6
   INTRODUCTION 6
   LC 1: Spotting lies: Listen, don't look 7
   LC 2: Meet Snuppy, the world's first cloned dog 8
   LC 3: Fifth-grade chorus becomes a YouTube hit 10
   LC 4: A Facebook tale: Founder unfriends pals on way up 12
   LC 5: Doctors urge research on cell phone-cancer issue 14
   LC 6: Study may tie food additives to hyperactivity 16
   LC 7: Homework: When dangerous animals attack 17
   LC 8: Teen T-shirt entrepreneur wins $ 10,000 19
   LC 9: Using music to mentor Venezuela's poorest youth 20
   LC 10: A real-life school of rock 22
   LC 11: New Hampshire split over high school cheating 24
   LC 12: Some spend thousands to save pets 26

READING COMPREHENSION 28
   INTRODUCTION 28
   RC 1: How to find out if food is still good to eat 29
   RC 2: Couch potato lifestyle versus smoking – which is worse? 32
   RC 3: Does e-mail distract? 34
   RC 4: For a shopper who has drunk alcohol, a mouse can be a dangerous thing 37
   RC 5: How the mobile phone is changing our lives 39
   RC 6: Yes, I'm an Internet addict 42
   RC 7: Why it's simply fun being rich 44
   RC 8: Animal experiments – one of the most controversial issues 47
   RC 9: What a dog's life 49
   RC 10: Teenage pregnancies: top or flop? 52
   RC 11: High School Prom – the best night of your life 55
   RC 12: Making your own music – creating your own style 58

WRITING 61
   Common linking words 61
   Informal (personal) letter 63
   Formal letter 65
   E-mail 69
   Story 71
   Article 74
   Reports 77
   Argumentative essay 79
   Opinion essay 82

VOCABULARY 84
   Housing and accommodation 84
   Music 88
   Animals 91
   Food 95
   Mobile phones 99
   Internet 102
   School 105

GRAMMAR 109
   Present tenses 109
   Present perfect tenses 115
   Past tenses 118
   Future tenses 125
   Modal verbs 127
   Irregular verbs 132

LANGUAGE IN USE 134
   What is it all about? 134
   False friends 134
   Exercises 136

TESTING SECTION 144
   TEST 1 144
   RC: The cool school 144
   Language in Use: Discovering British Breakfast 145
   Tenses 146
   LC: Seattle Program claims to treat Internet addiction 147

   TEST 2 148
   RC: My life in a flat-sharing community 148
   Language in Use: NRJ Music Awards 2010 149
   Tenses 150
   LC: Airline going to the dogs … and cats too 151

   TEST 3 152
   RC: Saving money – the "cheapest family" shows how 152
   Language in Use: Turning into a star: Christina Stürmer 153
   Tenses 154
   LC: The modern vampire: Bloodthirsty, but chivalrous 155

   TEST 4 156
   RC: A completely different sort of hero 156
   Language in Use: Child labour in India: Facing the truth 157
   Tenses 158
   LC: What's wrong with this snowflake? 159

   Titelverzeichnis Audio-CD 160

ALLGEMEINES

VORWORT

Willkommen in der 5. Klasse AHS, dem ersten Jahr in der Oberstufe! Nachdem du die Unterstufe gut hinter dich gebracht hast, fängt jetzt ein völlig neuer Abschnitt an. Ein Abschnitt, an dessen Ende die Matura steht. Natürlich ist der Weg dorthin noch ein langer, doch du wirst sehen, die Zeit vergeht schneller, als du denkst.

Schulisch wird sich mit dem Eintritt in die Oberstufe einiges ändern. Du wirst neue Schulkameraden bekommen haben, neue Fächer und wahrscheinlich auch neue Lehrerinnen und Lehrer. Die ersten mehrstündigen Schularbeiten warten auf dich und es gilt, sich neuen Herausforderungen zu stellen und diese zu bewältigen.

Doch was heißt das jetzt konkret für das Fach Englisch? Vielleicht hast du es schon bemerkt, aber in der Oberstufe wird das Hauptaugenmerk zusehends auf die Textproduktion gelegt. Während du in der Unterstufe mit der Grundgrammatik vertraut gemacht wurdest, geht es nun darum, eigene Texte zu produzieren, Briefe zu schreiben, deine eigene Meinung zu gängigen Themen auszudrücken und noch vieles mehr. Kurz, die erlernte Grammatik soll nun in der Textproduktion angewandt und der Weg zur Matura – langsam, aber doch – in Angriff genommen werden. DURCHSTARTEN für die 9. Schulstufe soll dich dabei bestmöglich unterstützen!

Was erwartet dich in diesem Übungsbuch?

Das Übungsbuch ist in fünf Abschnitte unterteilt, um möglichst viele der (in diesem Schuljahr und bei der Matura) geforderten Fertigkeiten abzudecken. Den Anfang machen die **Hörübungen** (*listening comprehensions*), die allesamt von *native speakers* mit verschiedenen Akzenten gesprochen wurden. Die Aufgabenstellungen hierzu **entsprechen bereits der standardisierten Reifeprüfung**. Das heißt, du kannst schon jetzt damit beginnen, dich auf die Matura und die vorgegebenen Testformate vorzubereiten. Gleichzeitig findest du aber auch noch „konventionelle" Übungen zu den *listenings*.

Gleiches gilt für den zweiten großen Abschnitt, die **Leseübungen** (*reading comprehensions*). Am Anfang speziell dieser beiden Abschnitte findest du eine Erklärung zu den Testformaten (wie kannst du dein Lese- bzw. Hörverständnis üben und überprüfen) sowie Tipps und Tricks, wie man am besten an die Sache herangeht. Lies dir diese kleinen Erläuterungen aufmerksam durch, denn damit vermeidest du Verwirrung bei den eigentlichen Übungen (welche ja doch im Vergleich zur Unterstufe sehr differenziert sind).

Der dritte Abschnitt widmet sich dem **Writing**. Hier findest du gängige Textformate, *linking words* und jeweils eine Sammlung wichtiger und hilfreicher Phrasen. Im Anschluss daran soll dir der **Vokabelteil** dabei helfen, deinen Wortschatz weiter auszubauen und zu verbessern. Zu einem gewissen Thema passend (**auf den Lehrplan der 9. Schulstufe abgestimmt**) findest du Vokabeln und Phrasen sowie ausreichend Übungen dazu.

Den vierten großen Teil bildet die **Grammatik**, die sich einerseits aus Grammatikübungen (samt Erklärungen) und andererseits dem *Language in Use*-Block (**wieder ein Teil der standardisierten Zentralmatura**) zusammensetzt. Grammatikalisch liegt der Schwerpunkt in diesem Buch auf den *English tenses*, ein Gebiet, bei dem auch gilt: Übung macht den Meister!

Als Anhang findest du vier **Probeschularbeiten**, welche du als zusätzliche Schularbeitsvorbereitung nützen kannst. Diese bestehen jeweils aus einer *reading comprehension*, einer *Language in Use*-Übung, einer Grammatikübung sowie einer *listening comprehension*. Mittels eines vorgegebenen Punktesystems kannst du dir deine Note errechnen und weißt somit ganz genau, bei welchen Teilbereichen du vielleicht noch ein bisschen üben musst.

Wie sollst du mit diesem Buch üben?

Grundsätzlich kannst du an jeder beliebigen Stelle dieses Buches zu üben beginnen. Es empfiehlt sich aber, die Art der Übungen abzuwechseln, damit nicht eine Fertigkeit mehr geschult wird als eine andere. Im Idealfall nimmst du also in einem bestimmten Zeitraum aus jedem Teilbereich eine gewisse Anzahl von Übungen durch. Auf diese Art und Weise kannst du sichergehen, dass dir keine Übungsart entgeht, und du hast viel Abwechslung beim Üben. Nachdem du eine Übung beendet hast, kannst du dich mittels des beigelegten **Lösungsheftes** selbst korrigieren. In diesem findest du die Lösungen zu sämtlichen Übungen, Muster- und Beispieltexte sowie die *Transcripts* zu den Hörübungen.

Allgemeines

Wie lernt man am besten?

Fördernde Aspekte:

- Achte darauf, dass du eine **positive Einstellung** hast. Alles, was man gerne macht, macht man auch gut. Wir wissen, dass das manchmal nicht so leicht ist, versuche es aber trotzdem!

- **Motiviere dich,** indem du deine **Ziele definierst**! Mach dir klar, warum du in der 5. Klasse AHS bist – höchstwahrscheinlich weil du die Matura machen möchtest. Auch wenn es immer wieder Tiefs und Rückschläge geben wird, sei dir bewusst, dass DU einzig und allein für dich und DEINE Zukunft lernst!

- **Belohne** und **entspanne** dich und achte stets auf eine gute Mischung von Arbeitszeit und Freizeit. Versuche fixe Lernzeiten festzulegen, damit du einen Lernrhythmus findest, nach dem du dich richten kannst. Wenn du alle deine Aufgaben erledigt hast (und damit sind nicht nur die Hausaufgaben gemeint), gönne dir Ruhe und einen guten Ausgleich.

- Schaffe dir eine **angenehme Lernumgebung**! Räume deinen Schreibtisch frei von unnötigen Dingen, damit du Platz hast, achte auf ausreichend Frischluft und Licht. Du sollst dich in deiner Lernumgebung wohlfühlen.

- Beachte deinen **individuellen Lerntyp**. Bist du der visuelle Lerntyp, der Lerninhalte sehen und schreiben muss, um sie zu behalten? Oder der auditive Lerntyp, der Lerninhalte hören und laut wiederholen muss? Oder bist du der kinästhetische Lerntyp, der Lerninhalte erfassen und begreifen will?

- Erstelle dir einen realistischen **Zeitplan** und halte dein **Zeitmanagement** unter Kontrolle. Um Lerninhalte dauerhaft zu behalten, musst du diese oft wiederholten. Dies funktioniert allerdings nur, wenn du genug Zeit hast. Fange also nicht erst drei Tage vor dem Test oder der Schularbeit zu lernen an, sondern tue dies zeitgerecht. Das spart dir (und wahrscheinlich auch deinen Eltern) viel Stress!

Hemmende Aspekte:

- Nur wenn du dich körperlich fit fühlst, kann dein Gehirn optimal arbeiten. Gründe, warum dies nicht der Fall ist, sind zum Beispiel zu wenig Schlaf, ein Mangel an Bewegung, ein zu voller Bauch, eine zu geringe Aufnahme von Flüssigkeit oder auch der Konsum von Suchtmitteln.

- Achte auch stets darauf, WAS du WANN lernst, denn wenn du dich zu lange mit demselben Stoff beschäftigst, kann das eher kontraproduktiv sein. Auch solltest du es vermeiden, ähnliche Stoffgebiete unmittelbar hintereinander zu lernen, denn das führt leicht zu Verwirrung.

Viel Erfolg, vor allem aber viel Spaß bei der Arbeit mit diesem Buch!
Sonja Häusler und *Katrin Pürer*

LISTENING COMPREHENSION

INTRODUCTION

Einer der Teilbereiche der *Four Skills Matura* ist das Abprüfen des Hörverständnisses, die sogenannte *listening comprehension* (LC). Die Art der Aufgabenstellungen orientiert sich an der *Cambridge First Certificate*-Prüfung. Innerhalb von **40 Minuten** musst du verschiedene Aufgabenformate zu vier unabhängigen Hörtexten lösen. Du darfst dabei kein Wörterbuch verwenden. Um positiv beurteilt zu werden, musst du **60 %** der **möglichen Punkte** erreichen. Folgende Aufgaben kommen auf dich zu:

	Mögliche Aufgabenstellungen
Multiple matching	Gezielt Informationen heraushören und den richtigen Fragen zuordnen
Multiple choice	Aus vier Antwortmöglichkeiten die passende finden
Note form	Fragen mit bis zu maximal vier Wörtern beantworten
Gapped text	Sätze mit maximal vier Wörtern vervollständigen

PRACTICING LISTENING COMPREHENSIONS

Die anschließenden Übungen sind so konzipiert, dass du anhand einer Fülle von unterschiedlichen Hörtexten dein Hörverständnis trainieren kannst. Weiters bieten sie dir die Möglichkeit, alle für die *Four Skills Matura* relevanten Aufgabenformate kennenzulernen und zu festigen. Hörübungen 1 bis 8 führen dich langsam an die diversen Formate heran, indem sie in kurzen Abschnitten verschiedene Übungsformate beinhalten. Um dir das **Finden der Hörtextstelle** zur jeweiligen Übung zu erleichtern, findest du die **Zeitangaben bei der jeweiligen Übung**. Somit kannst du jederzeit vor- und zurückspulen und dir die relevanten Stellen öfter anhören. Damit du dich inhaltlich auf die Hörtexte vorbereiten kannst, findest du am Anfang der Übung immer eine *introduction* und eine *pre-listening activity*. Lies dir die Einleitung gut durch und löse die erste Aufgabe. Sie dient der Aktivierung wichtiger Begriffe und Konzepte der Hörübung. Dann kannst du schon mit der Hörübung loslegen! Hörübungen 8 bis 12 entsprechen schon den Maturaformaten. In der folgenden Auflistung findest du noch ein paar hilfreiche Tipps:

	How to deal with listening comprehensions
Thinking Ahead	Lies dir die Überschrift der Hörübung sowie die Aufgabenstellung gut durch. Sammle und ordne so viel Information wie möglich, um dir eine Vorstellung des Inhalts der Hörübung machen zu können.
Understanding the Task	Lies dir die Aufgabenstellung gut durch, damit du genau weißt, was die Übung von dir verlangt.
Listening 1	Hör dir die Aufnahme aufmerksam an. Versuche so viele Fragen wie möglich zu beantworten. Bleibe ruhig, wenn du ein paar Antworten nicht gleich findest. Du hast noch eine zweite Chance.
Checking your Answers	Nach dem ersten Hören nimm dir Zeit, um deine Antworten durchzulesen und dir fehlende Antworten zu markieren.
Listening 2	Achte beim zweiten Hören auf Antworten, die dir noch fehlen.
Completing and Checking	Lies dir deine Lösungen nach dem zweiten Hören noch einmal genau durch und überprüfe, ob auch wirklich alle Fragen beantwortet sind.
Guessing the Answer	Löse immer alle Aufgaben, auch wenn du unsicher bist oder die Antwort gar nicht weißt. Eine geratene Antwort ist besser als gar keine Antwort!

Wie bereits oben erwähnt, dienen die folgenden Hörübungen vorrangig dem Trainieren und nicht dem Abprüfen deines Hörverständnisses. Deshalb darfst du selbstverständlich ein bisschen „schummeln" und dir Teile öfter anhören. Du kannst die CD nach jeder Übung kurz anhalten, um dich auf die nächste Aufgabe zu konzentrieren. Überprüfe die Richtigkeit deiner Lösungen aber erst, nachdem du alle Übungen abgeschlossen hast. Es ist auf alle Fälle empfehlenswert, wenn du nach dem Vergleichen die Hörübung noch einmal abspielst und das *Transcript* durchliest. So trainierst du dein Hörverständnis am besten.

Listening Comprehension

LC 1: SPOTTING LIES: LISTEN, DON'T LOOK

Introduction

You are going to hear a radio show on new methods in questioning and identifying criminals. Imagine a scene from CSI on TV when the police officer questions a suspect. What is the atmosphere like?

1. Pre-listening: Word matching

Match the words with the definitions by writing the numbers into the lines.

a. civilian — c) act of questioning a suspect

b. to fidget — d) another word for fear

c. interrogation — e) act of tricking and misleading someone

d. anxiety — b) to move nervously

e. deception — f) to force sb. to do sth.

f. to coerce — a) a person who is not a member of the police or army

g. inmate — g) an imprisoned person

2. True or false?

When a police officer makes a false decision about the suspect's guilt or innocence, it can

a. wreck the investigation. **F**
b. cost the police officer's job. **F**
c. let a guilty person go free. **T**
d. give a bad impression of the police. **F**
e. send an innocent person into a nightmare. **T**

3. Sentence completion Track 01 – 0:34

Fill in the missing words or phrases.

a. Liar's do not necessarily have troubles _making eye contact_.

b. The guilty don't fidget or _sweat_ more.

c. In fact, research shows that _innocent_ people can be just as nervous.

4. Multiple choice Track 01 – 0:48

Tick the correct answers.

a. From what we know from TV, we think that an interrogation starts with
  (A) a suspect making mistakes.
  B a suspect telling what happened.
  C a suspect defending himself.
  D a suspect tricking the police officers.

b. At the moment, the goal of interrogating suspects is to
  A find out as many details as possible.
  (B) trick them to confess to the crime.
  C gain their trust.
  D search for various possible answers.

c. A new approach of interrogating suspects is to
  A elicit information by confusing them.
  B look for signs of anxiety.
  C deceive the suspects with tricks.
  (D) see encounters as opportunities to get information.

Listening Comprehension

5. Who says what? Track 01 – 1:43

Find out who says which sentences. Write R for Sergeant Romeo de los Reyes
H for Dr. Cheryl Hiscock-Anisman
T for Dina Temple-Raston, the reporter

a. We've always learned that communication is 60 to 90 percent nonverbal.   R

b. Interviewers begin with a non-threatening question.   H

c. We asked them, "What was the first day like for you in prison?"   T

d. This question is very likely to get a truthful answer.   H

e. There's no need to lie about your first day in prison.   T

6. Answer the questions (key words). Track 01 – 2:45

a. What is the use of the first non-threatening question that a police officer asks the suspect?
_____

b. What is the next question about?
_____

c. What do the interviewers do with the two questions and answers?
_____

d. Which two criteria offer information on the truthfulness of a suspect's story?

   1. _____

   2. _____

e. What is the hard task that follows the second question?
_____

f. How much more detail do honest people tell compared to those who are lying?
_____

g. What's the San Diego Police Department's plan for the future of investigation?
_____

LC 2: MEET SNUPPY, THE WORLD'S FIRST CLONED DOG

Introduction

You may have heard of Dolly, the first cloned sheep, which became world-famous in the 1990s. The following report presents the story of Snuppy, the first cloned dog.

1. Pre-listening: Find the correct order of the words. The first letter is written in bold.

yemrob	early stage of a creature in its mother's womb
lcle	basic unit of a living organism
rsurgotea rmohet	woman/female animal carrying not her own baby to term (= *austragen*)
fofspingr	the babies, or descendants, of a person or animal
ngee	basic unit of heredity, a sequence of DNA

Listening Comprehension

2. Tick the correct sentences.

a. The first cloned dog's name is Snoopy. ☐
b. It is an Afghan hound. ☐
c. Five years ago, scientists cloned a sheep called Dolly. ☐
d. So far, scientists have also cloned mice, goats, pigs, rabbits, cats, rats, mules and horses. ☐
e. Dogs are very easy to be cloned. ☐
f. The team who has cloned the first dog has also cloned a human embryo. ☐

3. Find the correct order of the sentences. Track 02 – 0:45

Write numbers from 1 to 3 into the boxes provided in order to reconstruct the order of the sentences.

a. They inserted the DNA of a skin cell into a dog egg. ☐
b. The egg started dividing. ☐
c. The scientists took skin cells from an adult Afghan dog. ☐

4. Find out the numbers. Track 02 – 1:00

a. How many eggs did the scientists use for their experiment? _____
b. How many dogs served as surrogate mothers? _____
c. How many of those dogs got pregnant? _____
d. How many foetuses miscarried? _____
e. How many mothers carried to term? _____
f. After how many days did one puppy die of pneumonia? _____

5. Answer the questions (key words). Track 02 – 1:35

a. What does SNUPPY stand for?
_____

b. Why did the scientists choose a Golden Retriever as surrogate mother for an Afghan puppy?
_____

c. How can cloned animals help medical research and treatment? (2 aspects)
 1. _____
 2. _____

6. Sentence completion Track 02 – 3:00

Complete the sentences with the correct words or phrases (P = Palca, S = Simerly).

P Kraemer's team has abandoned a _____-_____ program to clone dogs, in part because _____ proved so difficult. Dogs have a unique physiology that makes their eggs hard to work with. But reproductive _____ Calvin Simerly of the University of Pittsburgh School of Medicine says even though the principles of cloning have been worked out, each species presents its own _____.

S You have to learn the uniqueness about that model and then design research around those unique properties. So it's just not _____ _____ _____ _____.

P Simerly knows that too well. He's spent years trying to _____ a monkey, so far without success.

Listening Comprehension

LC 3: FIFTH-GRADE CHORUS BECOMES A YOUTUBE HIT

Introduction

How often have you been to a performance of your school choir yet? Or – are you even a member of a chorus yourself? Then think of the biggest success the choir you know has had so far and the factors that made it so successful. Which ones, do you think, are the most important?

Hörübung: CD-Track 03

1. Pre-listening: Synonyms

Match the numbers with the letters by finding words having the same meaning.

1.	to adore	A	children with problems	1.	
2.	to captivate	B	to sulk, to complain	2.	
3.	to qualify for	C	idol	3.	
4.	to pout	D	to meet the criteria	4.	
5.	troubled kids	E	to fascinate	5.	
6.	role model	F	to love	6.	

2. True or false?

a. A school chorus of 11- and 12-year-olds has become famous on YouTube. ☐

b. Stars like Tori Amos love their music. ☐

c. The pupils attend Public School 22, Staten Island, New York. ☐

d. Gregg Breinberg is the headmaster of the school. ☐

e. They are practicing in Central Park for a performance. ☐

3. Multiple choice Track 03 – 0:45

a. Why is the current situation of the chorus "bitter-sweet"?

  A Because only half of the chorus wants to continue.
  B Because of budget cuts for Public School 22 in the next year.
  C Because the children will be leaving the school next year.
  D Because the choral director will be leaving the school next year.

b. What does the choral director say about the children's performance of "The World"?

  A That it's amazing.
  B That he wants more power and more feeling.
  C That he feels the beauty of the lyrics.
  D That he is questioning the performance.

c. What do we learn about the social background of the children?

  A That they only speak and understand English.
  B That they are all very helpful and like sharing with friends.
  C That they have very special qualifications.
  D That some are poor and have problems.

Listening Comprehension

4. List four statements Maimouna Faye makes about Mr. Breinberg (key words). Track 03 – 1:50

a. _____

b. _____

c. _____

d. _____

5. Who says what? Track 03 – 2:04

Read through the list of statements about Mr. Breinberg and find out who makes which statement. Write **B** for Mr. Breinberg himself and **A** for Mrs. Adler, the reporter.

a. He is non-traditional. ☐

b. He is intense. ☐

c. He is working hard for the chorus. ☐

d. He is trying to do the best for the chorus. ☐

e. He is a role-model. ☐

f. He is eccentric and emotional. ☐

g. He is passionate about music. ☐

h. He weeps at performances. ☐

i. He is a goofball. ☐

6. Tick the correct statements. Track 03 – 2:35

Being part of the chorus allows the children ...

a. to be and to express themselves. ☐

b. to be wacky and silly. ☐

c. to make mistakes. ☐

d. to go to places they have never been before. ☐

e. to let out their emotions and to show their feelings. ☐

f. to sing with Lady Gaga. ☐

g. to do things they couldn't do anywhere else. ☐

h. to meet many professional musicians. ☐

7. Sentence completion: Fill in the blanks with the missing words. Track 03 – 4:00

B There is something just magical about their _____. I think it's their selections. I think they

sing _____ people don't expect. I try to teach them that there's more to music than what they're

hearing necessarily on the _____ and to be open. And they bring their own thing to it. They have a

_____. And when you bring something unique to the table, yeah, that _____ people's interest.

A Despite success, Breinberg says the future of the chorus is _____. He's still waiting to hear if,

given education budget cuts in New York City, his chorus will be fully _____ this year.

Listening Comprehension

LC 4: A FACEBOOK TALE: FOUNDER UNFRIENDS PALS ON WAY UP

Introduction

It is a given fact that nowadays, the Internet offers diverse opportunities for communicating. You send e-mails, write blogs, chat with your friends and you are part of so called "social networks", like Facebook. The following interview tells the story of the inventor of this famous site. Have you ever heard his name?

Hörübung: CD-Track 04

1. **Pre-listening: Fill in the words from the box into the gaps.**
   The first letter may help you.

semisecret	froze	upset	prank	malicious	launch	investor
shed	dorm		salacious	geek		sophomore

   a. Young boys often play a **p**_____ on other people, like putting sugar into the salt shaker.

   b. As a **s**_____ you spend your second year at university.

   c. When you **l**_____ a business, you start a business.

   d. **S**_____ means that people have heard about it, but they don't know any hard facts.

   e. When my mum gets **u**_____ she yells at me and tells me to go to my room.

   f. An **i**_____ is someone who lends money for founding a new business.

   g. The bank **f**_____ my bank account! I can't get any money now.

   h. That's a **s**_____ story. It tells a lot of dirty details.

   i. A **g**_____ is someone who works a lot on his computer and focuses hard on studying.

   j. The **d**_____ room is the place where you sleep on the university campus.

   k. When you **s**_____ good friends, you dump them.

   l. A **m**_____ joke is a very nasty, wicked and mean joke played on someone.

2. **True or false?**

   a. Facebook has just signed up its 200 millionth user. ☐

   b. Mark Zuckerberg invented the program as a student at Stanford University. ☐

   c. The program was a project for a course at university. ☐

   d. The book "The Accidental Billionaires" by Ben Mezrich describes Zuckerberg's rise. ☐

   e. Zuckerberg dropped many friends who helped him on his way up. ☐

   f. Facebook started as a joke in summer 2003. ☐

   g. Zuckerberg was in his second year when he started a site called facemash. ☐

   h. Facemash was a hot-or-not site where you could vote for the hottest boys on campus. ☐

   i. Facemash was an immediate success. ☐

   j. However, Mark had to stop it because it nearly cost his place at university. ☐

   k. Mark started a site called The Facebook, where people could meet friends. ☐

   l. It was first only designed for students all over the US. ☐

Listening Comprehension

3. Answer the questions (key words). Track 04 – 1:35

a. Who is Eduardo?

_____

b. What are finals clubs?

_____

c. What kind of people become members of these clubs?

_____

d. According to Mezrich, what was Mark's initial idea behind creating The Facebook?

_____

4. Who did what? Track 04 – 2:00

Find out who did which things. Write **M** for Mark Zuckerberg, **E** for Eduardo Saverin or **S** for Sean Parker.

a. He had the idea of creating Facebook. ☐

b. He needed some money. ☐

c. He invested $ 1,000. ☐

d. He held 70 percent of the project. ☐

e. He went to California. ☐

f. He was the bad boy of Silicon Valley. ☐

g. He co-founded Napster. ☐

h. He stayed behind on the East Coast and then moved to New York. ☐

i. He tried to sell advertising for Facebook. ☐

j. He froze the bank accounts. ☐

5. Multiple choice Track 04 – 3:20

Tick the correct answers.

a. What did Peter Thiel do?
   - A He introduced Mark around Silicon Valley.
   - B He froze Eduardo out.
   - C He invested $ 500 000.
   - D He betrayed Mark.

b. Why did Mark, according to Mr. Mezrich, rid himself of all his friends who supported him?
   - A Because he was the one who had all the ideas.
   - B Because he focused so hard on his project that he did not care about other people.
   - C Because he felt like they had betrayed him.
   - D Because he didn't want to share the profit.

c. Which sentence describes Mark's attitude towards and contribution to Ben Mezrich's book best?
   - A He had time problems arranging interviews with Ben Mezrich.
   - B He was afraid of what Ben Mezrich would reveal in his book.
   - C He knew that Ben was one of the biggest proponents of Facebook.
   - D He wanted Ben to reveal the truth of the foundation of Facebook.

Listening Comprehension

6. Find the correct endings of the sentences. Track 04 – 4:55

a. Ben Mezrich sees himself as
   - A an opponent of Facebook.
   - B a danger to Facebook.
   - C the biggest supporter of Facebook.
   - D a neutral observer.

b. Ben Mezrich says that he writes
   - A funny fiction stories.
   - B true stories in an exciting, entertaining way.
   - C interesting movie scripts.
   - D frustrating critical reviews.

c. According to Ben, the basic information presented in the book is based on
   - A data received through interviews with Zuckerberg.
   - B invented scenes.
   - C Ben Mezrich's personal interpretation.
   - D sources like court documents and articles.

d. Elliot Schrage, Facebook's vice president of global communication, wrote that
   - A the book is just entertainment.
   - B the book is a lie.
   - C Mark Zuckerberg likes the book.
   - D the book gives a good account of reality.

LC 5: DOCTORS URGE RESEARCH ON CELL PHONE-CANCER ISSUE

Introduction

Hörübung: CD-Track 05

When you use your mobile phone, have you ever thought of the idea that your phone may cause harm to your health? The following radio show presents scientific facts on how dangerous cell phones really are.

1. Pre-listening: Find the correct order of the words.

tsohr-mter sexpoure	being exposed to/confronted with something for a short time
aincerse	to rise, to grow, to become more
paeln	a group of people discussing or studying a subject matter
tradiaino	the emission of waves produced by a mobile phone
gure	to force somebody to do something
reietraet	to repeat
evluntero	someone who offers to do something without being forced or paid
bga	to talk a lot

2. True or false?

a. The idea that cell phones may be linked to cancer is new. ☐
b. Most studies show that there is a connection between cell phones and cancer. ☐
c. There are numerous studies on short-term exposure to cell phones. ☐
d. Some studies found little increased risk within the first ten years of use. ☐
e. From 1987 to 2005, there was no upturn of brain cancer in the United States. ☐
f. Dr. Trichopoulos is a professor of cancer prevention at Oxford University. ☐
g. He says that there is no reason to be alarmed. ☐
h. Dr. Lawrence Challis is a British scientist. ☐
i. His panel did 25 studies on cell phone use and health effects. ☐
j. They found out that there is a big short-term health risk. ☐
k. British short-term studies show that the amount of radiation is not enough to cause harm. ☐
l. Challis says that there is certainty about long-term effects of cell phone use. ☐

Listening Comprehension

3. Answer the questions (key words). Track 05 – 1:40

a. How many cases of brain cancer did long-term studies identify?
_____

b. What other explanation than cell phone use is there for the cases of brain cancer?
_____

c. Name four options Dr. Challis offers people who want to minimize their risk of disease.

1. _____
2. _____
3. _____
4. _____

d. Which advice does the Stewart Committee give parents on cell phone use?
_____

4. Error correction: Find the mistake and correct the sentences. Track 05 – 2:40

a. During a hearing in the British parliament, the importance of restricting children's use of cell phones was repeated.
_____
_____

b. Ronald Herberman urged his family to limit cell phone use.
_____

c. Ronald Herberman can tell that cell phones are dangerous.
_____

5. Sentence completion: Fill in the blanks with the missing words. Track 05 – 3:13

A Herberman and his colleagues are asking _____ _____ in their efforts to get cell phone companies to release billing _____ for future studies. This is the strategy already under way in a _____-_____ European study. Lawrence Challis says it includes about 200,000 cell phone using _____ and loads of documentation from their cell phone bills. This way, researchers won't have to _____ _____ people's faulty memories about how much they _____ five years ago.

C Most of these volunteers will have used their phones for about five to ten years previously. So you've then got a much better calibration of how much they used.

A If lots of gabbing over time is predictive of any _____ risk of _____, in five years or so this study will show it. Allison Aubrey, NPR News.

LC 6: STUDY MAY TIE FOOD ADDITIVES TO HYPERACTIVITY

Introduction

When you drink a soft drink, do you think of where its bright colour comes from? A new study has found out that there may be an interesting connection between chemicals added to our food and behavioural problems of children.

1. Pre-listening: Word matching

Match the words with the definitions. Write the correct numbers on the lines provided.

1. preservative   _____ substance added to colour edible products
2. food dye   _____ incapacity of concentrating, heightened need to move
3. concoction   _____ chemical substance added to conserve food
4. additive   _____ mixture of substances
5. elimination   _____ any chemical substance added to (edible) products
6. hyperactivity   _____ complete removal

2. Multiple choice

a. What is Sunset Yellow?
   A The name of a study on the effects of food additives on children.
   B A substance that dyes food.
   C A substance that preserves food.
   D A British medical journal.

b. What is the name of the preservative mentioned?
   A Sunrise
   B Lancet
   C Hyperactivio
   D Sodium Benzoate

c. In the course of the study, what kind of concoction did the researches serve to some children?
   A four types of preservatives mixed with juice
   B forty types of food dye mixed with juice
   C four types of food dye mixed with juice
   D four types of food dye mixed with a soft drink

d. What did the other children get served?
   A the same kind of juice without additives
   B water
   C nothing
   D the same kind of juice added with various kinds of preservatives

3. Answer the questions (key words). Track 06 – 0:45

Which aspects of children's behaviour were teachers and parents supposed to observe?

a. _____

b. _____

c. _____

d. _____

Listening Comprehension

4. Tick the correct statements. Track 06 – 1:00

a. Gene Arnold is a psychiatrist. ☐

b. He says that children who drank the spiked juice were more inattentive and impulsive. ☐

c. Shashank Joshi is an adult's psychiatrist. ☐

d. He says that the effect of additives on children is very strong. ☐

e. Joshi fully agrees with the press claiming that all food additives increase hyperactivity. ☐

f. According to Joshi, all children are affected in the same way by food additives. ☐

g. Children without behavioural problems show a very low sensibility to food additives. ☐

h. Existing behavioural problems are enhanced by food additives. ☐

5. Error correction Track 06 – 2:27

Find the mistakes and correct the following sentences.

a. Children who stop consuming food additives will immediately get rid of hyperkinetic behaviour.

_____

b. Some studies testing small amounts of dyes and preservatives have found out that there are massive harmful effects.

_____

_____

c. The remaining question is what kinds of additives at which doses may be worth worrying about.

_____

LC 7: HOMEWORK: WHEN DANGEROUS ANIMALS ATTACK

Introduction

In the following radio programme people talk about their personal experience. This time, two listeners tell us about their adventures with wild animals. Have you ever been attacked by an animal? How did you feel? Which animals, do you think, are the most dangerous?

Hörübung: CD-Track 07

1. Pre-listening: Complete the sentences with a word from the box.

rear end	trough	encounter	chomp	wheelbarrow	entanglements

a. I have never had a dangerous _____ with a wild animal in my life.

b. If an animal bites you into your _____ it bites you into your butt.

c. When people talk about their _____ with animals, they mean adventures.

d. When an animal bites you, you feel a _____.

e. When a zookeeper feeds animals, he puts the food into a _____.

f. A _____ is a device that helps you to carry things.

Listening Comprehension

2. True or false?

a. Two weeks ago, listeners were asked to tell stories about their experiences with animals. ☐

b. The listeners present entanglements with their pets. ☐

c. Avner Ussan worked as a zookeeper at the Tel-Aviv Zoo. ☐

d. The incident happened while he was feeding the big monkeys. ☐

e. A monkey grabbed Avner by the hair and he got pinned to the bars. ☐

f. Someone from the audience tried to help him. ☐

g. Avner threw a tomato at the monkeys, but it hit the bar and splashed into a visitor's face. ☐

3. Sentence completion: Fill in the blanks with the missing words. Track 07 – 1:30

Susie: So I _____ _____ in the Dry Tortugas off of the tip of Florida and I was with a man and a teenage boy. And the man suddenly _____ down and _____ up a three-foot-long nurse shark. (music) And the shark was _____ and it wanted to attack the first thing that it could see. And unfortunately, I was the first thing that it _____. And so the shark is coming at me and I was whirling side-to-side trying to get away from it. And suddenly I feel this chomp and the nurse shark _____ very hard into my rear end. The shark bite _____ a perfectly round scar that lasted for many years.

4. Answer the questions (key words). Track 07 – 2:35

a. What kind of problems does the presenter of the show want to discuss the next time?
_____

b. Which examples of problems does the presenter give?

1. _____

2. _____

c. What is the number of the homework hotline?
_____

d. What does the presenter ask the listeners to do when they call the hotline?
_____

Listening Comprehension

LC 8: TEEN T-SHIRT ENTREPRENEUR WINS $ 10,000

Introduction

You are going to listen to an interview with a young man who started his own business. First you will have 45 seconds to study the task below, then listen to the recording. While listening, choose the correct answers (A, B, C or D) for questions 1–7. Put a ☒ in the correct box. The first one (0) has been done for you.

Hörübung: CD-Track 08

After the first listening, take 45 seconds to check your answers. Then listen again.

0 Kalief Rollins won a prize at the
- A 2007 National Youth Entrepreneurship Competition.
- B 2009 Californian Youth Entrepreneurship Contest.
- C 2009 National Youth Entrepreneurship Competition.
- D 2009 National Youth Business Competition.

Q1 The major target group of Kalief's business is
- A successful white businessmen.
- B people who want to support their urban leaders.
- C people who love funny prints.
- D black politicians.

Q2 The next best seller is probably going to be
- A the Obama shirt.
- B The PHREE KOUNTRY print.
- C the one showing Malcolm X.
- D the one reading "Caution: Educated Black Male".

Q3 10 000 $ is
- A the amount Kalief and his brother had to invest to start their business.
- B the money they won at the competition.
- C what Kalief and his brother need to buy a new machine for their business.
- D what Kalief and his brother earned in their first year running their business.

Q4 The two young entrepreneurs are planning to
- A buy a new heat press.
- B have a big party to celebrate their success.
- C invest all the money they won back into the company.
- D use most of the money they won to enhance their business.

Q5 Roscoe's Chicken and Waffles
- A is a famous place in L.A.
- B is the place where Kalief and his brother celebrated their success.
- C serves the best frappuccino in town.
- D is too expensive for Kalief and his brother.

Listening Comprehension

Q6 Phree Kountry Clothing
- A is located at the Rollins' family house.
- B has two staff members, Kalief and his brother.
- C is supported financially by Kalief's mum.
- D now needs an accountant.

Q7 Kalief's mum
- A hired a CFO for Kalief's company.
- B worked as CFO for a big company.
- C works in her son's business without claiming money.
- D works in accounting.

After the second listening, take 45 seconds to check your answers. Then, tick the correct boxes and compare them with the solutions.

	A	B	C	D
0	☐	☐	X	☐
Q1	☐	☐	☐	☐
Q2	☐	☐	☐	☐
Q3	☐	☐	☐	☐
Q4	☐	☐	☐	☐
Q5	☐	☐	☐	☐
Q6	☐	☐	☐	☐
Q7	☐	☐	☐	☐

LC 9: USING MUSIC TO MENTOR VENEZUELA'S POOREST YOUTH

Introduction

Do you play an instrument? If yes, what do you like about it? Perhaps you have been to a concert recently. Why, do you think, do people like making or listening to music? What is music's secret power? The following radio show illustrates how music can change the lives of young people.

1. Pre-listening: Find the correct order of the words.

dcoornuct	someone who directs an orchestra
otuedx	man's formal suit of clothes (BE: "black tie")
uabse	misuse or maltreatment of a person, doing harm to a person
umatityr	psychological state of displaying responsibility, acting "grown up"
radveysit	misery, problematic circumstances
edeirs	state of really wanting something

2. You are going to listen to a recording about unusual young musicians. Take 45 seconds to study the task below, then listen to the recording. While listening, complete the sentences (1–9) using a maximum of 4 words. Write your answers in the spaces provided on the next sheet. The fist one (0) has been done for you.

Listening Comprehension

After the first listening, take 45 seconds to check your answers. Then listen again.

0	El Sistema or The System is a Venezuelan programme that teaches _____ .
Q1	The stage _____ .
Q2	The biggest concert hall outside seats _____ .
Q3	Diana Tardes plays the contrabass because she wanted to _____ .
Q4	What makes El Sistema unique is that 70 percent of those in the programme _____ .
Q5	Ulysis Acano, a principal director, says that he is like _____ .
Q6	The maturity the kids display is largely due to the discipline _____ .
Q7	19-year-old Clarinet player Miguel Rodriguez says he _____ .
Q8	Most young people start out in El Sistema _____ .
Q9	Susan Simon says that the kids like to do it because they _____ .

Write your answers in the spaces provided below.

After the second listening, take 45 seconds to check your answers.

0	classical music to kids
Q1	
Q2	
Q3	
Q4	
Q5	
Q6	
Q7	
Q8	
Q9	

Now, check your answers with the solutions.

Listening Comprehension

LC 10: A REAL-LIFE SCHOOL OF ROCK

Introduction

You are going to listen to a very special school. First, you will have 45 seconds to study the task below, then you will hear the recording. While listening, answer the questions (1–10) using a maximum of 4 words. Write your answers in the spaces provided on the next sheet. The first one (0) has been done for you.

1. After the first listening, take 45 seconds to check your answers. Then listen again.

0	What kind of award did The Flaming Lips win?
Q1	What can the students attending the Academy of Contemporary Music earn?
Q2	Where is the school based?
Q3	What is Steven Drozd going to teach at the Academy?
Q4	What do you have to send in to apply for this school?
Q5	On which instruments should you be able to perform?
Q6	Why does the first semester focus on playing rock?
Q7	What else do students learn, apart from playing better?
Q8	What kind of musical training did Steven Drozd have?
Q9	Apart from good training, what do you need to become a rock star?
Q10	Why does Steven suggest playing "Stairway to Heaven"?

Write your answers in the spaces provided below.

After the second listening, take 45 seconds to check your answers.

0	a Grammy
Q1	
Q2	
Q3	
Q4	
Q5	

Q6	
Q7	
Q8	
Q9	
Q10	

Now, check your answers with the solutions.

Listening Comprehension

2. Complete the sentences with a word from the box.

| degree | accredited | train hard | scholarship | quit | drop out | aspiring | launch |

a. An _____ university programme is an officially tested and accepted program.

b. If you _____ high school early, you will not be able to go to college or university.

c. Pupils who earn a _____ do not have to pay for school or university.

d. An _____ musician is someone who really wants to become a musician.

e. People who want to earn a college _____ have to _____ _____.

f. Another word for not finishing high school is to _____ _____ early.

g. If you want to _____ a new school, you have to find qualified teachers.

3. Error correction

Find the mistake and correct the following sentences.

a. Members of The Flaming Lips are attending the new school of rock.

_____

b. Students are going to earn a university degree at the new school of rock.

_____

c. Steven Drozd is the band's manager.

_____

d. Scot Booker is going to teach a master class at the new academy.

_____

4. True or false?

a. There are three paths to get admission to the new rock academy. ☐

b. The first path is performance. ☐

c. The categories of performance are guitar, bass, keys and vocals. ☐

d. Interested students send in a demo tape. ☐

e. Scot Booker hopes some people have sent in tapes not playing themselves. ☐

f. The first course started last Monday. ☐

g. The second path to get into the college is production. ☐

h. Your band must have a very high level to enter the course. ☐

Listening Comprehension

LC 11: NEW HAMPSHIRE SPLIT OVER HIGH SCHOOL CHEATING

Introduction

You are going to listen to an interview about a cheating scandal at a school in New England. First, take 45 seconds to study the task below, then listen to the recording.
While listening, match the speakers (1–5) with the sentences they say (A–H). There are two extra sentences that you should not use. Write your answers in the boxes provided on the next sheet. The first one (0) has been done for you.

Hörübung: CD-Track 11

1. After the first listening, take 45 seconds to check your answers. Then listen again.

	Speaker
0	Tovia Smith
Q1	Mike Rotch
Q2	Ethan Forhour
Q3	Jim Kenyon
Q4	Dillon Gregory
Q5	Aine Donovan

	Sentences
A	I'm as guilty as anyone.
B	I think they know they did make a mistake.
C	There are some who don't see it as such a serious issue.
D	Some teachers don't classify that as cheating.
E	Many say the kids do deserve to be punished.
F	They're criminals.
G	Cheating is bad, but it's not like this is unheard of.
H	It' a different kind of orientation about morality.

Write your answers in the spaces provided below.

0	Q1	Q2	Q3	Q4	Q5
E					

After the second listening, take 45 seconds to check your answers. Then check with the solutions.

Listening Comprehension

2. Answer the questions (key words). Track 11 – 1:16

a. How could the students break into the college?

_____

b. What exactly did they steal to cheat?

_____

c. According to Mike Rotch, who should punish the students?

_____

d. What exactly were the students charged with?

_____

e. Which consequences does this charge carry?

_____

f. Which punishment could the students have faced if charged with burglary?

_____

g. What does Ethan Forhour consider as unfair?

_____

3. Multiple choice Track 11 – 2:12

Find the best answers to the questions.

a. How do other students react?
  - A They all consider having taken the students to the police unfair.
  - B They are extremely furious and want to attack the students.
  - C Some want the nine students to be punished, some think that the punishment is too hard.

b. What is extremely important for young people in Hanover?
  - A To drive an expensive car as status symbol.
  - B To attend a good college.
  - C To deal with the pressure put on them.

c. According to Jim Kenyon, why is treating the nine students like criminals not a solution?
  - A Because cheating is a mass phenomenon and needs broader actions to be fought against.
  - B Because he, as a father, only wants the best for his child.
  - C Because other students also profited from the stolen papers and should be punished too.

d. In how far is the cheating scandal also the teachers' fault?
  - A The pressure the teachers put on the pupils is simply too high.
  - B As teachers do not look after the exam papers carefully enough, they can be stolen too easily.
  - C They do not have common standards when it comes to classifying and punishing cheating.

e. According to Aine Donovan, what has changed in the students' attitude towards honesty?
  - A Being faced with a performance-oriented society, they have lost any set of morality.
  - B Due to the downloading business, they have lost the meaning of honesty.
  - C They have developed their own standards of right and wrong.

Listening Comprehension

LC 12: SOME SPEND THOUSANDS TO SAVE PETS

Introduction

Has your pet ever been sick? How did you feel when you saw your pet suffering? In the USA, there are people spending thousands of dollars on saving their pet's life. How far would you go for an animal? How much money would you be prepared to spend for the life of your cat, your dog or your horse?

Hörübung: CD-Track 12

1. Pre-listening: Find the correct order of the words.

rcance	disease that causes an abnormal growth of cells
erysurg	another word for operations
tiordiana	high energy, like X-rays or gamma rays, used to kill cancer cells
theapcheorym	therapy used to fight cancer
atmtreent	general term for fighting a disease
goran tsprantlan	medical treatment where an organ is transferred to a body

2. You are going to listen to a recording about how far people would go for their pets. First, take 45 seconds to study the task below, then listen to the recording. While listening, match the beginnings of the sentences (1–9) with sentence endings (A–L). There are two sentence endings that you should not use. Write your answers in the spaces provided on the next sheet. The first one (0) has been done for you.

After the first listening, take 45 seconds to check your answers. Then listen again.

0	Boswell has had cancer twice,
Q1	Vicki Constantine Croke wrote about Boswell the goose
Q2	Even though his owner is squeamish about it,
Q3	I met plenty of people
Q4	Very often, 10 or 15 years of relationship have elapsed,
Q5	I saw that yesterday,
Q6	One study that I do know of
Q7	But if your dog comes into the room,
Q8	So, increasingly, we are beginning to think
Q9	Three quarters of married respondents say

Listening Comprehension

A	he spent $20, 000.
B	never imagining the bill that would come down the line.
C	and he's had surgery, radiation, chemotherapy.
D	who can afford this kind of treatment.
E	that they greet the pet in coming in through the front door first before their spouse.
F	and the many medical options now open to pet owners.
G	that maybe a pet is not a replacement for a human.
H	showed that in a stressful situation, your blood pressure obviously goes up.
I	your blood pressure goes down.
J	and people feel very dedicated to saving their pets.
K	was done at the Animal Medical Center in New York.
L	the New York Times Sunday Magazine has a big cover story on animal pharm.

Write your answers into the spaces below.

0	Q1	Q2	Q3	Q4	Q5	Q6	Q7	Q8	Q9
C									

After the second listening, take 45 seconds to check your answers. Then check with the solutions.

READING COMPREHENSION

INTRODUCTION

Einer der Teilbereiche der *Four Skills Matura* ist das Abprüfen des Leseverständnisses, die sogenannte *reading comprehension* (RC). Innerhalb von 60 Minuten musst du verschiedene Aufgaben zu vier unabhängigen Texten lösen. Bei der RC dürfen keine Wörterbücher verwendet werden. Welche Aufgabenstellungen könnten (und werden) konkret nun auf dich zukommen?

- **Multiple matching**
  Gezielte Informationen im Text müssen gefunden und den richtigen Fragen zugeordnet werden. Hierbei ist es oft hilfreich, die Schlüsselwörter in den Fragen zu unterstreichen, um so die Suche nach den richtigen Antworten zu erleichtern. Mach dir bewusst, nach welcher Information gesucht wird.

- **Multiple choice**
  Verständnisfragen zum Textinhalt werden gestellt und vier Antwortmöglichkeiten (welche einander teilweise ziemlich ähnlich sind) gegeben. Du musst die richtige Antwortmöglichkeit finden, wobei es immer nur EINE richtige Antwort gibt.

- **Gapped text**
  Fehlende Wörter, Sätze oder Absätze müssen an den richtigen Stellen im Text eingefügt werden. Fülle zunächst jene Lücken, die für dich völlig klar sind, denn je vollständiger dein Lückentext wird, desto kleiner wird die Anzahl der noch offenen Lösungsmöglichkeiten.

- **Note taking**
  Auf eine gestellte Frage musst du – in nicht mehr als VIER WÖRTERN – die richtige Antwort geben. Hierbei kommt es nicht auf grammatikalische Richtigkeit (zB Verwendung der falschen Zeit) oder die richtige Rechtschreibung (*address* statt *adress*) an, sondern dass du zeigst, welche die wichtigen vier Wörter sind, um die Frage korrekt zu beantworten.

- **Matching headlines**
  Passende Überschriften müssen entsprechenden Textpassagen zugeteilt werden. Meist gibt es zwei Überschriften mehr, als du brauchst.

- **True/False tasks mit justification**
  Eine Frage/eine Aussage wird mit „wahr" oder „falsch" beantwortet (angekreuzt). Danach muss genau der Satz im Text gefunden werden, der deine *true/false* Annahme bestätigt. Von diesem Satz werden die ersten vier Wörter in das Feld *justification* eingetragen.

HOW TO DEAL WITH READING COMPREHENSIONS

Gehe die folgenden Punkte aufmerksam durch, sie sollen dir helfen, bei der Bearbeitung einer *reading comprehension* richtig vorzugehen. Wichtig ist auch, dass du dir ausreichend Zeit nimmst, damit sich keine „Schlampigkeitsfehler" einschleichen.

1. **Guess what the content could be about**
   Bevor du mit dem eigentlichen Lesen des Textes beginnst, solltest du dir einen Moment Zeit nehmen, um Vermutungen über den Inhalt des zu bearbeitenden Textes anzustellen. Lies dir in Ruhe die Überschrift (auch eventuelle Unterüberschriften) durch und schau, ob es vielleicht auch Bilder gibt (bei der Matura ist das in der Regel der Fall). All das hilft dir, eine ungefähre Idee davon zu bekommen, welches Thema dich in diesem Text erwarten wird.

2. **Understand the task**
   Lies dir nun die eigentliche Aufgabenstellung durch und versichere dich, dass du genau weißt, was zu tun ist. Die unterschiedlichen Aufgabenstellungen wurden oben ja bereits erörtert.

Reading Comprehension

3. Read the text

Widme dich nun dem Lesetext. Dies machst du am besten in zwei Etappen: Lies dir den Text zunächst überblicksmäßig durch, noch ohne irgendetwas auszufüllen oder einzusetzen. Halte dich auf keinen Fall mit einzelnen Wörtern auf, deren Bedeutung dir unklar ist. Oft wird durch das Weiterlesen der Kontext klar und es spielt keine Rolle, dass du ein Wort nicht verstehst. Nach diesem ersten Lesedurchgang wird dir klar sein, worum es in dem Text geht. Im zweiten Durchgang geht es an das genaue Lesen – jetzt konzentrierst du dich auf die Details und versuchst gedanklich Lücken zu füllen/Fragen zu beantworten/usw. (je nachdem, was gefragt ist).

4. Choose the correct answer/eliminate the wrong answer(s)

Mit dem genauen Textwissen im Hinterkopf machst du dich jetzt an die eigentliche Ausführung der Aufgabenstellung. Beginne immer mit den Lösungen, die dir eindeutig erscheinen, und suche im Text stets nach genauen Hinweisen und Schlüsselwörtern. Sind mehrere Antwortmöglichkeiten angeboten (zB bei Multiple-choice-Aufgaben), versuche die falschen Antworten logisch auszuschließen (warum kann es die eine oder andere Antwort NICHT sein?).

5. Last check

Überprüfe nun noch einmal, ob du alles ausgefüllt und bearbeitet hast. Ein kleiner Tipp zum Schluss: Statt eine Frage unbeantwortet oder eine Lücke ungefüllt zu lassen, weil du die richtige Lösung einfach nicht herausfinden kannst, ist es auf jeden Fall besser zu raten. Du kannst dadurch nur gewinnen, denn es macht keinen Unterschied, ob eine Antwort völlig fehlt oder diese falsch ist.

And now, it's your turn! Im nachfolgenden Teil findest du eine Reihe von *reading comprehensions*. Versuche dich bei deren Bearbeitung an die oben genannte *guideline* zu halten. Zu jedem Lesetext findest du unterschiedliche Übungstypen, und zwar nicht nur jene, die für die Matura relevant sind, sondern auch noch zusätzliches Übungsmaterial. *Have fun and enjoy!*

RC 1: HOW TO FIND OUT IF FOOD IS STILL GOOD TO EAT

Task 1 Pre-reading

Think about the following:

How is food stored at your home? Which food goes into the fridge and which does not?

Have you ever felt sick because you ate something wrong?

Task 2 Reading

Read the text to find out if you store food at your home correctly. Then do the tasks below.

Are you a slave to the sell-by date? Do you bin perfectly good food because it's a day over the limit on the label? If yes, then you might be perfectly happy to hear that yesterday, Britain's Government issued guidelines to reduce the 1,000 tons of food waste people in Great Britain throw out every day. One of the most important of these guidelines was stated by UK's environment Minister Hilary Benn, who said that we should ignore use-by dates and sniff food to see if it is OK to eat. But how can you tell if that wrinkly tomato, which has been lying around in your kitchen for more than one week, will make a tasty sauce or give you a nasty food poisoning? Nutritionist Angela Dowden reveals how to work out if it should go on your plate or in the bin.

MEAT: it's okay to eat chicken a day or two after the use-by date on the packing if you have bought it from the supermarket. The general rule is to check if it still smells fresh and make sure it's not slimy. A touch test can check for that slimy feeling – but make sure you wash your hands afterwards. The expert recommends not to use chicken if it has lost any of its pink colouring. Lamb, pork chops and beef are a lot easier but they, too, should be checked on their smell before consumation.

Reading Comprehension

DAIRY PRODUCTS AND EGGS: you can't go wrong with cheese, even if it's after the use-by date. Cut off any mouldy bits and it's okay to eat. However, you have to be a bit more careful with soft cheese. Wrap it in foil and keep it in the fridge to be on the save side. As far as yoghurt is concerned it should be fine as long as it isn't blown out with the lid puffed up. Usually it can also be eaten up to three days after the use-by date. Just make sure to always store it in the fridge. Milk is a simple one – if it smells bad or has any floating bits in it, then don't drink it. However, it is not really going to make you ill if you do, and you wouldn't physically be able to drink milk that has gone off for a long time as the smell would make you sick. Let's take a look at eggs. They should be fine a day or two after the use-by date. A great test is to put an egg with the pointy-end down into a glass of water. If it sinks it's OK, if it floats it's not and might contain salmonella.

FISH: it goes off quickly and should be eaten within two days of buying. Bin it if it is very fishy-smelling. With a whole fish, dull and sunken eyes are a bad sign and it should not be eaten. Shellfish, such as prawns and crab, can give you food poisoning if left too long. This is because of toxins that are not killed off by cooking. So always stick to use-by dates and cook according to the instructions.

VEGETABLES and SALAD: if tomatoes have gone really soft and wrinkly, then I wouldn't eat them in a salad, but you could fry them or use them in a soup. Potatoes are very durable. Even wilted ones are fine to eat, but cut out bruises and green shots. Mushrooms go off when they lose their firmness and go brown. You could fry them, but if there is any mould, bin them immediately. Lettuce is very delicate and can contain bacteria. Any browning is a tell-tale sign. An unopened pack of salad may be okay a day past its use-by date, but red discolouration on the cut surfaces indicates microbial growth.

But what can actually be done to keep food save? Here are useful tips that might help you to avoid nasty diseases: use any leftovers within two days, don't let flies get on food, wash your hands with hot and soapy water before handling food, always clean cooking surfaces before and after putting food on them, always store fresh or frozen food in the fridge or freezer, don't overstock the fridge as it may not cool food properly and finally don't put opened tins in the fridge but transfer their contents to an airtight container.

Task 3 Vocabulary work

Find synonyms (words with the same meaning) for the following words and phrases taken from the text. If you don't know what a word means, read the respective text-passage again and find out from the content.

to bin food _____

it was stated _____

to reveal _____

to buy _____

to keep it _____

ill _____

durable _____

immediately _____

unopened _____

disease _____

nasty _____

to ignore _____

to reduce _____

to sniff _____

to work out _____

to check _____

usually _____

quickly _____

firmness _____

lettuce _____

to indicate _____

tasty _____

guidelines _____

to touch _____

Reading Comprehension

Task 4 — Multiple choice

For the following questions, choose the answer (a, b, c or d) which you think fits best according to the text:

1. What is a sell-by date?
    a. It tells you when the product must arrive at the supermarket.
    b. It tells you the exact day when the product must be sold in the supermarket.
    c. It tells you important nutritional values.
    d. It tells you until which time, at the latest, the product must be sold in the supermarket.

2. What should you do if you see that a product is one day over the limit on the label?
    a. You can consume it without thinking about it because there is no risk anyway.
    b. You should sniff the food to check it.
    c. It should be thrown away immediately because it cannot be consumed any longer.
    d. The colour of the food should be checked to see if it is still okay.

3. How can you find out if chicken is still good for consumption?
    a. Ask in the supermarket where you bought it.
    b. Touch the meat to check how hard it is.
    c. Touch the packing to check if it is slimy.
    d. Check if the meat has lost the pink colour.

4. What is a use-by date?
    a. It tells you the date when you have to buy the product.
    b. It tells you the day on which you have to consume the product.
    c. It tells you the time span within which you have to consume the product.
    d. It tells you how long the product can be stored in the supermarket.

5. How do you handle cheese that is after its use-by date?
    a. You better throw it away.
    b. You eat half of it and then you throw it away.
    c. You check it by smelling it and then you eat it.
    d. You cut away bits and pieces that don't look good and then you eat it.

6. How can you find out if an egg is still good for consumption?
    a. You drop it into a glass of water.
    b. You pour a glass of water over it.
    c. You put it into a glass of water and see if it sinks.
    d. You put it into a glass of water and see if it floats.

7. What do dull eyes of a fish mean?
    a. That the fish is not fresh any longer and should not be consumed.
    b. That the fish is perfectly ready to be eaten.
    c. That the fish has swum in deep and dark rivers.
    d. Only very big fish have dull eyes and they don't mean anything special.

8. What should you take care of when handling lettuce?
    a. That you put it into the freezer immediately after having it bought.
    b. That brown and reddish parts are a sign of not consuming it any longer.
    c. That you should always wash it with boiling water.
    d. That it should be eaten five times a day.

Reading Comprehension

Task 5 — Jumbled expressions

Which adjective goes together with which noun? Write down the correct constructions:

ADJECTIVES	NOUNS
slimy, delicious, brownish	colour, fridge, disease
nasty, durable, dangerous	tomatoes, tin, guidelines
unopened, soft, dull	food, smell, toxins
bad, important, clean	potatoes, eyes, surface

_____   _____
_____   _____
_____   _____
_____   _____
_____   _____
_____   _____

RC 2: COUCH POTATO LIFESTYLE VERSUS SMOKING – WHICH IS WORSE?

Task 1 — Pre-reading

- What do you think is a couch potato lifestlye? Try to define a couch potato, what is he/she like? Come up with a few adjectives describing this person. Do you know a couch potato or are you a couch potato yourself?
- Why is being a couch potato so bad? Why is smoking so bad? What are the risks on both sides? And which do you personally think is worse: being a couch potato or smoking? Why?

Task 2 — Reading / Fill in the sentences

Read the text, ignoring the gaps with the numbers. Below the text you will find eight sentences (A–H). Six out of these eight sentences belong to the text. Try to find out which ones they are and match them with the correct gap (numbers 1–6).

Only a few weeks ago the AHL, the *Association for Healthy Lifestyle*, published a shocking survey in their monthly newsletter. The message was basically that a poor diet and a lack of exercise cause more serious illnesses than smoking. You don't believe that? Then just go on reading!

When being interviewed last month, Dr. Maylin Jankins of the Royal Washington Hospital, announced that in EU countries the couch potato lifestyle has overtaken smoking as the major cause of ill-health for the first time.

1 _____ According to Dr. Jankins, every second person does too little or even no exercise which is, and that goes without saying, a disaster.

By now it should be clear that doctors and governments must take the issue of diet and exercise more seriously. 2 _____ The main purpose is to inform people about how to live a healthy lifestlye and to encourage them to train at least two times a week. "Most people do know about healthy food and a healthy diet anyway, but they fail to make it part of their daily lives," says Dr. Jankins. Unfortunately, that is really the sad truth.

3 _____ Taking out ready-made microwave meals is much easier and takes you less time. That's at least what the majority thinks. Dave Miller, cook at the famous *Starship Restaurant*, says that simple and healthy meals are easy and fast to prepare. You just have to have some basic knowledge about cooking and that's it. And, of course, you must be willing to try out something new.

Reading Comprehension

Coming back to the couch potato lifestyle, we have to ask ourselves what is actually so bad about it.

4 _____ "About 25–35 per cent of these cancer cases could be prevented through better diet," Dr. Jankins says. That is undeniably an enormous number. Additionally, obesity is another problem created by the couch potato lifestyle. Obesity in adults is up to 30–40 per cent and is also escalating among children, increasing their future risk of suffering from diabetes and of cardiovascular diseases. These days parents even start to outlive their obese children, and this is something that's definitely abnormal.

So does that mean that people can go on smoking without bad conscience as long as they live a healthy lifestlye and exercise regularly? Of course not!

5 "_____ I am saying that diet is as important and we have to get that through and into people's minds because it is not understood at the moment," Dr. Jenkins explains. The above-mentioned study showed that smoking causes nine per cent of all chronic diseases in the EU while physical inactivity and poor diet are responsible for 9.7 per cent.

6 _____ Summarizing it can be said that the key to a long and happy life is most probably the combination of a healthy diet, an active lifestyle, no addictions (like smoking or drinking alcohol) and a fulfilled life, meaning having a nice job, good friends and the like. Well … sometimes it can be so easy.

One problematic aspect is that the main conditions caused by bad diet and no exercise are heart diseases, followed by cancer.	A
However, it should also be mentioned that drinking too much alcohol can lead to illness, too.	B
It seems as if these figures speak for themselves and as if it is time for the people to become active and to do something.	C
Consequently, the start of a campaign is being planned at the moment.	D
I am not saying that smoking plays no part in ill-health. Surely it does!	E
This is of course shocking and the number of people living a couch potato lifestyle must not be underestimated any longer.	F
Eating vast amounts of fast food can lead to high colesterol and therefor to problems with your liver.	G
New figures show that most people are simply too lazy to go shopping for fresh food and to cook a proper meal for themselves and their family.	H

Task 3 Comprehension

Answer the questions in full English sentences:

- What are the dangers of a poor diet and too little exercise?

_____

- Why did the government start a campaign? What was the purpose of it?

_____

- What can be done to live a healthy life?

_____

- What is the problem with obese children these days?

Reading Comprehension

Task 4 Gapped text

Read the summary of the text above and complete it with the words given. Note that there are more words than you need!

> lead to – in contrast – keen on – additionally – reminds – survey – hardly – harm – involves – discussion – nearly – lazy

According to a new _____, a couch potato lifestyle is worse than smoking.

Defining such a couch potato lifestyle is quite easy: these are people who do not do any (or _____ any) exercise and who are rather _____. They are simply not very _____ training and doing sports. They prefer sitting at home, in best case in front of the TV, the computer or a Playstation, not doing anything. At least nothing that _____ physical activity.

_____, these people also have quite bad eating habits. They mostly live on junk food and ready-made food that is unhealthy and that damages your health if you eat too much of it. This is because this type of food contains too much sugar, salt and fat – things our body does not need a lot of. But of course smoking is also bad for our health as it can _____ lung cancer, for example. But compared with a couch potato lifestyle, smoking – paradoxically – does not _____ the human body that much. Incredible, isn't it?

RC 3: DOES E-MAIL DISTRACT?

Task 1 Pre-reading

Think about the following aspects:
- How often do you check your e-mails? Just once a day or several times?
- How many e-mails do you write? Do you only write mails if you need some information or do you also write them to communicate and chat with your friends?
- Are spam mails a problem for you? Do you know what they are?

Task 2 Reading

Read the following interview between Joseph Steward, journalist at the Daily Mirror, and Nigel Newman who is a clinical psychologist specialized on attention deficit disorders and time management.

Daily Mirror: Mr. Newman, you work as a clinical psychologist who focuses on time and stress management. Am I right in guessing that this is a widespread problem nowadays?

Newman: You're absolutely right. One aspect why people suffer from stress more and more often is the fact that they spend a very long time in front of their PCs. What they do most of this time is easy to explain: surfing the Internet and, primarily, checking and writing e-mails. Especially at work this can turn into a problem.

Daily Mirror: Can you explain that in more detail?

Newman: Sure. Most of the people who work on a computer permanently check their e-mails. They do so because they are either waiting for important business mails or they simply write mails related to private affairs. The problem is that they honestly believe that checking mails does not distract them. But in fact that is complete nonsense.

Daily Mirror: Why?

Newman: Because it is proven that the human mind cannot work and concentrate on two things simultaneously. That means if I check my mails while I am working, I interrupt one action (in that case the work) to concentrate and focus on another action (reading the mail). To summarize it again, we are constantly interrupting one task to attend to another task. And in the long run this leads to cognitive fatigue.

Daily Mirror: That doesn't sound good. Are there any positive aspects related to e-mail checking as well?

Newman: Well, actually there are. Some psychologists claim that e-mail interruptions can enhance creativity and therefore also productivity.

Daily Mirror: What does that mean?

Newman: If we receive work-related e-mails it might be the case that certain parts of our brain (the creative centre to be more accurate) are stimulated and consequently we are better at problem solving. But here again a problem comes up because who tells us how many mails stimulate our creativity and at what point we are simply overloaded?

Daily Mirror: That's absolutely true. So, should people try to limit the number of times they check their e-mails during the day or is there any other solution to this dilemma?

Newman: Ideally yes, it would be perfect to limt this number. But let's be honest, that's hardly possible because especially in your job nobody has the right to tell you when to check your e-mails. Besides, in urgent cases that might put people under even more stress and pressure and consequently that would only halve solve the problem.

Daily Mirror: I see. But what can people actually do when their in-box is overflowing?

Newman: Well, there are several possibilities. At first you best scan the messages to figure out which ones you can answer easily and immediately. Another option would be to use a so-called preview function. That means that you can read the first line or two of a message and decide whether this mail is important or not. If not, then just delete the message at once.

Daily Mirror: Doesn't Microsoft Outlook also offer a feature called "e-mail management system"?

Newman: That's correct. This is another way how you can prioritize your messages. Outlook offers colour-coded flags which then tell you the status of a message. A red flag, for instance, reminds you that certain messages have not been answered yet. That might sometimes be quite helpful.

Daily Mirror: Alright Mr. Newman. Thank you so far. Are there any last pieces of advice you can give our readers?

Newman: There's only one more thing I'd like to point out: never forget that the fewer messages you send, the fewer you are likely to receive and the more time you have for the really important things in life.

Task 3 Combining sentences

Take a look at the following sentence halves and combine them by drawing lines.

Writing e-mails is as popular as	don't have access to the Internet is very small.
Spam mails might	at handling computers than adults.
Photos and other data	it might be advisable to set it up again.
Writing and using e-mails has been	can easily be sent via e-mail.
Your computer should regularly be	to check your mails regularly.
Your boss must not forbid you	endanger your computer and can carry a virus.
The number of people who	also send invitations via mail.
Sometimes children are better	sending short messages from your mobile.
These days it's popular to	updated for new anti-virus-programs.
If you buy something online,	you will get a confirmation via mail.
If your computer carries a virus,	popular for many years now.

Reading Comprehension

Task 4 True/False/Justification

After having read the interview, decide whether the statements are true (T) or false (F) and put a cross in the correct box. Then identify the sentence in the text which supports your decision (justification). Write the first four words of this sentence in the space provided. The first one (0) has been done for you.

	T	F	JUSTIFICATION
0. If you work as a clinical psychologist, clients frequently consult you.	X		You're absolutely right …
1. Most people only and exclusively write e-mails for private purposes.			
2. The majority believes that they can concentrate on two things at the same time.			
3. Unfortunately most people do no have the ability to work on two things simultaneously.			
4. It is a fact that the human brain can only really concentrate on one thing after the other.			
5. If we permanently interrupt one action for another one, our creativity will be stimulated.			
6. Work-related e-mails only disturb the working process and hinder further progress.			
7. In best case it should be limited how often you check your e-mails.			
8. Limiting the times how often people check their mails during work doesn't lead to further stress.			
9. In case your inbox is full of mails, there is nothing you can do except delete them all.			
10. Preview functions allow you to read the beginning of e-mails.			
11. The Microsoft Outlook "e-mail management system" tells you which mails are important.			

Task 5 Word formation

The following verbs are taken from the interview. First find the noun that goes together with the given verb and then translate the noun.

VERB	NOUN	GERMAN TRANSLATION
to explain	*explanation*	
to distract		
to concentrate on		
to interrupt		
to receive		
to decide		
to remind		
to stimulate		
to reduce		

Reading Comprehension

RC 4: FOR A SHOPPER WHO HAS DRUNK ALCOHOL, A MOUSE CAN BE A DANGEROUS THING

Task 1 Pre-reading

- Have you ever bought anything via the Internet? If yes, what was it and how did you pay for it?
- How did you feel while shopping online? Do you prefer it compared to "normal" shopping?
- Do your parents or other family members sometimes purchase goods online?
- What do you think is the biggest advantage of online shopping?

Task 2 Reading

Read the text, ignoring the missing headlines:

1 _____

John Silvans remembers exactly how he felt on that chilly spring evening when he returned home from a business party. It was already past midnight and he had had a few glasses of whiskey too much. But he was in such a good mood that, spontaneously, he decided to buy a present for his girlfriend. "I logged on to this luxury jewelry Web site and I bought her a pair of $ 1,200 earrings, or at least I thought that this would be the correct price", says Mr. Silvans. "Maybe my vision was blurred or I just missed a decimal point, but the earrings turned out to be a more expensive present than actually planned because in fact they were $ 12,000."

2 _____

Fortunately John Silvans realized his mistake on the next morning and was able to cancel his order. So apart from the shock, no real harm was done. But not everybody is that lucky. The number of people who order goods after having drunk too much is higher than one would think. And in most cases they do not even realize what they did while they were drunk. Mostly the damage is only realized when the goods and the credit-card bill arrive. And at that point, it's far too late to do anything so not everyone gets away without damage.

3 _____

But how come that a phenomenon like that has developed? Experts use to call it "sip and click" and it is one of the latest and strangest side effects of our high tech age. Like the 24-hour availability of shopping channels, the growth of the at-home Internet access has provided the background for attracting many would-be shoppers. There is nothing easier than logging in, choosing the goods, entering your credit card number and finally clicking the button "purchase". And the best thing is that you can do that any time, day or night. Above all, the rapid spread of high-speed Internet access contributes to browsing and buying in the privacy of your own home.

4 _____

As mentioned before, paired with alcohol this phenomenon can turn out to be quite dangerous. "Actually it's very embarrassing", a 42 year-old woman explains, "because you don't want other people to think you might have an alcohol/shopping problem. But it simply can happen that, under the influence of alcohol, you do things you can't remember later on. I do know how surprised I was when the postman rang my doorbell to deliver a package from Amazon. Obviously I had ordered several books and DVDs and I had no idea about it."

5 _____

So all in all, does this unlimited and constant access to the world of commerce mean an irresponsible buying behaviour? "Not necessarily", says Dr. Fulton, professor at the Golden Gate University in San Francisco. "People shop while being under the influence of a lot of things, not just alcohol. These days shopping might be used to deal with obsessions, loneliness, boredom or friendship issues. Clicking while under the influence of alcohol is, however, relatively new."

6 _____

One – and probably the only – reasonable solution to the problem would be to set up a complicated alpha-numeric password for your computer to prevent yourself from further impulse purchases. Another one that might be even more effective, but probably difficult to carry out, would be to stop drinking alcohol at all …

Reading Comprehension

Task 3 **Matching headlines**

In the text there are six gaps for the headlines of the paragraphs. Take a look at the headlines below and decide which headline (A–H) goes together with which paragraph (1–6). Mind that there are two headlines that do not fit.

Better and enhanced technology being the reason	A
Why people go shopping at all	B
How to avoid the dilemma?	C
In most cases the harm must not be underestimated	D
The human shopping behaviour	E
A dangerous combination	F
Who is responsible?	G
Personal nightmare	H

Task 4 **Finding the summary**

Read through the following sentences and put them into the correct order to get a short summary of the article. Number the sentences from 1–8, the first one has already been done for you.

The tricky aspect is that often these people don't remember having bought the goods in question.	
It is difficult how to handle a problem like that.	
This means that once people have drunk too much, they are more likely to purchase goods online.	
A solution is to install a password on your computer to stop yourself from buying unnecessary stuff.	
They only realize their fault once the articles are delivered or they receive their credit card bill.	
One of the most recent ones is called "sip and click".	
With the development of new technologies, new problems come up.	1
Unfortunately, nothing can be done at that point.	

Task 5 **Correcting sentences**

Choose the correct alternative in *italic* in these sentences.

- Online shopping *is becoming / has become* more popular during the last years.
- The majority *don't / doesn't* remember having bought goods online.
- A woman says that she can't *remember / remind* having bought books at Amazon.com.
- According to a psychologist, drunk people tend to buy unnecessary *staff / stuff*.
- It's so easy to buy something online: you just have to *pull / push* the "purchase" button.
- I remember I bought earrings after I *had returned / have returned* home from a party.
- While Marylin was drinking cocktails, she *searched / was searching* the Internet for special offers.
- "Sip and click" is a problem that *need not / must not* be underestimated.

Reading Comprehension

RC 5: HOW THE MOBILE PHONE IS CHANGING OUR LIVES

Task 1 Pre-reading

- How important is your mobile phone for you?
- Could you imagine to live a life without it?
- How do you feel if you forget it at home? Does that make you feel uncomfortable? Why?
- Does everyone in your family have a mobile phone?

Task 2 Reading

Everyone knows

Does the following situation sound familiar to you? You are sitting on the train or in the bus and a mobile phone lets off its mostly very annoying melody, making everyone aware of its presence. The owner pulls it out of his or her pocket, answering it with a loud "hello". Sometimes the owner of the phone says that he or she can't talk right now but is at home in ten minutes anyway. In most cases, however, the owner starts chatting as if being alone and in privacy.

Disturbed privacy

So how has the mobile phone changed our lives? The most significant change is definitely the fact that mobiles let us have personal and private conversations in public places. We let strangers in the street participate in our lives by talking about our feelings, worries, school, our job, family, friends and thousands of other things. Usually we talk as if being at home, not even taking into consideration the presence of others. We share personal feelings with them when we quarrel on the phone or tell our beloved ones how important they are for us. We completely open up ourselves.

Freeing yourself

The existence of mobile phones has brought about an enormous freedom. In former times people were dependent on the Post Office for the installation and use of telephones. But this has changed completely. Nowadays only a small number of people still use fixed phone lines. Most use cell phones and enjoy all advantages offered which means being free to buy and use a mobile whenever and wherever you want.

Safe and cared for

Another way mobile phones have altered our lives is that they make us feel safe. You never know when your car breaks down and you might need to call help. Or how often have you missed the bus and were happy to be able to phone your parents to pick you up from the train station? When we think back to September 11th, thousands of phone calls were made shortly before the World Trade Centre collapsed. People used their last chance to call their families telling them that they loved them.

Safety turning into control?

But there is another way how cell phones convey a feeling of security. Just think about worried parents who are able to call their daughter or son on a night out. Mobiles also give you the chance to call your husband or wife, boyfriend or girlfriend any time you feel like. Because of that they may make us feel being cared for. But out of the same reason they may also make us feel being controlled.

Not only positive

Certainly, there is no advantage without disadvantage, and in the case of the mobile phone this is clearly the health aspect. Experts are not a hundred percent sure, but many feel mobile phones pose a risk to your health. What can be said, however, is that mobiles emit radiation and radio waves. If they enhance the risk of cancer or not, cannot be analysed exactly. In any case, cell phones should only be used in urgent or emergency situations and not for chatting with your best friends for several hours a day.

Task 3 Matching

Take a look at the following phrases and combine them by drawing lines.

to charge	online aps
to download	cover on your mobile
to search your way	the ringtone and volume
to put a colourful	via Google maps
to adjust	the battery of your mobile

Reading Comprehension

Task 4 Note taking

Answer the questions related to the text in <u>not more than four words</u>. You need not answer in full sentences, key words are enough. The first one has been done for you as an example.

A	Which is the most striking change mobiles have brought about?	*private conversation in public*
B	If we talk on the mobile in the street, which relation do we build up with strangers?	
C	Why do mobile phones give us a feeling of freedom?	
D	When talking about telephones, which type is on the verge of dying out?	
E	Give two reasons why mobiles have changed our lives positively.	
F	At what point can safety and care turn into something negative?	
G	Concerning the health, why do some people consider cell phones as risky business?	
H	What do experts say about possible health risks?	

Task 5 Guessing the facts

Test your knowledge about mobile phones and guess whether the following facts are true or false. But mind that this is only a guessing activity. So, there is no use to check with the text.

	TRUE	FALSE
1. 90% of Britain's population have a mobile phone.		
2. About 30% of British children aged between 7 and 16 possess a mobile.		
3. 40% of the US population have a mobile phone.		
4. China has less mobile phone users than the US and Canada together.		
5. Only 3% of Africans have mobiles.		
6. One in six people in the whole world has a mobile phone.		
7. 33% of mobile phone users say their phone is for emergencies only.		
8. Drivers' reactions are two times slower when talking on a mobile.		
9. In Austria it's no obligation to use a hands-free set when you go by car.		

Reading Comprehension

Task 6 My first mobile phone – tense exercise

Read the text about Lou Anne and how she remembers when she bought her first mobile phone. Fill in the verbs in the correct tenses.

Well, I can remember it very well, it was a Saturday afternoon many years ago. At that time mobiles _____ (not be) very common and only few people _____ (possess) them. I was the first in my family who bought one, no-one _____ (have) one before me. At first my parents _____ (not understand) my wish to have a mobile. So I _____ (try) to convince them by telling them all the advantages. That they could reach me while I _____ (enjoy) myself out, for example. But all that _____ (not help).

Anyway, I _____ (buy) my mobile phone and I was very proud of it. By and large also the other members of my family _____ (become) friends with this new invention and by now everyone _____ (have) his/her own mobile phone.

Nowadays I can't imagine living without it, of course. I _____ (need) it every day and it _____ (have) and enormous importance for me. It's funny that a little thing like that _____ (become) so popular over the years. I'm curious how this whole development _____ (go on) and I am sure that many new features for mobile phones _____ (invent) in the future.

Task 7 Apple iPhone – adjective exercise

Read this description of the Apple iPhone and complete it with the missing adjectives (either comparative or superlative).

According to Apple's website, the brand new iPhone 4G is the _____ (schnell) and _____ (stark) iPhone ever. The technical features are numerous. There's nothing _____ (einfach) than shooting a video and editing it directly on the phone. Searching across your iPhone by using spotlight search is definitely one of the _____ (gut) characteristics because it helps you spare time. The handling of the iPhone is _____ (wenig) complicated than with other mobiles as you can make a call or play music via the voice control. One of the _____ (unerwartet) features is the compass that points you the right direction. But that's by far not all. The iPhone works like an iPod that can show music videos, movies, TV shows and much _____ (viel). There's yet another feature that is _____ (beeindruckend): it's the multitouch interface. You can make calls by just tapping the number or name in your contacts or favourites. Well, sounds like a little computer in itself …

RC 6: YES, I'M AN INTERNET ADDICT

Task 1 Pre-reading
- Do you know what it means if somebody is addicted to something?
- What do you think people can be addicted to?
- Do you believe that one can also become addicted to the Internet? How is that manifested?
- How often do you use your computer and the Internet? How many hours a day do you spend in front of your PC?

Task 2 Finding prepositions

to be addicted _____   to be good _____

to be interested _____   to be famous _____

to be prepared _____   to subscribe _____

to suffer _____   to pay _____

to be responsible _____   to get along _____

to be bad _____   to write _____

Task 3 Reading / Fill in the sentences

Read the text about Calvin, a 15 year old Internet addict. While reading ignore the gaps with the numbers. Below the text you will find eight sentences (A–H). Six out of these eight sentences belong to the text. Try to find out which ones they are and fill them into the correct gap (numbers 1–6).

Yes, it's true. I'm an addict. Not in the classical sense, which means being addicted to drugs, alcohol, cigarettes, food, shopping or other stuff. I'm addicted to using the Internet. I'm 15 and I have been addicted for almost one year now.

Everything started when I got my own computer for my bedroom. **1** _____ I could finally do some Internet research for my home-exercises and I even had some time left to chat with friends. **2** _____ At first I didn't realize that I began to spend more and more hours in my room and in front of my computer. I started to search for different kind of information, pop groups, football results, checking Wikipedia, googling friends and so on. I also logged-in at various interactive forums where I could e-mail other teenagers with similar interests. **3** _____ My bedroom was the place where I felt most comfortable.

It took my parents a very long time to realize that I had a problem. **4** _____ And by that time they were mostly tired and didn't really pay attention to what I had done during the day. I always told them that I had done all my work for school and that was it.

My mum actually found it out when she fell ill, shortly before Christmas. **5** _____ She soon became suspicious as I stayed in my room all day long. At some point I didn't even come out to join her for lunch. So she started to carry food into my room which I ate while I was chatting and surfing. The Net fully captured all my concentration and was my sole interest.

The moment when I stopped eating at all – because I simply was no longer interested in it and I had the feeling that I didn't need it – my mum took me to a psychologist. **6** _____ For me, and in my little world, everything was fine – at least as long as I could turn on the computer and log in to the Internet. The doctor, however, helped me to find out that nothing was fine and that I really did need help.

I have been in therapy now for a few months and, of course, my parents removed the computer from my bedroom. They now allow me to use the Internet for some two hours a day to do my homework but not more. I have started to go outside again, joining "real life", so to speak. And I have to confess that I like it.

Reading Comprehension

At the same time I also stopped meeting "real" friends, going outside with them, playing football or just hanging around.	A
She had a nasty cold and so she had to stay at home in bed for almost two weeks.	B
I didn't really know how I should have handled the problem or what I could have done.	C
That was really gorgeous and the best birthday present I have ever got.	D
It was simply fascinating and amazing to have access to so many different types of information and I never got tired of searching the Net.	E
It goes without saying that I didn't want to go there because I didn't see the need to do so.	F
They both work long hours and only come home in the afternoon or early evening.	G
But somehow things got out of control.	H

Task 4 Correcting sentences

Choose the correct alternative in *italic* in these sentences.

- I have always been *interesting / interested* in working with the Internet.
- After having gone to the psychologist I really felt *embarrassed / embarrassing*.
- The way my addiction developed was definitely *surprising / surprised* for me.
- There was a time in my life when meeting my friends made me feel *boring / bored*.
- Before my mum had found out about my addiction she was *annoying / annoyed* by my behaviour.
- When my parents returned from work they always asked what I *had done / did* all day long.
- I never thought that a thing like that *could happen / could have happened* to me.
- Many teenagers *have worked / have been working* with computers for all their lives.
- So far I *didn't meet / haven't met* anybody with the same addiction.
- After I *had started / have started* to meet friends again, I felt much better.

Task 5 Multiple choice

For the following questions, choose the answer (a, b, c or d) which you think fits best according to the text:

1. How did Calvin's addiction start?
    a. He borrowed his parents' computer to work with it.
    b. He got his own computer for Christmas and got hooked on working with it.
    c. He regularly used the computers available at school.
    d. He got his own bedroom computer as a birthday present.

2. Why did Calvin's parents not immediately realize their son's problem?
    a. Because they didn't ask whether he had a problem or not.
    b. Because they were busy with work and didn't come home early.
    c. Because they didn't know that a thing like Internet addiction existed.
    d. Because his mother was ill and couldn't care about her son.

3. At which point did Calvin's mother decide to go to a psychologist with him?
    a. When he stopped doing his home-exercises.
    b. When his grades at school became worse.
    c. When he stopped eating lunch with his mother.
    d. When he didn't eat anything at all.

Reading Comprehension

RC 7: WHY IT'S SIMPLY FUN BEING RICH

Task 1 Pre-reading

You are going to read an interview with Jennifer Ryan, the 15-year-old daughter of an Australian millionaire. Read what her life is like to find out about the following aspects:

- Do you know anybody who is rich?
- Do you think being rich is funny?
- Would you like to be rich? Why / Why not?
- If you had a lot of money, what would you do with it?

Task 2 Reading

Steven Jillings: Hello Jennifer. First of all, thanks a lot for doing this interview here with our *"Famous Teens"* magazine. You are 15 years old and you range among the "hundred wealthiest teens in the world". How does that feel and what does that mean exactly? Are you still able to live a "normal" life?

Jennifer Ryan: Well, living a normal life in the ordinary sense is of course difficult. As you have already mentioned, my dad is very famous and he has made a great fortune in his life, so simply because out of that fact my life differs from that of most teenagers my age.

Steven Jillings: Certainly. So what are the most significant of these differences? Could you outline them for our readers, please?

Jennifer Ryan: Sure, I can. My day starts working early in the morning, so far there's nothing unusual. I attend a private school in Perch, that's about half an hour's drive away from our villa. Our driver takes me there and also picks me up every day. School starts at half past eight a.m. and ends at four p.m. But that differs as it depends on whether you attend additional courses or not. I attend the Jazz-dance club that takes place two times a week, always Mondays and Wednesdays. I like exercising and doing sports and I am particularly keen on dancing, you see.

Steven Jillings: Alright. So what does your home look like? Could you fill us in on some details?

Jennifer Ryan: Well, I'd say that our villa is quite ordinary but others would probably not. It's a four-storey house, each floor having about 200 square meters. We do have a wonderful garden leading into a small park with a pond. A gardener takes care of it, mows the lawn and plants and waters the flowers. We have an in- and an outdoor swimming pool. On hot summer days I love lying on an airbed, floating around in the pool. If I ask Carmelita, our maid, to bring me an ice-tea, I even feel like one of the famous Hollywood stars. It's awesome, I can tell you.

Steven Jillings: That does indeed sound very good. Can you describe your house and your room to us?

Jennifer Ryan: Well the house itself is very nice and my mum has decorated it really beautifully. I sometimes feel that it is almost too big but I generally love having enough space. We have a huge living room with an enormous red velvet couch. If I have to read something for school, I often stretch out on the sofa and do the things I have to do. There is an oversized flat TV opposite the couch and this is clearly the preferred place of my little brother. He spends whole afternoons and evenings sitting in front of the TV and playing the newest and hottest PS3 games. Crazy, isn't it? Anyway, from the living room you can directly go into the library. Most of the books there belong to my father and I often ask myself whether he has read all of them or not. I tried to ask him twice but I kind of didn't really get an answer. So he probably has not ...

Steven Jillings: What about your room then, Jennifer. What does that look like?

Jennifer Ryan: My room is on the third floor and of course it's very big, too. When you enter it, you have a nice balcony to your right. My bed is on the left side of the room. It's a wonderful four-poster bed with numerous pink and purple pillows on it. Oh I love it and it's so comfortable. In the middle of the room there is a wall with a flat TV-set hanging on it. I try not to watch too much TV and sometimes my mum comes into my room to check whether I work for school or watch TV. She has already caught me many times not working for school ... However, at the end of the room there is a door leading into my bathroom.

Reading Comprehension

Steven Jillings: Wow, you have a bathroom of your own? That's great and probably something most of our readers would like to have, too.

Jennifer Ryan: Yeah it's fine, even though mine is relatively small. I have my own bathtub with a whirlpool function as well. I particularly like that in winter when it's cold outside. Next to the bathtub there is my washbasin with an integrated cupboard for my cosmetic stuff. There is also a toilet in the left corner of my bathroom.

Steven Jillings: Jennifer, what does it feel like to be rich and wealthy? Do you think that you live the perfect life?

Jennifer Ryan: It's difficult to answer because I have always lived the way I live right now. And of course it's great because my parents never have to worry about money and I always get the things I want to have. If there is a new i-pod or a new smartphone and I want to have it, I just tell my dad and he buys it for me. It's so simple.

Steven Jillings: But are there also negative aspects?

Jennifer Ryan: Sure there are. You never know who your true and real friends are, for example. I always have to ask myself whether other people like me because of being the person I am or because of the fact that my dad has a lot of money. That can be quite nasty from time to time.

Steven Jillings: Thank you for giving this interview, Jennifer. I wish you all the best for your future.

Task 3 True/False/Justification

After having read the interview, decide whether the statements are true (T) or false (F) and put a cross in the correct box. Then identify the sentence in the text which supports your decision (justification). Write the first four words of this sentence in the space provided.

	T	F	JUSTIFICATION
1. Jennifer's life is not different to the one of ordinary teenagers.			
2. Jennifer's dad is listed among the "hundred wealthiest people in the world".			
3. Jennifer's parents don't have to pay for her daughter to attend school.			
4. Jennifer goes to school by car, the family's driver takes her.			
5. The 15-year-old girl is a single child and doesn't have any siblings.			
6. The house where Jennifer lives has about 800 square meters.			
7. Jennifer feels like a star when the maid brings her something to drink into the pool.			
8. There is no need for Jennifer to use her parents' bathroom.			
9. Jennifer's brother loves watching TV and playing games on the flat TV in the living room.			
10. The girl has a big number of colourful pillows on her bed.			
11. According to Jennifer life is not always easy when you have rich parents.			

Reading Comprehension

Task 4 Describing people

The following words are jumbled adjectives. Put the letters into the correct order to find the adjectives describing Jennifer Ryan. The first letter of the word is always **bold**.

1. t**o**ryps _____
2. **y**thewal _____
3. **e**inc _____
4. **t**solip _____
5. **n**yfrleid _____

6. **e**lentiligtn _____
7. **v**eatci _____
8. **h**ric _____
9. **o**uygn _____
10. **o**peilt _____

Task 5 Being rich / Correct the if-sentences

1. If Jennifer would not be rich, she would not have her own bathroom.
   _____

2. Jennifer's mum sometimes is angry, if Jennifer watches TV in her room instead of doing her homework.
   _____

3. If the family didn't have such a big flat TV, Jennifer's brother didn't play PS3 games all the time.
   _____

4. Would Jennifer's live be better if her dad had even more money?
   _____

5. If Jennifer's dad didn't work hard when he was young, he would not have become rich.
   _____

6. If you entered the library through the living room you will be amazed by the number of books.
   _____

7. Jennifer would not have been spoilt if her parents were not rich and did not have a lot of money.
   _____

Task 6 Combining sentences

Take a look at the following sentence halves and combine them by drawing lines.

1. Every day Jennifer is taken	to be a little bit arrogant and snobbish.
2. It is almost unbelievable that	to find out who her real and true friends are.
3. It is often difficult for Jennifer	that has got four large floors.
4. For Jennifer, being rich is great because	to school by the family's driver.
5. Wealthy people sometimes tend	Jennifer has got a bathroom of her own.
6. Jennifer and her family live in a wonderful house	living in a luxurious villa.
7. The 15-year-old girl absolutely enjoys	she always gets the things she wants to have.

Reading Comprehension

RC 8: ANIMAL EXPERIMENTS – ONE OF THE MOST CONTROVERSIAL ISSUES

Task 1 Pre-reading

Before you read this article about animal testing, think about the following aspects:

- What do you know about animal experiments? Do you think they are important and justified?
- Are there any alternatives to avoid tests on animals?

You might also study the vocabulary section in this book to learn some new words!

Task 2 Reading

1 _____

Carrying out animal experiments has always been and will always be a controversial and widely discussed topic. Clearly, opinions are divided as far as an issue like that is concerned. There are people who consider it important and necessary and, of course, the opponents who think that it's brutal and cruel. But what do the facts actually say?

2 _____

According to Wikipedia, "animal testing or animal experimentation is the use of non-human animals in scientific experimentation". The reason why tests like these are carried out is easy to explain: research is done to see whether products (shampoos, shower gels and many others) harm humans and are consequently dangerous. In most cases the testing is carried out in universities, medical schools, pharmaceutical companies or commercial facilities.

3 _____

It is difficult – if not impossible – to really find out how much animals suffer when they are subject to animal testing. From a moral and ethic point of view, procedures causing animals to feel pain should therefore be forbidden as questions like "who gives us the right to do things like that?" come up and remain unanswered.

4 _____

But it cannot be denied that animal testing is important and also presents positive aspects. It provides scientists and doctors with fundamental and significant knowledge, for example. Knowledge about how the human body reacts in connection with certain substances, for instance. And this kind of knowledge might be life-saving and essential.

5 _____

But is it always only black or white or do alternatives exist? Well, not really. The so-called "three Rs" are tried to be carried out, which means **r**educe (limiting the number of animals), **r**eplace (trying to use non-animal methods) and **r**efine (minimizing potential pain and suffering). But in the end, it's almost always animals that are involved.

Task 3 Matching headlines

In the text there are five gaps for the headlines of the single paragraphs. Look at the headlines below and decide which headline (A–G) goes together with which paragraph (1–5). Mind that there are two headlines that do not fit.

What are we actually talking about?	A
Not only negative	B
Animal testing – a rather new topic	C
Pointing out the controversy	D
Do alternative ways exist?	E
Describing the alternative	F
Simply not justified	G

Reading Comprehension

Task 4 Finding out people's opinions

Read through the short comments people give on the topic of animal testing. Then decide which of the three statements (A, B, or C) best summarises the person's opinion.

Hilary Jones: *Animal testing, well, that's difficult. I'd say that is a topic everyone should be interested in and everyone should have an opinion on. Mine is that it is useful and necessary. Just think about all the cosmetic products – I simply don't want to imagine what would happen if these tests didn't exist.*

- A Mrs Jones thinks that everybody should be in favour of animal testing.
- B She believes that it's important to test products on animals first.
- C She doesn't consider it important to have an opinion on animal experimentation.

Brian Jackobson: *I have to confess that I'm not really interested in a topic like that. To tell the truth, I don't even have a lot of knowledge about animal experiments and I don't really care if there are rats or rabbits in laboratories that suffer or not. At least not as long as I am directly concerned.*

- A Brian Jackobson knows a lot about animal experimentation.
- B He is concerned about the rats and rabbits in the laboratories.
- C Mr Jackobson is ignorant towards the topic of animal testing.

Julie Miller: *We talked about animal testing only last week. At school, in our biology lessons, we also watched a documentary about the conditions under which these test animals are kept. Very cruel, I can tell. Most of the time I couldn't even look at the screen because it was so disgusting. And the animals are so poor.*

- A Julie thinks that the living conditions of the test-animals could be improved.
- B The girl generally feels sorry for animals.
- C Julie feels sorry for the test-animals and thinks that their living conditions are bad.

Rob Johnson: *From a purely scientific point of view I can only tell you that animal testing is absolutely fundamental. It provides us with an enormously valuable general knowledge and allows us to test treatment and medication for ill people.*

- A In Mr Johnson's opinion, animal testing is only valuable for ill people.
- B He thinks that the knowledge gained through animal testing is extremely important.
- C Mr Johnson believes that there's nothing more important than animal testing.

Clair Welsh: *I've been a member of "FTA – Free Tested Animals" for five years now and I have to say that I am absolutely against animal experimentation. Nobody is allowed to harm animals and to make them suffer and feel pain. Some people claim that the animals don't feel the pain but that's nonsense of course.*

- A Mrs Welsh is angry that there are people (doctors, scientists) who make animals suffer.
- B According to her opinion only scientists have the right to harm test-animals.
- C She is convinced that the animals don't really feel the pain.

Mike Tailor: *I'd say there is no use in being against animal testing because it will be done anyway. And scientists will always do it in the name of the greater good. So why being against it?*

- A Mr Tailor is not sure what to think about animal testing.
- B Mike Tailor believes that scientists only carry out the tests for themselves.
- C He's in favour of it but only because the tests are going to be carried out anyway.

Reading Comprehension

Task 5 — Gapped text

Read the text about animal experimentation and then look at the verbs given. Try to put them into the correct gap but be careful to use the correct tense as well (including passive voice). Mind that there are three verbs which you don't need.

provide – describe – improve – use – isolate – born – forget – call – be – be – find – lose

The history of animal testing

The earliest references to animal testing _____ in the fourth century. Since then animals _____ throughout the history of scientific research. One of the best-known scientists working with animals _____ Ivan Pavlov. He used dogs to _____ classical conditioning.

Dogs, however, have always been important test animals. Insulin, for example, _____ first _____ from dogs in 1922 and it consequently _____ the treatment of diabetes. In 1957, a Russian dog that _____ Laika was sent to orbit the earth. That was an enormous breakthrough as well.

The following decades were devoted to finding out how to change the genetic code of animals. The ultimate success came in 1996 when Dolly, the sheep, _____. It _____ the first mammal to be cloned from an adult cell.

RC 9: WHAT A DOG'S LIFE

Task 1 — Pre-reading

- Look at the vocabulary section of this book and study the vocabs.
- Try to find out advantages and disadvantages of having a dog (or a pet in general).
- If you don't have a dog, would you like to have one? How would you call it?

Task 2 — Reading

Read this article about what it's like to have a dog, then do the tasks below. While reading, ignore the gaps in the text.

Have you ever asked yourself what it's like to have a dog? If not, then just read this article and learn some more about the responsibilities and the duties of being a dog owner.

I really love dogs. When I think back to the time when I still was a child, I always wanted to have a dog. **1** _____ I thought about that – once I have my own apartment – I would definitely have one. A big one. I even thought about names. Maybe *Ronny* or *Joe*. However,

2 _____ Which was kind of clear anyway, wasn't it? When I moved into my apartment I started to work and I soon found out that keeping and caring for a dog takes a lot of time. And when I came home from work, usually late in the afternoon, I was really grateful for NOT having a dog because I had time for myself and my hobbies. So years went by and, from a rational point of view, I decided that it's simply easier to live without a dog.

But destiny held an unexpected surprise for me. I got to know an interesting guy. **3** _____ We met while I was in a bar with one of my best friends. And we sympathised with each other at once. Anyway, that's another story I think. What's far more important here is the fact that this guy had a puppy. It was a female puppy, about four months old, and she was called *Mara*. **4** _____ I immediately fell in love, but not only with the dog if you know what I mean …

Reading Comprehension

I became a couple with this guy which also meant, by and large, that I started to spend a lot of time with *Mara*. I went jogging and for walks with her and of course also took her into my garden and my apartment. Unfortunately that was the point when I found out that I was not fit for having and keeping a dog. Why?
5 _____

The duties which you have when keeping a dog, are enormous. You have to go for walks at least two times a day. In best case these walks are long so that the dog can run around enough. Before going to bed you have to take care that the dog "goes on the loo" again, no matter if it's already shortly before midnight and you are tired and would urgently need some sleep. In the morning you immediately get a wet "good morning kiss", something you definitely not want to start your day with. Then it's time to go out again, ignoring the fact that you are already late for work, the weather might be more than poor and you'd actually do anything for an undisturbed cup of coffee.

6 _____ For me, a person who absolutely loves cleanliness, it was most horrible when *Mara* shook herself so that a thousand brown and white dog hairs landed on the floor that I would have liked to sponge up immediately. I can also remember when *Mara* once took a wooden stick with her into my apartment. She started to gnaw on it until there were uncountable pieces of wood lying around in the living room. And until I was completely desperate, fetching the vacuum cleaner. Which was the second time on that day ...

Anyway, *Mara* definitely enriched my life because she was like a good friend for me and I often had lots of fun with her. But she also meant a lot of stress for me, as I was simply not able to handle this cleanliness-affair with enough ignorance and calmness. I don't really know whether I would have become happy with her or not. This question, however, remains unanswered as the cute guy and I have split up in the meantime.

Task 3 Sentence matching

Six out of the following eight sentences are taken from the text above. Find out which ones they are and fill the correct sentence (A–H) into the corresponding gap (1–6). Mind that there are two sentences which you don't have to use.

Things developed differently.	A
It has always been my greatest wish to have a dog.	B
I can tell you, that was the sweetest puppy I've ever seen.	C
Besides you must also not forget that dogs make a lot of dirt.	D
Probably like every child.	E
Well, that's easy to explain.	F
I couldn't tell whether the guy or the dog was sweeter.	G
Fortunately he was very handsome and cute.	H

Reading Comprehension

Task 4 — Vocabulary work

Explain the following words and terms in English, trying to take care to express yourself correctly.

responsibilities _____

apartment _____

afternoon _____

to be grateful _____

surprise _____

immediately _____

puppy _____

at least _____

undisturbed _____

cleanliness _____

Task 5 — Word classification

Classify the words taken from the text according to the categories given.

always – hobbies – split up – myself – midnight – urgently – afternoon – run – live – yourself – duties – moved – usually – enriched – destiny – immediately – rational – walks – take care – definitely – enormous – couple – sympathised – often – grateful – unfortunately

ADVERBS OF FREQUENCY	NOUNS	VERBS	ADJECTIVES	REFLEXIVE PRONOUNS

Task 6 — Matching words and definitions

to sympathise with somebody	to clean/hoover something
to become a couple	to be frustrated
to sponge up something	too many to count, numerous
to gnaw on something	to immediately like somebody very much
uncountable	to influence another person's life positively
to be desperate	to bite on something (e.g. a bone)
to enrich somebody's life	to start a love relationship with someone

Reading Comprehension

RC 10: TEENAGE PREGNANCIES: TOP OR FLOP?

Task 1 — Pre-reading / Vocabulary work

Look at the following English and German words and match the correct translations.

to be pregnant	Verhütungsmittel
pregnancy	ein Kind bekommen/gebären
to have a baby	Abtreibung
to raise a baby	der Vaterschaftstest
maternity leave	das Kleinkind
paternity leave	ein Kind aufziehen/großziehen
abortion	schwanger sein
contraceptive	Mutterschaftsurlaub/Karenz
toddler	die Schwangerschaft
paternity test	Vaterschaftsurlaub/Karenz

Task 2 — Reading

Read this article about teenage pregnancies to find out what happened in a High School in Louisville, Canada.

Fourteen pregnant students at one school. Did they have a pact or were they copying a Hollywood movie? Report by Susan Lorence.

Teachers at the local Canadian Louisville High School were shocked when they found out that fourteen of their students were pregnant in one year. Teenage pregnancies are neither new nor unusal in a big school like that, but according to the headmaster they usually had about three to five pregnancies per year. Another striking aspect was the fact that almost all of the young girls were under the age of 16. For the headmaster, the teachers and of course the parents, the question came up why this sudden baby boom among the teenage girls took place. The answer might be provided when checking the cinema program.

Towards the end of the year 2007 *Juno*, a Hollywood movie, was released which featured Juno, a witty teenager from Minnesota, who gets pregnant the first time she sleeps with her boyfriend Bleeker. Fortunately, her parents are very liberal and understanding and therefore she gets all the support and help she needs to endure the pregnancy and to find a good home for her baby. For sure, the movie is characterised by a happy ending as Juno and Bleeker get together again.

"Movies and other media do have an effect on young people that must not be underestimated", says Joseph Ribton, professor for sociology at the Standford University, England. "Especially films like *Juno* make having a baby look all too easy. Unfortunately these films convey the wrong message because they do NOT present real life, with all its ups and downs, difficulties and challenges. So teenagers simply get a wrong picture of what life is like … or is actually not like."

But let's put the focus back on life at the Louisville High School. When the fourteen pregnancies were first discovered, the headmaster claimed that the teenage girls had made a pact to have children and to raise them together. The girls, however, denied all that but it is certain that at least some of them wanted to have a baby. Anyway, the principal felt that something should be done to prevent more kids from having babies. The result was a school-wide campaign where information brochures and condoms were distributed among the students. Some time will have to elapse in order to find out if that was the key to success.

There is, however, one last open question that might be worth discussing: what about the role of the teenage fathers? One of them is a homeless man in his 20s, the others might be students themselves, or a bit older. It's difficult – if not impossible – to really find out what their motivation was. One teenage boy in Louisville had a very simple explanation for the baby boom. He told a reporter from the town's local magazine: "It was a cold and long winter. And for teens it's sometimes quite boring around here in a town like that. Nothing to do." Well … there isn't anything left to say, is there?

Reading Comprehension

Task 3 — Note taking

Answer the questions related to the text in <u>not more than four words</u>. You need not answer in full sentences, key words are enough. The first one has been done for you as an example.

A	Why were teachers at the Canadian Louisville High School shocked?	*14 pregnancies same time*
B	What is the average per-year number of pregnancies at that school?	
C	Who was wondering about the high number of pregnancies at the school in question?	
D	When talking about this high number of pregnancies, what role does the movie *Juno* play?	
E	What is bad about films like *Juno*?	
F	What was the headmaster's first suspicion concerning the pregnancies?	
G	What was the headmaster's reaction to all the pregnancies?	
H	Which reasons did one of the teenage boys in Louisville give for the pregnancies? Name two!	

Task 4 — Verb practice

The following verbs are taken from the text above. Put them into the tenses given.

1. they **were shocked**: present perfect simple _____
2. the question **came up**: past perfect simple _____
3. the boy **told** that: present tense progressive _____
4. the headmaster **claimed**: going to future _____
5. people **must not**: past simple tense _____
6. the result **was**: will future _____
7. Condoms **are distributed**: present perfect tense _____

Reading Comprehension

Task 5 Summarising the text

Which of the three statements (A, B or C) best summarises the article about teenage pregnancies?

A *Juno* is a film about a teenage girl who got pregnant. It's the story of her pregnancy and how she finally becomes a couple with her boyfriend Bleeker again.

B The fact that Hollywood movies influence the behaviour of today's teenagers is often underestimated. Films like *Juno* do neither present life the way it really is, nor do they contribute to children's general education.

C During one school year the number of teenage pregnancies in a Canadian school rose significantly. That was probably due to the release of Hollywood movie *Juno* which presents life in a very positive way.

Task 6 Correcting mistakes

Laura Witson, the mother of one of the pregnant teenage girls, has written a letter about her daughter's pregnancy. Unfortunately there are some mistakes in her letter (all in all 15). Can you find and correct them?

Dear Auntie Mary Lou!

How are you? Hope things are fine with you and uncle George had already recovered from his illness. Is he allright again or does he still need you to look after and care for him? In any case, send my love to him and say him I hope he is fine soon.

Just imagine! I've got surprised and unexpected news to tell you. You better sit down before you go on reading because this might be a little bit of a shock for you. Helen is pregnant! Yes, you had read correctly! She told us about it at the end of last week. At first she wasn't sure about it herselfe. So I arranged an appointment at the doctor and he confirmed the pregnancy.

At the beginning we really were shocked. Jack had no idea how to react to that whole topic. His first impulse was to shout at her, how she could do a thing like that. At her age. But then I tryd to calm him down, telling him that NOW it's too late anyway. So he calmed down a little bit. Later on we had a serious talk with Helen, asking her how she imagines her live to go on. She told us that she wanted to get the baby and that an abortion is no option for her. Of course we accepted her wish. She also informed us that, under any circumstances, she want to finish school later on. And she hopes for our support.

We are certainly going to support her and buy now the shock is not that big any longer. I have to confess that I even look forward to the baby. We already arranged the next appointments at the doctor and the baby is expected for the end of September. Of course we don't know yet whether it will be boy or a girl but Helen is already thinking about names. Cute, isn't it?

However, I'm curious to hear your opinion for that topic and I hope you soon find the time to drop me a line. In the meantime don't let yourself be dragged down by uncle George.

All the best and all my love, Laura

RC 11: HIGH SCHOOL PROM – THE BEST NIGHT OF YOUR LIFE

Task 1 Pre-reading / Vocabulary work

Match the words with their corresponding definitions:

to hire something	a small flower
to date somebody	a tailor, a person who produces clothes
carnation	a short evening dress which you wear at parties
a cocktail dress	part of your body where you usually wear a watch
a ball gown	a formal dinner suit
a dressmaker	to pay money to borrow something
a tuxedo	a golden rim which is worn by queens on their heads
wrist	to meet somebody who you like very much
a crown	a very elegant, usually long, dress for balls

Take a few minutes time to think about the following questions:

- What do you think has been the best night of your life? Why?
- What do you imagine a High School Prom to be?
- In Austria are there comparable events to American High School Proms?
- If you were planning the perfect night, who would be with you (friends, family, girlfriend, boyfriend …)?

Task 2 Reading

Read the text about High School Proms in order to get some more detailed information.

1 _____

Going to a High School Prom means having a party in the junior and senior years of high school. It is considered to be an important American tradition and annually millions of teenagers look forward to this great happening. There's no need to say that it's a special night for the teens involved. A night they plan carefully and will probably never forget for the rest of their lives.

2 _____

The High School Prom season starts at the beginning of April and lasts until the end of May. Preparations and planning, however, already start in February. That's also the time when magazines and shops start selling and promoting their prom fashions. In general, organizing this evening takes longer than one would expect.

3 _____

So where do proms take place? That's quite different. Rather old-fashioned schools have their proms in their own school gymnastic halls. More modern schools normally rent hotels or country clubs where the proms take place. The teens then go there and enjoy themselves in a surrounding not connected to school.

4 _____

Needless to say that – especially for the girls – the dress is one of the most important aspects of an evening like that. As fashions change from year to year, a lot of time and also money is devoted to the choice of the right dress. Fashions range from cocktail dresses to glamorous ball gowns, guys are supposed to wear tuxedos. Some girls even have their dresses tailored by dressmakers so that they really have the perfect dress that fits a hundred percent. In any case, proms call for formal and elegant clothes.

5 _____

Before dealing with the dress-code, you have to do something even more important: find a date. This doesn't have to be a regular boyfriend or girlfriend but it should be someone who you would like to spend this important night together with. American teenagers must take care to have a date in time because otherwise somebody else might have already asked the boy or girl you actually wanted to ask. For sure, nobody wants to go to the prom alone and sometimes teens can get really upset if they don't find a date.

Reading Comprehension

6 _____
At the night of the prom, everybody is extremely excited. Parents sometimes allow their kids to have a party at their home before they go to the prom. They can eat something and lots of photos are taken (sometimes also by professional photographers). As a rule, the boy picks up the girl from her house. He enters the house, greets the girl's parents and then he puts a carnation around the girl's wrist. Some more pictures are taken and then off the couple goes. In some cases two or three couples rent a limousine with which they go to the location of the prom. Clearly, a special night needs special procedures.

7 _____
Sometimes at a prom, students elect a so-called prom king and queen. These two are the most important and most prominent couple of the year. Crowns are given to them and they lead the dancing when the music starts again. Well, sounds like a nice tradition, doesn't it?

Task 3 Matching headlines

In the text there are seven gaps for the headlines of the single paragraphs. Look at the headlines below and decide which headline (A–I) goes together with which paragraph (1–7). Mind that there are two headlines that do not fit.

The correct season	A
Who to go with	B
The place to be	C
The girls' dresses	D
What to wear	E
Getting the facts straight	F
The night of the nights	G
How to behave during the prom	H
What else	I

Task 4 The correct behaviour

Read through the phrases and put them according their categories.

wear your date's carnation – drink too much alcohol – wear dirty shoes – wear short trousers – be nice – spill your drink on another girl's dress – flirt with another person's date – wear a nice necklace – refresh your make-up – chat with your friends – be angry because your date doesn't dance – amuse yourself

Things you do during a prom	Things you don't do during a prom

Reading Comprehension

Task 5 True/False/Justification

After having read the text, decide whether the statements are true (T) or false (F) and put a cross in the correct box. Then identify the sentence in the text which supports your decision (justification). Write the first four words of this sentence in the space provided.

	T	F	JUSTIFICATION
1. For most American teens the night of the prom is their most exciting night.			
2. Proms take place every year.			
3. The High School Prom season typically lasts for two months.			
4. There is no need to start the preparations for the night of your prom early.			
5. Only senior High School students are allowed to go to the prom.			
6. Finding the right clothes for this special night is a very big business.			
7. There is no official dress-code for the boys.			
8. Sometimes it's more difficult than expected to find a date for the prom.			
9. It's good behaviour of a boy to fetch his date from her parents' house.			
10. All teenagers go to the prom by limousine.			

Task 6 Gapped text / Filling in the correct information from the text

Going to the prom is an important _____ tradition which teenagers really love. Already in _____ first preparations start. By then people may also already go shopping to check the latest and hottest trends. The beginning of the prom season is usually in _____.

The _____ where proms take place can vary significantly. Some schools organise proms in their own school, others rent a _____ or a _____. Far more important than the location are the dresses. Girls are supposed to wear _____ or _____ while boys must wear _____. You must not, however, wear _____ clothes and the dress-code is usually rather strict. There is another thing that must be done before going to the prom: checking a _____. This should of course be someone you like. The night of the prom is extremely special, not only for the teenagers but also for the parents. They sometimes organise a _____ for their kids where they can eat something and where _____ are taken. The boys are supposed to pick up the girls from home. It is an old tradition that the boy then puts a carnation onto the girl's _____. Some couples organise themselves in little groups and hire a _____ that takes them to the correct location. At the prom, people sometimes choose a prom _____ and _____.

Reading Comprehension

RC 12: MAKING YOUR OWN MUSIC – CREATING YOUR OWN STYLE

Task 1 — Pre-reading / Jumbled expressions

Write down the correct constructions, combining the words from box A with those from box B.

A	B
fantastic – favourite – meaningful	the drums – MTV – voice
watch – participate in – good	lyrics – band – concert ticket
expensive – listen – romantic	love song – live performance – band
playing – band – school	a band contest – leader – to music

_____   _____

_____   _____

_____   _____

_____   _____

Study the vocabulary section about music to find out about the different types of music.

- Do you have a favourite band? If yes, what characterises this band?
- Do your preferences concerning music change from time to time?
- Do you sometimes download music on your MP3 player?
- How important is listening to music for you?

Task 2 — Reading

Read this interview with four guys from Gloustershire (England) who started out as a school band and who have become rather successfull in the last two years.

Nils Barkley: Hello Gloustershire, hello England. My interview partners today are four guys who have managed to realise their dream of creating their own band and becoming popular. I heartily welcome Tom, Phil, Tobi and John. So first of all, how old are you and when did you start making music?

Tobi: Well we are 16 now and we already started very early, I think it must have been at the age of eleven. During Junior High School however, at the age of 13, we decided to set up our own band and try to become popular with our music.

Nils Barkley: Alright, your band is called *Rampax* and I guess that most of our readers have already heard about you. Could you nevertheless tell us how the roles in your band are distributed?

Phil: Sure. Tom is the singer. He also writes the lyrics himself. That's at least what he does most of the time. Sometimes, when motivation is tough, he asks us to help him and then we do it together. But most of the time he writes the songs on his own and then presents them to us. In most cases we only have to do minor changes so that the lyrics really fit to the rhythm.

Nils Barkley: I see. What about the rest of you?

Phil: Tobi plays the guitar. He has been playing it since he was a baby, I guess *(laughs)* and he is really good at it. Occasionally he tries out solos and he's really keen on that. The girls love that, too, so no wonder that they are crazy about him.

Nils Barkley: What is your part Phil? And, are the girls also crazy about you?

Reading Comprehension

Phil: I play the drums. I started when I was eleven. At that time my parents were shocked when I told them that my only wish for that year's Christmas was getting drums. My mother worried about the noise and that I would soon lose the interest in it, but luckily my dad supported me a lot. He's really cool. The girls ... well ... I split up with my girlfriend only two weeks ago. So at the moment I'm not that fond of girls, if you know what I mean.

Nils Barkley: Poor you, I can imagine that you have enough for some time now. John, what about you?

John: Well, I play the bass and I am the one who organises gigs and live concerts. That can somtimes be quite stressful because the event managers usually give you the details very late. So we often don't know until the very end where exactly we play and if there are other bands that play, too. But of course it also makes a lot of fun and you meet loads of interesting people. I always try to stay in touch with them because, you know, networking is half our life.

Nils Barkley: Do tell me, how did *Rampax* actually start?

Tom: We got to know each other when we entered Junior High and we soon found out that not only our sympathy for each other, but also our love and passion for music united us. It was pure coincidence that all of us played different instuments so we thought we might give it a try and meet for our first rehearsal. It took place in our garage. I can remember it as if it was only yesterday.

Tobi: Yea, me too. Thinking back I have to confess that, fortunately, we really improved our performance. But nevertheless, it was great fun at that time. It didn't really take us long to become better. We regularly rehearsed two or even three times a week and we soon managed to be part of the school band.

Tom: *(laughs)* That was also the time of our first "gigs", playing at school festivals and our only fans being our classmates. But it was indeed funny.

Nils Barkley: So things have obviously changed and by now you do have more fans than only your classmates. How did that come?

Phil: We got the chance to participate in a band contest organised by the local government. The winner would get the opportunity to play at a charity concert in London. Luckily the boss of a famous music label was there and liked our music. So after the show he asked us whether we would also like to play at other concerts. Of course we agreed and by now we have played some 15 concerts all around England.

Nils Barkley: Sounds good. But how do you manage playing concerts and touring around while still attending school?

John: Good question ... but somehow it works *(laughs)*. No honestly, school is very important for us and we all want to take our A-levels. We are happy that we are successful right now but we can't be sure that our success will last. We will see whether we go to university after High School or not. That's something to be considered over the next two years.

Nils Barkley: Ok guys, thanks a lot for talking to us. I wish you all the best for your future and hope that things will work out the way you want.

Task 3 Comprehension

Answer the following questions in full sentences.

1. Who belongs to *Rampax* and which instruments do the boys play?

___

2. How often did they meet for rehearsals in Junior High?

___

3. Why is Phil fed up with girls at the moment?

___

4. At what occasion did *Rampax* get popular?

___

Reading Comprehension

Task 4 Multiple matching

For the following questions, choose the answer (a, b, c or d) which you think fits best according to the text:

1. Who are Nils Barkley's guests?
   a. Four guys who play in the school band.
   b. Four guys who have become popular with their music.
   c. Four guys who had a hit-single when they were in Junior High School.
   d. Four guys who want to make music after finishing school.

2. For how many years have they been making music now?
   a. For 3 years.
   b. For 4 years.
   c. For 5 years.
   d. For 6 years.

3. For how many years has *Rampax* existed?
   a. For 1 year.
   b. For 2 years.
   c. For 3 years.
   d. For 4 years.

4. How often does Tom need help when writing the lyrics of the songs?
   a. He almost always needs help.
   b. He hardly ever needs help.
   c. He constantly needs help.
   d. He occasionally needs help.

5. Why is Tobi popular with girls?
   a. Because he plays awesome guitar solos.
   b. Because he flirts a lot with them.
   c. Because he looks very handsome.
   d. Because he likes being the centre of attention.

6. How important is finishing school for the four guys?
   a. It's rather important.
   b. It's not important at all.
   c. It's more or less important.
   d. It's extremely important.

Task 5 Word order / Sentences about Rampax

1. rarely/The/bad/have/performances/only/guys.

   _____

2. rather/was/Phil's/when/wanted/mother/sceptical/he/have/drums/to.

   _____

3. hardly/John/a/Tobi/miss/ever/rehearsal/and.

   _____

4. perfect/nearly/in/on/Tom/is/writing/lyrics/his.

   _____

WRITING

In der Oberstufe wird die Textproduktion, also das Verfassen verschiedenster Texte wie Briefe, E-Mails, argumentative Aufsätze, Geschichten usw. immer wichtiger. Dabei solltest du nicht nur die korrekte Anwendung der englischen Grammatik im Griff haben, sondern auch ein gutes und abwechslungsreiches Vokabular aufweisen und vor allem deine Texte gut und übersichtlich gliedern. Unterschiedliche Textsorten weisen einen unterschiedlichen Aufbau auf, eines haben aber alle gemeinsam: Absätze (*paragraphs*).

Schon beim Anschauen deines Textes sollten diese *paragraphs* ersichtlich sein. In der Regel hast du jeweils einen Absatz für die Einleitung (*introduction*), einen Absatz für den Hauptteil (*body* – dieser kann sich, je nach Länge deines Textes, wieder in mehrere Absätze gliedern) und schließlich einen Absatz für den Schlussteil (*conclusion*).

Um einen richtig guten Text zu schreiben, verwendest du im Optimalfall auch noch sogenannte *linking words* (Verbindungswörter und Phrasen). Im Anschluss findest du eine Auflistung gängiger *linking words*, welche du in deine Texte einbauen kannst, um sie stilistisch und sprachlich ein bisschen „aufzupeppen". Ein letzter wichtiger Aspekt noch: Bitte überlege dir, BEVOR du zu schreiben beginnst, was du überhaupt schreiben möchtest. Sammle deine Gedanken in Stichworten, lege eventuell eine *mind map* an (*brainstorming*) und erst dann fang mit der eigentlichen Textproduktion an. Nichts ist schwieriger, als einen Text zu schreiben, wenn du eigentlich gar nicht weißt, WAS du schreiben sollst oder willst.

COMMON LINKING WORDS

Addition (Zusatzinformation geben)			
also	ebenso	*too*	auch
and (then)	und (dann)	*equally*	gleichermaßen
further(more)	außerdem	*indeed*	tatsächlich
in fact	tatsächlich	*moreover*	außerdem
in addition (to)	zusätzlich (zu)	*what is more*	außerdem

Comparison (Vergleich)			
compared with	verglichen mit	*in comparison with*	im Vergleich zu
let's compare	vergleichen wir	*likewise*	gleichermaßen
similarly	gleichermaßen	*in the same way*	gleichermaßen

Contrast (Gegenüberstellung)			
but	aber	*however*	wie auch immer
in contrast to	im Gegensatz zu	*instead (of)*	anstelle (von)
naturally	natürlich	*nevertheless*	trotzdem, dennoch
although	obwohl	*even though*	obwohl
of course	natürlich	*on the contrary*	im Gegenteil
on the one hand	einerseits	*on the other hand*	andererseits
still	immer noch	*whereas*	wohingegen

Enumeration (Aufzählung)			
first(ly)	erstens	*second(ly)*	zweitens
in the first place	als erstes	*next*	als Nächstes
last	schließlich	*to end with*	abschließend

Giving examples (Beispiele geben)			
for example	zum Beispiel	*for instance*	zum Beispiel
such as	so wie	*as evidence of*	als Beweis für

Writing

Summary (Zusammenfassung)			
all in all	alles in allem	on the whole	alles in allem
to sum up	zusammenfassend	in conclusion	zusammenfassend
in brief	kurz gefasst	in short	kurz gefasst

Time (Zeitausdrücke)			
after (a while)	nach (einer Weile)	afterwards	danach
at the same time	gleichzeitig	meanwhile	in der Zwischenzeit
next	als nächstes	last	zum Schluss
before (that time)	vor (dieser Zeit)	then	dann
so far	bis jetzt	up to (then)	bis (dann)

Result (Ergebnis)			
as a result	als Ergebnis	consequently	folglich
for that reason	aus diesem Grund	that's the reason	das ist der Grund
hence	daher	therefore	daher
thus	daher	so	daher

Read the text below and complete the gaps with suitable linking words:

Famous people like Angelina Jolie or George Clooney often complain and critizise that newspapers print too many details about their private lives, _____ newspapers say that they simply write what their audience wants to read about. Let's consider these different points of view.

_____, it seems that famous people want as much media attention as possible, especially at the beginning of their careeres. _____ as soon as they are popular enough, _____, most of them really get upset if newspapers give away personal information which they would prefer to keep secret. This was the case with Britney Spears, _____.
_____ the stars' attitude, newspapers say that publicity has a right to know how celebrities spend their money and what they do in their free time. _____, the majority of the readers wants to know who the stars are in love with. That really seems to be a hot topic.

_____, I believe that the public should be told what the lives of the stars are like. _____ stars should have some privacy, especially to protect their families. This means that we should have clear rules about what the media should be allowed to publish.

Writing

INFORMAL (PERSONAL) LETTER

Informal letters sind an Personen gerichtet, die man kennt. Daher gibt es beim Layout nicht so strenge Vorgaben und auch eine *informal language* (also eher umgangssprachliche Ausdrucksweise) ist erlaubt. *Slang* sollte jedoch vermieden werden. Hier eine kurze Checkliste, was bei einem *informal letter* erlaubt ist:

- Abkürzungen (**There's** something else **I've** forgotten.)
- informelle Ausdrücke (**Thanks** for your last letter.)
- informelle Anrede (**Hi** Tim, **Hello** Sarah)
- unvollständige Sätze (Great news about your brother … in diesem Satz fehlt zB das Verb)
- informelles Vokabular und *phrasal verbs* (**go on** statt continue, **mate** statt friend)
- direkte Fragen (What was your holiday like?)
- viele aktive Phrasen (They've built a new cinema.)
- informelle *sentence linkers* (**Well**, I think that's about all I wanted to say.)
- Rufzeichen setzen, um etwas zu betonen (I'm going out with this amazing guy!!)
- Gedankenstriche, um Erklärungen abzugeben (I'm so busy – you know what it's like.)

Aufbau und Layout von *informal letters*

> Adresse (aber nicht Name!) des Absenders:
> Hausnummer und Straßenname
> Name der Stadt und Postleitzahl
> Datum
>
> Dear …, *
>
> *Introduction:* Solche Briefe werden durch einen kurzen Verweis auf ein vorangegangenes Treffen oder Telefonat eingeleitet. Man bedankt sich für erhaltene Post und/oder Neuigkeiten oder erinnert sich an vergangene Treffen oder Erlebnisse. Wenn man länger nichts von sich hat hören lassen, entschuldigt man sich und erklärt normalerweise den Grund dafür.
>
> *Body:* Das ist der Hauptteil deines Briefes, er bezieht sich auf die genannte Aufgabenstellung. Wichtig ist, dass du dir diese immer ganz genau durchliest und auf **alle** angeführten Angabepunkte auch eingehst. Behandle alle Angabepunkte entsprechend ausführlich, aber „verzettle" dich nicht bei einzelnen Aspekten, damit dir für den Schluss genügend Zeit bleibt. Achte auch auf eine entsprechende Gliederung (*paragraphs*) und leite jede neue Idee oder jeden neuen Gedanken auch durch einen neuen Absatz ein. Verbinde diese durch entsprechende *linking words* und achte stets auf die korrekte Verwendung der Grammatik. Erkläre eventuell auch, was du dir als Reaktion auf deinen Brief erwartest.
>
> *Conclusion:* Hier kannst du deine Vorfreude oder Erwartungshaltung auf die Antwort oder Reaktion auf deinen Brief ausdrücken. Gegebenenfalls kannst du Grüße an gemeinsame Freunde oder Bekannte übermitteln. Es ist auch möglich, den Brief unter Angabe einer noch durchzuführenden Tätigkeit zu beenden (zB man muss noch für die Englisch-Schularbeit lernen und kann daher leider nicht weiterschreiben).
>
> Yours, …

---

* ACHTUNG – im Englischen kommt hier ein Beistrich und kein Rufzeichen!

Useful phrases and expressions for *informal letters*

Introduction: Hi! How are things? How are you? How's it going?
Thanks a lot for your letter. It was good to hear from you and I'm happy that you're fine.
I'm really sorry I haven't written for such a long time.
I just haven't been able to get round to writing recently because …
I have been so busy at school because …
Sorry it's been so long since I last wrote/since we last heard from each other but …
Sorry/glad to hear about …

Writing

Body:
Listen, did I tell you about ...?
Anyway, I'm writing to tell you ...
You'll never believe what happened last weekend/yesterday/...!
Oh, and another thing I must absolutely tell you: ...
Believe it or not but ...
Guess what! ...
Before I forget, ...
That reminds me to (phone Sarah) / of (our last school trip)
What's more ...
Plus ...

Conclusion:
Well, got to go now because my mum has just come home.
Write back soon and maybe we can arrange a meeting next weekend.
Do write again soon. Drop me a line soon.
Look forward to seeing you soon.
Give my regards to ...
Give my love to ...
Say hello to ...

Signing off:
Love/Lots of love/Love and kisses/All my love,
Best wishes/regards,
Take care,

It's your turn! Complete the letter with suitable expressions:

28 Beech Avenue
Bristol BR 9 8SV
28th September 20 . .

Dear Michael,

_____ your postcard from Spain, sounded as if it was a great holiday. Did you go to Madrid in the end or did you spend all the time playing volleyball at the beach? Last year my uncle went to Spain too and he also enjoyed it very much.

_____ , I'm writing to ask you if you would like to go to the *Lady Gaga* concert with me. She's going to perform in Vienna at the end of October. I think it's the 23rd but I have to check that first. Have you ever been to one of her concerts _____ ? My brother once was and he said it was absolutely great. Good show and perfect performance! By the way, that _____ me to buy her new single that is called "Poker Face". That's one of her best!

Oh, and _____ I must absolutely tell you. Jenny, this girl from 5A asked me if I wanted to go out with her. At first I wasn't sure what to say _____ I suggested going to the cinema together. So we're going to watch this vampire movie next Saturday – I think it's called "Twilight". Of course I will keep you updated!

_____ , I must finish now because I haven't tidied up my room yet and if mum sees that she'll be angry with me. It's always the same. Drop me _____ soon or call me. As you like but let's stay in contact. Give my _____ to Paula.

All the best, Kevin

Writing

Task 1

Write an informal letter to one of your best friends telling him/her about your last summer holidays. Tell him/her where you went, what you did there, what the hotel and the food was like and what you liked best.
Write the letter in about 150 words, don't forget to structure it and to use appropriate linking words.

Task 2

Imagine that you have an Asian pen friend living in China. As these two cultures are completely different you explain to your pen friend how Christmas is celebrated in Austria. Inform him/her about how Austrians spend that day, when exactly they celebrate, what they eat and what the most important aspects of this festival are. Write your letter in about 150 words.

Task 3 (Mustertext im Lösungsheft)

Last Friday you were invited to your best friend's birthday party. It was one of the best parties you have ever been to. You now write a letter to another friend of yours, explaining why you liked the party so much, what the people were like and why the whole evening was so funny for you. At the end of your letter ask him/her to meet you next weekend. Write again about 150 words.

FORMAL LETTER

Formelle, höfliche Briefe (*formal letters*) sind meist an unbekannte Personen gerichtet und erscheinen auf den ersten Blick vielleicht ein wenig kompliziert. Das liegt daran, dass ihr Layout, also ihr Aufbau, etwas anspruchsvoller und der sprachliche Ausdruck weitaus höflicher sind, als dies bei *informal letters* der Fall ist. Es gibt verschiedene Arten von *formal letters*, hier ein kleiner Überblick:

- *letter of complaint* (Beschwerdebrief)
- *letter of application* (Bewerbung)
- *apology* (Entschuldigung)
- *request for information/inquiry* (Anfrage)
- *business letters* (Geschäftsbriefe)

Eines haben all diese formellen Briefe allerdings gemeinsam: den sprachlich höflichen Ausdruck (*formal language*). Das heißt, umgangssprachliche Ausdrücke werden gemieden, die Sätze sind meist lang und haben einen eher unpersönlichen Ton. Auch Abkürzungen (zB *I'd like to* im Gegensatz zu *I **would** like to*) kommen bei den *formal letters* **nicht** vor. Schau dir einmal folgende Beispiele an und entscheide, was davon *formal language* und *informal language* ist:

What is formal? Underline the formal expressions:

1. a. It gives me great pleasure to ...
   b. I'm very pleased to ...
2. a. We might arrange a meeting next Wednesday.
   b. Let's meet next Wednesday.
3. a. Please give my regards to your parents.
   b. All the best to your mum and dad.
4. a. Thanks a lot for helping me.
   b. I am very grateful for your help.
5. a. I look forward to hearing from you soon.
   b. I'm happy to hear from you soon.
6. a. Would you be so kind to send me ...
   b. Please send me ...
7. a. Please will you ...
   b. We would be grateful if ...
8. a. Just tell me if you need anything.
   b. In case you need anything, please inform me.
9. a. Let me ask you something else.
   b. Another question I would like to ask is ...
10. a. Is it a problem if ...
    b. Would you mind if ...
11. a. I apologize for the delay in writing.
    b. Sorry, I haven't written earlier.
12. a. We'd like to order ...
    b. We would like to order ...
13. a. Great – I meet all my mates next weekend.
    b. I am very happy to meet all my friends next weekend.
14. a. Could you please hand over the English book.
    b. Pass me the English book, please.
15. a. There's something I've forgotten.
    b. Something has been forgotten.

Writing

Aufbau und Layout von *formal letters*

Adresse (aber nicht Name!) des Absenders:
Hausnummer und Straßenname
Name der Stadt und Postleitzahl
Datum

Dear Sir or Madam (Sir/Madam), *

Introduction: Die Einleitung wird eher kurz gehalten und beinhaltet den Grund deines Schreibens. Für den Empfänger deines Briefes muss bereits nach der Einleitung klar sein, warum du diesen Brief geschrieben hast und was dein Anliegen ist. Je klarer und eindeutiger du das machst, desto besser.

Body: Lies dir die Aufgabenstellung genau durch, denn sie entscheidet darüber, welche Art von *formal letter* du schreiben musst. Sollst du dich nach etwas erkundigen (einer Unterkunft, einem Preis, Aktivitäten ...) oder sollst du dich beschweren oder gar für einen Ferienjob bewerben? Auch hier müssen alle Angabepunkte erfüllt, dein Brief logisch in Absätze gegliedert und diese durch *linking words* verbunden sein. Zusätzlich zu sprachlicher und grammatikalischer Richtigkeit muss nun auch noch auf den richtigen sprachlichen Stil (*formal language*) geachtet werden. Der *body of letter* wird dadurch beendet, indem du erklärst, was du dir als Reaktion auf deinen Brief erwartest.

Conclusion: Dein Brief wird durch höfliche Floskeln beendet, welche deine Vorfreude/deine Erwartungshaltung auf eine Antwort oder Reaktion ausdrücken. Am besten ist es, wenn du einige dieser Floskeln einfach auswendig lernst, denn sie sind bis zu einem gewissen Grad standardisiert und bei *formal letters* immer wieder gut verwendbar.

Yours faithfully/Yours sincerely, ...

---

* ACHTUNG – im Englischen kommt hier ein Beistrich und kein Rufzeichen!

Useful phrases and expressions for *formal letters*

Introduction:
- I am writing to ...
- I am interested in ...
- I would like to ask a few questions/inform myself about/receive some information about ...
- It would be helpful if you could ...
- Would you be so kind as to ...
- I am writing to apologize for ...
- I am interested in applying (*bewerben*) for the post of ...
- I am writing to express my concern about ...
- I am writing to complain about ...

Body:
- Firstly, secondly, thirdly ...
- Another question I have is about ...
- Could you also tell me if/when/whether ...
- Could you be so kind to ...
- Would you mind sending me some information about ...
- I would be (very) grateful/thankful if you could ...
- I would like to know more about ...
- Finally, lastly ...

Conclusion:
- I hope you will ...
- I look forward to hearing from you soon.
- I look forward to receiving your answer as soon as possible.
- I thank you for giving me all the details and look forward to your reply.
- Thank you for your attention and I look forward to your answer.

Writing

Task 1

It's your turn! Complete this request for information with suitable expressions:

36 Milton Beach Drive
Ludlow SP 3 4GM
15th October 20 . .

Dear Sir/Madam,

I have decided to spend my upcoming Christmas holidays in Canada and I _____ in going skiing at the *Lake Side Resort* in Canada. As I have never been to Canada before, I _____ in order to receive some important information.

_____, and this might be the most essential question, do you still have a free bedroom left? I would arrive the week before Christmas and stay for seven days. I would _____ a calm and comfortable room. Secondly, is there a possibility to make ski-tours as well? If yes, could you be _____ to supply me with relevant information so that I can plan my tours ahead? Thirdly, what is the weather like at that time of the year? As I said, this is my first journey to Canada _____ I am not sure what to take with me. What are the average temperatures? If I do believe some friends of mine, the temperatures are far below zero.

Another _____ I have is about the price of the hotel room. On the Internet it said that the price would be 45 Euros per day. Is that per person or per room? And could you also tell me _____ breakfast is included in the price and where we can have dinner? Are there any good restaurants nearby?

There is another question I would like to _____ you: does your hotel offer a wellness and spa area? If yes, is it included in the price or does that _____ extra?

Finally, I _____ to know more about a possible transfer from the train station to the hotel. Does the possibility of such a transfer exist or should I rather take a taxi? If I go by taxi, how long do you think that will take me?

I would be very _____ if you could answer all these questions as they are very important for me to properly plan my journey.

I look forward to _____ your answer as soon as possible.

Yours faithfully,

Jim Novis

Writing

Task 2

Now read the answer of the hotel manager and fill in suitable VERBS (taking care of the tense) to complete the letter:

> 248 Wellington Road
> Canada VC 87 6 DT
> 24th October 20..
>
> Dear Mr Novis,
>
> Thank you very much for your letter dated 15th October. I am very pleased to _____ (*übermitteln*) you all the information requested.
>
> First of all, we do have a double room left for the desired period. It is a cosy and comfortable room and I am absolutely sure that you _____ (*genießen*) your stay in our hotel. Secondly, even though the area here is very famous for skiing, you can also _____ (*machen*) ski-tours as there are several good and also difficult ways you can go. Enclosed you _____ (*finden*) some brochures. Thirdly, the weather is usually very cold. On average we have about minus 18 degrees but there is usually a lot of sunshine so that the freezing temperatures do not feel so cold. Anyway, I would _____ (*empfehlen*) to take warm clothes with you.
>
> In your letter you also _____ (*erkundigen*) about the prices. As the time around Christmas is high season the 45 Euros are per person but breakfast is _____ (*eingeschlossen*) in the price. We _____ (*anbieten*) a breakfast buffet with various national and international dishes. Apart from that you can _____ (*wählen*) between different drinks, too. As far as dinner is concerned you can choose between eating in our restaurant (which either offers buffet or à la carte) or going out to Littleton, the next city where you find several exquisit and delicious restaurants.
>
> The *Lake Side Resort* is equipped with a nice and big wellness area which provides our guests with sauna, a whirlpool and separated relaxing areas. All these features are included in the price. If you wish, you can also have a massage but this, however, must be _____ (*bezahlen*) extra.
>
> Concerning the transfer we offer a shuttle service that directly _____ (*bringen*) our guests from the train station to the hotel. The journey only _____ (*dauern*) about 25 minutes and once you _____ (*ankommen*) at the hotel, a welcome drink is waiting for you. Just let me know whether you want me to book you for the transport.
>
> I hope I could _____ (*versorgen/ausstatten*) you with all the relevant information and I look forward to hearing from you and welcoming you in our *Lake Side Resort*.
>
> Yours faithfully,
>
> Robert Logdon

Writing

Task 3

You are going to take part in a students exchange programme next year. You have already received the name and address of your host family in New Jersey. You now write a letter to them, introducing yourself and asking all relevant questions. Write the letter in about 150 words. Don't forget to be polite because you want to make a good first impression.

Task 4 (Mustertext im Lösungsheft)

Imagine you bought a new Apple Laptop which, unfortunately, doesn't work properly now. So you decide to write a letter to the Apple Help Service, informing them about your problem and asking for help. Write the letter in about 150 words, inventing all the necessary details (e.g. which problems your laptop has).

Task 5

You have signed up for taking part in a sports competition. Because of having fallen ill some days ago, you now cannot join this competition and so you write a letter to your trainer, informing him/her about your illness and the fact that you do not participate. Again, write the letter in about 150 words and make sure you ask your trainer to understand your situation.

E-MAIL

E-Mails sind eine gute, einfache und oft genutzte Möglichkeit zu kommunizieren. Sie sind meist relativ kurz, haben formal einen einfachen Aufbau und sind durch eine eher informelle Sprache gekennzeichnet, vor allem wenn sie an Freunde und Bekannte geschickt werden. Nichtsdestotrotz sollten sie höflich formuliert, in Absätze gegliedert und diese durch *linking words* verbunden sein. Abkürzungen (*shouldn't* statt *should not*) und Gedankenstriche (*One more thing – can you tell Joana about the party?*) sind in Ordnung und können in E-Mails ruhig verwendet werden. Adresse (in diesem Fall die E-Mail-Adresse) und Datum müssen nicht extra geschrieben werden, da diese ja ohnehin aufscheinen. Sehen wir uns nun einmal den theoretischen Aufbau einer E-Mail an:

Aufbau und Layout von E-Mails

Greeting: Die Anrede in der Begrüßung ist informell und kann – wenn das Mail an mehrere Personen geschickt wird – auch eine allgemeine Formulierung beinhalten (zB *Hi there*). Eine Einleitung im eigentlichen Sinn gibt es nicht, man kommt gleich zum Hauptteil und damit zum Grund des Mails.

Short message: E-Mails sind kurz und beschränken sich auf das Wesentliche. Im Gegensatz zu den *formal letters* kann man hier auf sämtliche höfliche Floskeln verzichten und kommt *straight to the point*. Sollte dein Mail eine Antwort auf ein bereits vorangegangenes Mail sein, dann achte darauf, dass alle eventuell gestellten Fragen beantwortet wurden. Selbstverständlich kannst auch du direkte Fragen in deinem Mail stellen. Die Kommunikation via E-Mail ist ein reines Mittel zum Zweck, um Informationen auszutauschen. Je direkter das gemacht wird, desto besser und unmissverständlicher sind deine Mails.

Signing off: Auch hier werden wieder informelle Wendungen benutzt, welche sich möglicherweise auf ein zukünftiges Ereignis beziehen (zB *I hope to see you there* oder *We wait to hear from you*). „Unterschrieben" wird mit dem Vornamen, es ist aber auch durchaus üblich, nur seine Initialien als Unterschrift unter das Mail zu setzen. Das kommt einerseits darauf an, was dir persönlich lieber ist, andererseits, wie gut du die Person kennst, der du schreibst.

Writing

Useful phrases and expressions for *e-mails*

Greeting: Hi, Kate/Peter/Susan/…
Hi,
Hi there,
Hello everybody,

Short message: Just thought I'd remind you that …
I don't know if you remember but …
One thing I'd like to ask you is …
Another thing I want to know is …
One more thing that's important to know is …
One last thing – can you …
By the way – …
I just wanted to tell you …
Of course you can / we must …
The most important thing really is …
That's fantastic, isn't it?
How about meeting next …?
We must meet up next …!
I'll definitely be around when you get here.

Signing off: I hope to see you there.
See you (soon).
Hugs and kisses,
Love,

Task 1

Take a look at the following e-mail conversation between Caroline and Lydia. Read the mails and put them in the correct order:

A
Hi Lydia,
Yea, I know what you mean – my two little brothers also annoy me! It's nasty. Yes, you do have to dress up, I think that's quite funny. I'm going to be a witch – mum has already bought the costume. It's awesome! As I already said – the party is on the 31st of October, it starts at eight in the evening and will probably last until midnight. But we'll see … :-)
Hugs and kisses,
Caroline

B
Hello Caroline,
Thanks a lot for the invitation. Hallowe'en parties are always great fun! I'm fine but I really have a lot of work with school. And Jamie, my little brother, keeps going on my nerves … – I guess you know what I mean.
Sure I come to your party! But there's one thing I'd like to know: do I have to dress up?
Waiting for your answer,
L.

C
Hi,
Cranberry muffins?? That would be fantastic!! I love them!!
I don't know if you remember but Monica Mayers dressed up as ghost at last year's Hallowe'en party and that was really great. So if you don't have any other ideas, you might dress up as ghost, too. But you'll see …
So see you then on the 31st of October. …
And don't let your brother go on your nerves … :-)
See you,
Caroline

D
Hi Caroline,
Eight o'clock sounds good. I've already asked my mum, she can take me to your house and pick me up again. I haven't decided about a costume yet, but luckily there's still some time left …
One last thing – shall I take something with me? I could bake some cranberry muffins, they are usually very tasty.
Love,
L.

E
Hi Lydia,
How are things going? I organise a Hallowe'en party on the 31st of October and want to invite you. Just tell me whether you can come and if yes, I'm going to give you all the details.
Love,
Caroline

Writing

Task 2

Now answer the questions related to the mails:

1. Why and when does Caroline organise a party?

   _____

2. Which costumes do the two girls choose?

   _____

3. What does Lydia take with her to the party?

   _____

4. Which are the two English expressions for the German *jemandem auf die Nerven gehen*?

   _____

5. In the e-mails, both the will-future and the going-to-future are used. Explain the difference in German words.

   _____

6. Can you tell another English word for *whether*?

   _____

Task 3

Imagine that you are going to celebrate your 15th birthday in two weeks. Your parents allow you to have a big party so you write an e-mail to all your friends, inviting them to this great event. Tell them everything they have to know (why/when/where/what to take with them/if they can take friends with them/…) and express your hope that they celebrate with you. Write the mail in about 120 words.

Task 4

Your friend has invited you to visit him/her in Bristol, England. You now write an e-mail asking him/her everything that is important for you and the things you want to know (e.g. about weather/what you'll do/which clothes to take with you …). Write the mail in about 120 words.

Task 5 (Mustertext im Lösungsheft)

You went to the cinema with a beautiful girl/a handsome boy and you've just come home. You promised your best friend to write him/her a mail about what the evening was like, as soon as you return. Write the mail (again about 120 words) telling him/her whether the evening was top or flop and why!

STORY

Eine *story* zu schreiben kann eigentlich ganz schön spannend sein – vorausgesetzt man weiß, was man schreiben will. Daher ist es auch bei dieser Textsorte unerlässlich, sich zunächst einmal Gedanken über den Inhalt zu machen. Nur wer einen Plan hat, also einen roten Faden, wird es schaffen, eine gute und mitreißende Geschichte zu schreiben. Der Hauptgrund, warum *stories* geschrieben werden (abgesehen davon, dass die Lehrerin/der Lehrer sie aufgibt …) ist es, die Leserin/den Leser zu unterhalten. Das heißt, dass du beim Schreiben einer (Kurz-)Geschichte deiner Kreativität und Fantasie freien Lauf lassen kannst. Klingt doch gut, oder nicht?

Vom Schreibstil her sollten *stories* eher neutral sein, das heißt, dass weder besonders formelle noch besonders informelle (umgangssprachliche) Ausdrücke verwendet werden. Eine sogenannte *descriptive language* wäre perfekt; das bedeutet, dass du möglichst viele *adjectives* und *adverbs* in deine Geschichte einbaust, um sie spannender, dramatischer und einfach interessanter zu machen. Je genauer du Details beschreibst, desto besser kann sich die Leserin/der Leser in die Handlung und die Szene hineinversetzen.

Writing

Nachdem du deine Geschichte geschrieben hast, überprüfe bitte auch nochmals die Verwendung der Zeiten. *Stories* sind fast immer in der *past tense* geschrieben – hier musst du auf den korrekten Einsatz von *past simple* (kurze Handlung, Erzählzeit) und *past progressive* (lange Handlung, Beschreibung der Rahmenbedingungen, genaue Zeitangabe) achten.

Besondere Bedeutung kommt beim Schreiben einer *story* auch den Absätzen (*paragraphs*) zu. Sie gliedern und unterteilen deine Geschichte und verhelfen zu einem sinnvollen Aufbau und einer logischen Handlungsabfolge. Überlege dir wieder **vor** dem Schreiben, wie deine Geschichte beginnen soll, wodurch du den Hauptteil spannend und lesenswert gestalten kannst und wie deine Geschichte endet. Auch hier kann ein *brainstorming* vorab sehr hilfreich sein. Nicht unerwähnt bleiben sollte an dieser Stelle auch wieder die Verwendung der *linking words*, um eine gelungene Überleitung zwischen den einzelnen Absätzen zu sichern. Doch wie wird eine *story* nun aufgebaut?

Aufbau von *(short) stories*

Setting the scene: Bevor du zu schreiben beginnst, solltest du dir einmal ganz aufmerksam die Angabe durchlesen. Hast du vielleicht einen Anfangs- oder Endsatz vorgegeben und musst deine Geschichte diesem anpassen? Wenn ja, dann tu das auch bitte wirklich und schreibe keine *story*, die mit der Angabe eigentlich gar nichts zu tun hat. Sollte kein Anfang oder Ende vorgegeben sein, dann gehe ganz genau auf die Aufgabenstellung und das damit verbundene Thema ein. Beschreibe dann als erstes die Rahmenbedingungen (das heißt das WANN und WO deiner Geschichte). Wer sind die handelnden Personen? Stelle sie vor und beschreibe sie. Oder hat deine Geschichte einen Ich-Erzähler? Dann stelle auch diesen vor. Ziel dieser „Einleitung" ist es, die Leserin/den Leser zum Lesen deiner Geschichte zu motivieren. Gelingt dir dies in dieser Anfangsphase nicht, dann hat der Beginn deiner *story* zu wenig vielversprechend geklungen.

Development of the narrative: Das ist der eigentliche Hauptteil, welcher sich wiederum in mehrere Absätze gliedern kann. Jeder neue Gedanke und jede neue Handlung sollte durch einen neuen Absatz eingeleitet werden (auch hier sollten die *paragraphs* optisch auf den ersten Blick ersichtlich sein). Die Haupthandlung wird nun genauer beschrieben, versuche dies durch den richtigen Einsatz von *linking words*, *adjectives* und *adverbs* möglichst abwechslungsreich und interessant zu gestalten.

Conclusion: Jede Erzählung braucht natürlich auch ein Ende. Nütze dies, um die Gefühle der Hauptpersonen abschließend zu beschreiben oder einen eventuellen Ausblick in die Zukunft zu geben.

Useful phrases for story writing

One Saturday afternoon / On a warm spring evening / It was a rainy day in September when ...
At first / The first thing that happened was ...
Next / Then ...
Suddenly / All of a sudden ...
After a while / After some time ...
Meanwhile / In the meantime ...
While / When ...
In the end / Finally / Eventually (ACHTUNG: das heißt nicht „eventuell" sondern „schließlich"!)
A few days later / About one week later ...

Useful adjectives that might make your story more exciting			
afraid	ängstlich	*frightened*	verängstigt
brave	tapfer	*courageous*	tapfer
desperate	verzweifelt	*injured*	verletzt
proud	stolz	*trapped*	gefangen
unconscious	bewusstlos	*surprising*	überraschend
reckless	rücksichtslos	*amazing*	außergewöhnlich
relieved	erleichtert	*reliable*	verlässlich
unbelievable	unglaublich	*unexpected*	unerwartet

Writing

Task 1

Study the following *story* and fill in the correct form of the tense: past tense (simple or progressive) and past perfect tense:

It _____ (*be*) a sunny but rather cold day in late August last year when I _____ (*leave*) for my tennis holiday camp. It was the first time that I _____ (*go*) on holiday alone and I was really looking forward to it. On my 15th birthday, which _____ (*be*) the month before, my parents _____ (*tell*) me that I was allowed to go there. I was really happy and excited and thought that it would be the best week of my life ever. However, I _____ (*not expect*) a thing like that to happen.

During the first days everything was fine and I _____ (*enjoy*) myself a lot while playing tennis and going swimming. Anyway, after some time something really exciting and unexpected _____ (*happen*). While I _____ (*lie*) close by the lake, a little girl _____ (*fall*) into the water and immediately _____ (*start*) to scream. I _____ (*stop*) reading, _____ (*drop*) my book, jumped up _____ (*run*) to the water as fast as I could. Meanwhile several people _____ (*stand*) around, watching the helpless, little girl but not doing anything. Without thinking I _____ (*jump*) into the deep water and _____ (*rescue*) the poor girl who was already completely exhausted. We _____ (*swim*) back and with all my strength I _____ (*pull*) her out of the water. That was really hard work. In the meantime somebody _____ (*call*) an ambulance and I could already hear the loud siren in the distance. While the little girl _____ (*take*) into the ambulance, I could see people pointing and staring at me. At first I _____ (*feel*) a little bit uncomfortable but then a police officer _____ (*come*) to me and thanked me that I _____ (*rescue*) the drowning girl. A few days later my parents picked me up from the camp and they _____ (*be*) very proud.

Task 2

Now take a look at the adjectives taken from the story above and find the opposite

sunny _____

late _____

happy _____

best _____

close _____

deep _____

little _____

loud _____

cold _____

alone _____

excited _____

unexpected _____

fast _____

helpless _____

exhausted _____

uncomfortable _____

Writing

Task 3 (Mustertext im Lösungsheft)

Write a story starting with the following sentence:

When I woke up on that foggy November morning I was tired and exhausted and I would have never thought that a thing like that could happen.

You can write any type of story (romance, adventure, science fiction, action, comedy, ...) as long as you divide it into paragraphs, use linking words and make it interesting and worth reading. Write about 150–180 words.

Task 4

Write a story which ends with the sentence given:

Lying in bed that evening I thought about what had happened that day and I just had to smile.

Again, the type of story is free for you to choose but make sure you write an exciting story! Write 150–180 words.

Task 5

Write a story about one day in your life which went completely wrong. Write 150–180 words and don't forget to give the reasons why that day was such a disaster!

ARTICLE

Articles sind Texte, welche in Zeitungen, Zeitschriften oder Magazinen erscheinen und der Leserin/dem Leser auf interessante Art und Weise Fakten und Ideen vermitteln. Um einen guten und gelungenen *article* zu schreiben, musst du die Antworten auf folgende Fragen im Hinterkopf haben:

- **Where will your article be published?**

    Schreibst du einen Artikel für die Schülerzeitung oder für ein Jugendmagazin? Wie sind Stil und Sprache dieser Zeitung bzw. Zeitschrift (eher formal oder informell)?

- **Who will read the article?**

    Wer liest deinen Artikel eigentlich? Sind es die Schülerinnen/die Schüler einer ganzen Schule (also von 11–18 Jahren) oder nur Jugendliche oder Gleichaltrige? Bedenke auch immer, was deine Zielgruppe über ein bestimmtes Thema eventuell schon weiß. Es ist daher immer wichtig zu wissen, wer die Zielgruppe ist, auch deshalb, damit du deinen Wortschatz und deinen Ausdruck an die Leserin/den Leser anpassen kannst.

- **What information should you include?**

    Baue in deinen Artikel auf jeden Fall persönliche Erfahrungen ein, aber auch Ideen und Gedanken, mit denen sich deine Zielgruppe (also zB Jugendliche) identifizieren kann, und die als aktuell, zeitgemäß und interessant empfunden werden.

- **What is the purpose of the article?**

    Sinn eines *articles* ist es, die Leserin/den Leser über ein bestimmtes Thema zu informieren, und zwar auf eine mitreißende und unterhaltende Art und Weise. Es sollen einerseits Fakten, aber – wie oben bereits erwähnt – auch persönliche Ideen und Erfahrungen gegeben und dargestellt werden.

- **What style should I use?**

    Der Stil hängt natürlich davon ab, wo dein *article* veröffentlicht wird (also vom Medium) – und das bringt uns wieder zur ersten Frage zurück. Meist werden Artikel, welche in Schüler- oder Jugendzeitschriften publiziert werden, eher in einem saloppen (aber nicht umgangsprachlichen) Ton geschrieben. Abkürzungen sind daher durchaus in Ordnung und dürfen verwendet werden.

Writing

Aufbau von *articles*

Headline: Jeder Artikel braucht eine Überschrift – und zwar eine gute, denn sie entscheidet darüber, ob die Leserin/der Leser den Artikel liest oder nicht. Denk nur daran, wenn du zB eine Tageszeitung durchblätterst. Welche Artikel liest du? Genau, jene, die eine für dich interessante und vielversprechende Überschrift haben. Ein Artikel kann durchaus neben der Überschrift auch noch eine Art von Unterüberschrift haben, das ist allerdings optional.

Proper text: Im „Kampf" darum, Leserinnen/Leser für deinen *article* zu finden, zählt nicht nur die Überschrift, sondern auch vor allem der erste Teil des eigentlichen Textes/Artikels. Dieser muss unbedingt das Interesse und die Neugierde des Lesers wecken, denn nur dann liest dieser auch wirklich weiter. Möglichkeiten, dies kreativ zu tun, sind unter anderem:

- der Leserin/dem Leser eine Frage zu stellen (*e.g. Have you ever eaten Indonesian food?*)
- das eigentliche Thema zu definieren – vielleicht sogar kombiniert mit einer Frage (*e.g. Have you ever asked yourself what "blogs" are? Well, here is the answer: that's the short form of the word "weblogs" and it's a frequently updated web-journal.*)
- ein bizarres oder besonders erstaunliches Statement zu geben (*e.g. Teenagers whose parents smoke are five times more likely to start smoking themselves*)
- ein Sprichwort zu formulieren (*e.g. The early bird catches the worm*) oder auch
- ein Zitat wiederzugeben (*e.g. To be or not to be, that's the question*)

Unterteile einzelne Gedanken und Ideen wieder in eigene Absätze und versuche das Interesse der Leserin/des Lesers weiterhin aufrechtzuerhalten. Eventuell in der Einleitung gestellte Fragen sollten in der eigentlichen Abhandlung beantwortet werden. Das heißt, stelle nicht am Anfang eine Frage wie *"What actually is bullying?"* und gib dann keine Antwort darauf.

Closing: Ein gelungener Abschluss hinterlässt einen guten Gesamteindruck. Hierfür könntest du inhaltlich an den Anfang deines *articles* zurückkehren, damit sich der Kreis schließt. Ebenso kannst du mittels einer kurzen Zusammenfassung nochmals die wichtigsten Aspekte hervorheben. Auch ein humorvolles oder gar provokantes Statement ist eine gute Möglichkeit für das Ende eines Artikels. Ganz egal, wofür du dich entscheidest, wichtig ist, auch den Schlussteil interessant und lesenswert zu gestalten.

Headlines

Überschriften sollten kurz und prägnant sein (*catchy*) und du kannst hier ruhig auf die Verwendung von Artikeln verzichten. Manchmal bestehen Überschriften auch nur aus einzelnen Wörtern und die Verben fehlen fast vollständig (*e.g. Teenager saved baby*). Durch das Lesen der Überschrift sollte man bereits eine Idee haben, wovon der Artikel handelt, sie sollten daher einen gewissen Grad an Information beinhalten.

Task 1

Match the following headlines with their corresponding opening lines

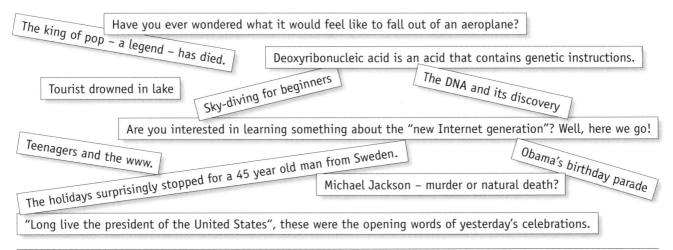

Writing

Useful phrases for writing an article

Adressing the reader:
Have you ever ...
What do you think about ...
You may be wondering ... / ask yourself ...
You may not agree with me, but I think ...

Describing experiences:
It happened to me when ...
This is what happened when ...
Here is what it feels like to ...
I'll never forget ...
I can remember (the day) when ...
It's hard to describe a feeling like that but ...

General expressions:
You can imagine ...
If you ask me ...
Another thing is that ...
It's also worth mentioning that ...
What shouldn't be forgotten is that ...

Task 2

Read the following article for a youth magazine and correct the 17 mistakes:

> Just crazy about rock climbing!
>
> You may be wondering why there are people which are crazy about something that can be quite dangerouse. Well ... some time ago I was wondering about it, to. And than I gave it a try ... Here is what it feels like to climb walls, fight your own fear and overcome your personel limits.
>
> I can remember the day when I dicided to go climbing for the first time. Of course I didn't know what to accept but I really felt thrilling. I went together with a friend of me, a guy who has climbed for almost all his live. He introduced the most important aspects to me, how to handel the rope and stuff like that. And then ... off I went.
>
> Surely, I did a bad job because I quickly found out that climbing is more difficult than I thought. I started to sweat on my hands which made it hardly possible to grab the stone and push my body upwards. But somehow I sueeded and I moved upwards a few meters. And that was the moment when I could feel the full sensation and the fascination.
>
> I've been climbing now for two years and it simply didn't let me go again. In a way I got stuck with the kick you get out of it. Besides it really keep you fit and you constantly meet new people with the same interrest as you.
>
> So, are you still wondering or do you already think about giving it a try yourself?

Task 3

After having read the article, try to answer the following questions:

- How does the writer try to interest the reader?
- In which paragraph does the writer give reasonable arguments for rock climbing?
- What is significant about the article's end?

Writing

Task 4

An English-language magazine for students is running a series of articles entitled *"Just crazy about ..."* in which young people can write about their interests and hobbies. Write an article for the magazine in about 180 words but don't forget to catch the reader's attention!

Task 5

Your school is currently running a competition about writing interesting articles related to the topic of school trips. You have decided to take part in the competition and you now write the requested article (about 180 words).

Task 6 (Mustertext im Lösungsheft)

Imagine that your teacher has set the following homework: write an article entitled *"I've always wanted to ..."*. Don't forget to structure your article and to create interest. Your article should have about 180 words.

REPORTS

Einerseits schreibt man einen *report*, wenn eine sachliche Beschreibung einer Situation oder eines Ereignisses gefragt ist. Andererseits findet diese Textsorte auch dann Verwendung, wenn Empfehlungen für zukünftige Handlungen abgegeben werden sollen (zB Was kann getan werden, um deinen Heimatort jugendfreundlicher zu gestalten?). Auch beim Verfassen eines *reports* sollten folgende Fragen nicht offen und ungeklärt bleiben:

- **What's the purpose of the report?**

  Mach dir immer, bevor du zu arbeiten beginnst, bewusst, was die eigentliche Aufgabenstellung ist. Sollst du Empfehlungen abgeben, Vorschläge machen, Informationen weiterleiten oder eine Situation beurteilen? Nur wenn du weißt, was du zu tun hast, kannst du einen guten *report* schreiben.

- **Who will read it?**

  Normalerweise sind die Leser eines *reports* diejenigen, die den *report* auch in Auftrag gegeben haben, also Arbeitskollegen, ein Arbeitgeber oder eine übergeordnete Institution. Ein *report* richtet sich entweder an eine Einzelperson oder an eine Gruppe von Personen – in jedem Fall ist die Leserin/der Leser aber mit dem Thema vertraut. Das heißt, im Gegensatz zum *article* muss hier das Thema nicht extra vorgestellt werden.

- **What style should be used?**

  Reports sind gekennzeichnet durch die Verwendung eines sachlichen und eher unpersönlichen Stils. Aussagen in der Ichform (*I think that ...*) sollten wenn möglich vermieden werden. Stattdessen findet das Passiv (*passive voice*) hier oft Verwendung und trägt dazu bei, einen neutralen Tonfall zu treffen. Beim Verfassen eines *reports* gilt in jedem Fall: In der Kürze liegt die Würze. Lass also unnötige Details und Ausschweifungen weg und konzentriere dich auf das Wesentliche.

- **What information should be included?**

  Alle in der Aufgabenstellung enthaltenen Fragen müssen beantwortet werden. Vorschläge können ergänzend eingefügt sein und Beschreibungen enthalten.

- **How to structure it?**

  Klare und eindeutige (aussagekräftige) Überschriften helfen der Leserin/dem Leser sich zu orientieren. Jede neue Idee bzw. jeder neue Gedanke muss durch einen neuen Absatz gekennzeichnet und gegliedert sein. Bei der Aufzählung einzelner Ideen kann man zum Beispiel auch Aufzählungszeichen verwenden. Abschließend solltest du deine Empfehlungen nochmals zusammenfassen.

Writing

Aufbau von *reports*

Introduction: Das Ziel des *reports* ist es, ein Thema kurz und prägnant zu präsentieren. Nach dem Lesen dieser Einleitung muss klar sein, warum dieser *report* geschrieben wurde und worum es eigentlich geht.

Proper text: Was im Hauptteil deines *reports* steht, hängt natürlich ganz stark von der Aufgabenstellung ab. Du kannst hier eine Aufzählung positiver/negativer Aspekte geben oder Vorteile/Nachteile darstellen. Ebenso kannst du *facts and figures* beschreiben oder die Konsequenzen möglicher Pläne skizzieren. Vielleicht musst du aber auch Lösungsvorschläge für ein bestehendes Problem aufzeigen. All das kommt ganz darauf an, wie die Themenstellung lautet.

Conclusion: Der Schlussteil ist eine kurze Zusammenfassung der wichtigsten und bereits genannten Aspekte. Ebenso sollst du am Ende deines *reports* eine Empfehlung abgeben. Drücke dich auch hier wieder so klar wie möglich aus.

Useful phrases for writing a *report*

Introduction:
- This report intends to …
- The aim of this report is to …
- This report will consider/analyse/compare …
- The reason for having written this report is to present/discuss …

Proper text:
- We would suggest …
- It might be a good idea to …
- Possible consequences must be discussed.
- One will have to wait what the consequences of this project are.
- For this reason …/for these reasons …
- A possible solution would be …
- Another option worth considering would be …
- As the problem has not been solved yet, one could think about …
- Let's not forget that …

Conclusion:
- Summarizing it is to say that …
- Eventually it can be said that …
- All in all it can be summarized that …
- Finally it should be mentioned that …
- In the end we must not forget that …

Task 1

Study this sample report, then do the task

Introduction:
The aim of this report is to present possible advantages and disadvantages of offering healthy food at schools.

Advantages:
First of all, providing children and teenagers with healthy food can never be wrong. It is proven that the right type of food stimulates people's motivation and their ability to concentrate. Let us not forget that this aspect is essential in schools.

Disadvantages:
Of course, there are also negative aspects related to this topic. One of these is definitely the fact that healthy food is usually more expensive. Parents might not be willing to pay more – even if it is for their children's health. Another problem is that children and teenagers are very keen on junk food like pizza or fries. They might not be happy with the "new" and healthy food that is on offer.

Conclusion:
It is difficult to say whether the introduction of healthy food at schools will be successful or not but summarizing it is to say that it would be a highly reasonable action that should be given a try.

Writing

Take a look at the adjectives taken from the report. Put them into the comparative and the superlative and finally find the opposite

adjective	comparative	superlative	opposite
healthy			
negative			
expensive			
happy			
new			
difficult			
successful			
reasonable			

Task 2

Imagine that your school is running a so-called "buddy project". This means that each student from a 5th form (that means your age) has to take care of a 1st form student. This should be the case especially at the beginning of the school year to make the start for the little ones easier. Your headmaster has now asked you to write a report discussing advantages and disadvantages of this project. Write your report in about 150 words.

Task 3 (Mustertext im Lösungsheft)

A group of students from Portugal is coming to stay in your town as part of an exchange programme. Your Spanish teacher has asked you to write a report suggesting places the group should visit and funny or interesting activites they might take part in during their seven-day stay. Write again about 150 words.

Task 4

A cosmetic company has asked you to try out their new hair shampoo. You did so and now they have asked you to write a report (including your personal experiences) which should then be published in their consumer's magazine.

ARGUMENTATIVE ESSAY

Ein *argumentative essay* (*discussion essay, discursive composition*) ist ein erörternder Texttyp, das heißt, ein Thema/ ein Sachverhalt oder ein Problem wird von beiden Seiten beleuchtet und alle Vor- und Nachteile werden diskutiert (und zwar zu ungefähr gleichen Teilen). Abschließend gibt die Verfasserin/der Verfasser noch seine eigene, persönliche Meinung bekannt. Die Schwierigkeit bei einem *argumentative essay* liegt am ehesten im Sammeln der Argumente bzw. Gegenargumente. Das funktioniert natürlich nur, wenn man als Verfasserin/Verfasser ein gewisses Sachwissen zum betreffenden Thema hat. Solltest du zu einem Sachthema überhaupt keine Ahnung haben, empfiehlt es sich auch, das Internet kurz zu konsultieren und sich ein wenig zu belesen. In jedem Fall erleichtert ein *brainstorming* vor dem Schreiben den eigentlichen Schreibprozess ungemein. Leg dir eine Liste an mit Vor- und Nachteilen (Plus und Minus) beziehungsweise Argumenten dafür und dagegen. Versuche bereits im Vorfeld deine Gedanken zu ordnen, denn ein logischer Aufbau und eine logische Abhandlung der Argumente sind bei diesem Texttyp unerlässlich. Mit einer guten und sinnvollen Gliederung hast du bereits einen großen Schritt in die richtige Richtung gemacht. Achte stets auf formale Sprache. Schauen wir uns aber nun einmal an, wie so ein *argumentative essay* aufgebaut wird:

Writing

Aufbau eines *argumentative essay*

Opening paragraph: Das Thema wird vorgestellt und die Hauptgedanken bzw. die Diskussionsfrage (*e.g. Are animal experiments justified?*) dargelegt. Hier können fachliche Hintergrundinformationen beschrieben und zB die aktuelle Situation aufgezeigt werden. Konkrete Beispiele haben hier jedoch noch keinen Platz. Wie immer sollte deine Einleitung interessant geschrieben sein und damit die Leserin/den Leser zum Weiterlesen verlocken.

Advantages: Die eine Seite des Themas (die Vorteile) wird nun im Detail diskutiert. Jeder Aspekt wird in einem eigenen Absatz behandelt und auch hier gilt es wieder, nicht auf die *linking words* zu vergessen.

Disadvantages: Nach einem kurzen Überleitungssatz wird nun die gegenteilige Seite (die Nachteile) erörtert. Auch hier bekommt jeder neue Gedanke einen neuen Absatz. Natürlich hast du auch die Möglichkeit, die Reihenfolge von *advantages und disadvantages* umzudrehen. Das ist ganz egal, solange du zuerst die eine Seite und dann die andere Seite bearbeitest.

Closing paragraph: Nachdem du nun nach bestem Wissen und Gewissen die beiden Seiten präsentiert hast, gilt es, die wichtigsten Argumente nochmals kurz in ein bis zwei Sätzen zusammenzufassen und zu wiederholen. Das Ende deines Aufsatzes bietet auch die Möglichkeit, deine eigene Meinung kundzutun. Tue dies aber so klar und eindeutig wie möglich. Eine zufriedenstellende Schlussfolgerung (falls möglich) rundet deinen Aufsatz ab.

Useful phrases for writing an *argumentative essay*

Opening paragraph:
The aim of this essay is to discuss ... / to point out / to present ...
The following composition will focus on ...
In the course of the following essay I would like to present ...
As ... is a very controversial topic, it shall be discussed in this essay in detail.
The purpose of this composition is to ...

Stating somebody's opinion:
Scientists argue / claim / say / state ...
Many people / most people believe ...
The majority / minority thinks that ...
According to ...
The public opinion is for / against ...

Stating one's own opinion:
In my opinion ...
I (do) believe that ...
I am (absolutely) convinced / sure that ...
On balance, it seems to me that ...
I am tempted to say that ... *(Ich bin versucht zu sagen, dass ...)*
I am in favour of ... / against ...

Task 1

Do the vocabulary work: Match each phrase in the list below with its purpose (either A, B or C)

A to give additional information
B to give contrasting information (expressing a contrast)
C to summarize an argument

all in all		to sum up	
additionally		moreover	
in contrast to		in short	
to put it in a nutshell		nevertheless	
summarizing it can be said that		last but not least	
by contrast		finally	
what is more		apart from that	
in conclusion		let's not forget that	
on the whole		it must also be mentioned that	
as well as		besides	
furthermore		compared to	

Writing

Task 2

Take a look at the following argumentative essay about school uniforms and then fill in the words from the box. There are more words than you need.

> poor – positive – possibilities – impression – difficult – hate – express – afford – fashionable – save – disadvantages – prevent – related – easy – anybody – excluded – spend

In some schools they are obligatory, in others not. Some students love them, others _____ them. What is being talked about here, are school uniforms. They have always been, and will always be, a very controversial topic that will be discussed in greater detail in this essay.

One of the most _____ aspects about school uniforms is the fact that no student is discriminated or _____ because of not wearing brand clothes. Everybody wears the same and it doesn't matter whether the students are rich or _____ and whether they can _____ expensive and stylish labels or not.

Another advantage of school uniforms is that you do not have to think about clothes and what to wear in the morning. You just put on your uniform and that's it. That might _____ a lot of stress and energy.

But having to wear a school uniform can sometimes also be quite annoying so it is clear that there are not only positive aspects _____ to this topic. One of the biggest _____ is that the students more or less lose their individuality. Everybody looks the same and there are not many _____ to show one's own personality, look and style.

Furthermore, you cannot do anything if you do not like your school uniform or if you feel uncomfortable wearing it. It is an obligation students have to live with, no matter if they want it or not.

Summarizing, it is _____ to say whether school uniforms are good or not. Personally, I appreciate that I do not have to wear one because I have the _____ that – through clothes – I can _____ who I am.

Task 3

Imagine that you should write an argumentative essay for your school magazine, discussing how important it is for students your age to read daily newspapers. Make sure that you mention different aspects and that you look at the situation from different sides. Don't forget to briefly give your own opinion towards the end. Write your essay in about 200 words.

Task 4

According to a recent study, children and teenagers are three times more likely to start smoking if their parents smoke. Write an argumentative essay (about 200 words) discussing the topic of smoking and why so many teenagers start these days. Take care of the structure of your essay!

Task 5 (Mustertext im Lösungsheft)

Imagine your teacher has set the following task: Write and argumentative essay (again about 200 words) discussing the question: "How useful are home exercises?"

Writing

OPINION ESSAY

Wenn du einen *opinion essay* (oder eine *opinion composition*) schreibst, dann geht es darum, deine Meinung für oder gegen eine These darzulegen und deinen Standpunkt (durch Argumente, Beispiele und Fakten) zu untermauern. Zweck eines *opinion essays* ist es, die Leserin/den Leser durch fundierte Beweisführung von der Richtigkeit deines eigenen Standpunktes zu überzeugen. Am Ende deines Aufsatzes soll die Leserin/der Leser in der Lage sein zu entscheiden, ob deine Argumentationslinie überzeugend war oder nicht.

Natürlich muss auch diese Textsorte gut gegliedert und übersichtlich aufgebaut werden. Im folgenden Abschnitt kannst du dir den Aufbau eines *opinion essay* genauer anschauen.

Aufbau eines *opinion essay*

Opening paragraph: In der Einleitung wird wie immer das Thema – und zwar so präzise wie möglich – vorgestellt. Eventuell werden eine oder mehrere umstrittene Fragen/Aspekte in den Vordergrund gerückt. Wichtig hierbei ist wiederum, dass die Leserin/der Leser nach dem Lesen der Einleitung ganz genau weiß, welches der/die Hauptgedanken des Textes sind und was sie/ihn in diesem Aufsatz erwartet. Ebenfalls klar sein muss, welche Position DU als Verfasserin bzw. Verfasser des Textes zum betreffenden Thema hast.

Body: Der eigentliche Hauptteil gliedert sich wieder in mehrere Absätze (wie immer: pro Idee/Gedanke ein neuer Absatz). Bitte vergiss nicht auf die Bindewörter (*linking words*), um deinen Text einerseits übersichtlicher, andererseits aber auch sprachlich hochwertiger zu gestalten. Durch deinen Hauptteil muss sich auf jeden Fall wieder ein roter Faden ziehen, um zu gewährleisten, dass die in der Einleitung angekündigten Aspekte logisch strukturiert und genau abgehandelt sind.

Closing paragraph: Man soll beim Lesen spüren, dass der Text dem Ende zugeht und somit komplett ist. Dies kann durch eine neuerliche Formulierung des ursprünglichen Schreibvorhabens oder der eingangs formulierten These geschehen. Der Kreis zum Anfang deines Aufsatzes sollte sich im Idealfall wieder schließen und die Leserin/der Leser sollte spätestens jetzt von deinen Argumenten überzeugt sein.

Useful language for writing an *opinion essay*

Opening paragraph:	The aim of this essay is to point out / to present my opinion concerning …
	In the following composition my focus will be on …
	In the course of the following essay I will state my personal opinion about …
	In the course of the following paragraphs I will discuss my attitude towards …
	The purpose of this opinion composition is to …
Stating your opinion:	In my opinion …
	My personal attitude towards … is that …
	I (do) believe that …
	I am (absolutely) convinced / sure that …
	On balance, it seems to me that …
	I am tempted to say that …
	I am in favour of … / against …
	Personally, I am …
	I can imagine that …
Closing paragraph:	At the end of this composition I want to …
	Let me point out once more that …
	Summarizing, it can be said that …
	Considering all arguments mentioned so far, it can be said that …
	Last but not least it should be pointed out / mentioned / stressed that …
	Thinking again about all the aspects discussed before, I / one can say that …
	Finally, I come to the conclusion that …
	In conclusion, …
	All in all it can be said that …
	Finally, … is always a topic worth thinking about.

Writing

Task 1

Read this opinion essay about school uniforms and compare it (in style and tone) with the argumentative essay. What strikes you most?

> The **aim** of this essay is to present my personal **attitude** concerning school uniforms. In my childhood I spent some years in France where we had to wear school uniforms. Now, after my return to England, I no longer have to wear them. But thinking back, I have to confess that wearing school uniforms simplified my life enormously. Here are the reasons why:
>
> To begin with, wearing school uniforms is simply easy. In the morning you do not have to **check** your whole wardrobe, **just** to find out that there is nothing you really **like to wear**. Besides, you do not have to take care of the weather. Your uniform more or less always stays the same, you only have to decide **whether** you take a pullover with you or not.
>
> Secondly, rich and poor students, and the difference between them, will always exist. If there is no dress code because of school uniforms, poorer students are at a disadvantage because their parents cannot afford **expensive** designer clothes. Consequently, these pupils are judged by their clothes and not by their characters. Personally, I think that this is a pity and also a sort of discrimination.
>
> Finally, I do **think** that because of wearing school uniforms, teenagers can concentrate better on school. They are not distracted by what other classmates wear or by thinking about which top might **fit to** the new blue skirt. They can simply focus and concentrate on learning and paying attention.
>
> In conclusion, I do believe that wearing school uniforms presents a lot of **advantages** as it simply makes life easier.

Task 2

Can you find other English words (with the same meaning!) for all the bold words from the essay?

aim _____ attitude _____

check _____ just _____

like to wear _____ whether _____

expensive _____ think _____

fit to _____ advantages _____

Task 3

Imagine that your biology teacher has asked you to write an opinion essay about animal experiments and animal testing. Make sure you present your opinion in a clear and well-structured way. Write about 200 words.

Task 4 (Mustertext im Lösungsheft)

Nowadays almost everybody is connected with the World Wide Web (www.) and uses the Internet. Some experts, however, say that especially for young people and teenagers the Internet can be very dangerous. In an essay of about 200 words express your own opinion whether the Internet is a blessing or a curse (*ein Segen oder ein Fluch*). Don't forget to give examples for what you say.

Task 5

Sometimes, when people talk about the United States of America, they say that it is the country of unlimited possibilities and chances where poor people easily become rich and unknown people turn into stars. In an opinion essay say if you agree with this statement, also giving reasons why/why not. Do you think that life is easier in America than in Austria? Write again about 200 words.

VOCABULARY

HOUSING AND ACCOMMODATION

TYPES OF HOUSES/DWELLINGS	
apartment (AE)	Wohnung
apartment building (AE)	Wohnhaus
block of flats (BE)	Wohnhaus
condominium/condo	Eigentumswohnung
detached house (BE)	Einfamilienhaus
duplex (AE)	Zweifamilienhaus
flat (BE)	Wohnung
maisonette	Maisonette
mansion	Herrenhaus/Villa
mobile home (BE)	Wohnwagen
row house/town house (AE)	Reihenhaus
semidetached house (BE)	Zweifamilienhaus
single-family house (AE)	Einfamilienhaus
studio	Atelier
terraced house (BE)	Reihenhaus
trailer (AE)	Wohnwagen
two-family house (AE)	Zweifamilienhaus
villa	Villa

ROOMS IN A HOUSE	
attic	Dachboden
balcony	Balkon
bathroom (BE)	Badezimmer
bedroom	Schlafzimmer
cellar (BE)	Keller
children's room	Kinderzimmer
dining room	Esszimmer
garage	Garage
guest room	Gästezimmer
hall	Eingangsbereich
kitchen	Küche
landing	Flur
living room	Wohnzimmer
master bedroom	Elternschlafzimmer
restroom (AE) toilet (BE)	Toilette
(roof) terrace	(Dach-)Terrasse
staircase	Stiegenaufgang
utility room	Waschküche

Exercise 1 Word matching

Match the words with the correct definition. There are more words than meanings. Write the number next to the definition.

1. semidetached house
2. detached house   _____   **a.** BE: row of houses sharing side walls
3. duplex   _____   **b.** AE: moveable home
4. row house   _____   **c.** a flat comprising at least two floors
5. trailer   _____   **d.** AE: a house completely separated from neighbours
6. terraced house   _____   **e.** AE: house with two units on different floors
7. single-family house
8. maisonette

Exercise 2 Jumbled words

Rearrange the letters. The first letter of each word is written in bold. The clues after each jumbled word will help you.

tmsare ordeom**b**	a place where the owners of the house sleep
ytil**u**ti orom	a place to store the washing machine, brooms and other useful things
re**c**lal	the space under the house which is often used as storeroom
retomsro	an American word for sanitary facilities in a house
oorf recar**te**	a place on top of the house where you can enjoy the sun- or moonlight
tor**nf** nd**g**rae	a piece of green space most British but also Americans are especially proud of
gi**d**nni omo**r**	a place some houses have especially for having meals
lo**b**cyna	an open place attached to a room

Vocabulary

THINGS FOUND IN A HOUSE AND IN A GARDEN ...			
alarm clock	Wecker	*king-size bed*	großes Doppelbett
armchair	Lehnstuhl	*lawn*	Rasen
back door	Hintereingang	*laundry machine (AE)*	Waschmaschine
(bath)tub	Badewanne	*make-up table*	Schminktisch
bedside table	Nachttisch	*queen-size bed*	kleines Doppelbett
bedside lamp	Nachttischlampe	*(open) fireplace*	(offener) Kamin
blender	Mixgerät	*oven*	Backofen
bookshelf	Bücherregal	*printer*	Drucker
bunk-bed	Stockbett	*refrigerator (fridge)*	Kühlschrank
carpet	Spannteppich	*rug*	Vorlegeteppich
coffee table	Couchtisch	*sauna*	Sauna
cupboard	Kasten/Kästchen	*shower*	Dusche
curtains	Vorhänge	*shrubs*	Gebüsch
dining table	Esstisch	*single bed*	Einzelbett
desk	Schreibtisch	*sink*	Abwaschbecken
dishwasher	Geschirrspüler	*steam bath*	Dampfbad
flat screen	Flachbildschirm	*stereo*	Hi-Fi-Anlage
flower bed	Blumenbeet	*electric/gas stove*	E-Herd/Gasherd
fountain	Springbrunnen	*sofa/couch*	Sofa/Couch
four-poster	Himmelbett	*swimming pool*	Pool
freezer	Tiefkühler	*toaster*	Toaster
front door	Eingangstüre	*TV set*	Fernseher
games console	Spielkonsole	*walk-in closet*	begehbarer Schrank
garden gnome	Gartenzwerg	*wardrobe*	Kleiderschrank
hedge	Hecke	*(wash)basin*	Waschbecken
ice-cream machine	Eismaschine	*washing machine (BE)*	Waschmaschine
iPod docking station	iPod-Station	*whirlpool/Jacuzzi*	Whirlpool
kettle	Wasserkocher	*widescreen TV/monitor*	Breitbildschirm

Exercise 3 Creative matching

Which things would you like to have in your dream house? Fill in as many words as you can think of in the columns provided.

living room	sanitary facilities	your room	kitchen	garden/terrace

Vocabulary

Things to do in a house and a garden

VERBS			
to arrange	anordnen	to erect	aufstellen
to assemble	zusammenbauen	to fix	anbringen
to build	aufbauen, formen	to furnish	einrichten
to buy	kaufen	to inlay (a floor)	mit Parkett auslegen
to call	rufen, anrufen	to install	installieren
to carpet	mit Teppich auslegen	to lay (the foundation)	das Fundament legen
to celebrate	feiern	to paint	ausmalen, lackieren
to choose	auswählen	to plan	planen
to clean	reinigen, putzen	to plant (flowers)	pflanzen
to colour	färben	to sew	nähen
to connect	anschließen	to plaster (the shell)	(den Rohbau) verputzen
to cover	bedecken	to purchase	käuflich erwerben
to decorate	dekorieren	to renovate (a building)	renovieren
to dig	graben	to sow	säen
to draw	zeichnen	to take the measurements	abmessen
to employ	anstellen	to tile	verfliesen
to equip	ausrüsten	to wallpaper	tapezieren

Exercise 4

When you want to move into a new house, many things have to be done. Fill in some of the verbs from above which collocate with the nouns. Remember to use passive structures if necessary. Mind irregular verbs!

When a suitable lot of land _____ _____ by the future owner of the premises, a ground-plan _____ _____ by an architect. Then, the foundation _____ _____ by a building firm. Brick by brick, the walls _____ _____ and then the shell of the building _____ _____. When the exterior of the house is finished, the owners can start working on the interior design. The walls _____ _____, or they _____ _____. Then, the floors _____ _____, _____ or _____. In the bathroom and the kitchen, the electrical equipment, such as the fridge, the oven or the washing machine _____ _____. Very often, professionals _____ _____ for these little jobs because they can get quite tricky. Then, the cupboards, wardrobes and other pieces of furniture _____ _____, which sometimes turns out to be rather difficult. Most of the times, there is one important thing missing, like a bolt or a screw. When the rooms _____ _____ with all the furniture, they can _____ _____ with rugs, curtains, pillows and plants. In order to add a little bit of colour, pictures _____ _____ on the walls and flowers _____ _____ in vases. In the garden, the lawn _____ _____, flowers _____ _____ and, perhaps, a swing _____ _____. Finally, the house-warming party _____ _____ with family and friends.

Vocabulary

Exercise 5 — A song

Listen to the song "Our House" by a band called "Madness" and fill in the missing words.

Hörübung: CD-Track 13

Father _____ his Sunday best.
Mother's tired, she needs a _____.
The kids are playing up _____.
Sister's sighing in her sleep.
Brother's got a date to keep, he can't hang around.

Our house, in the middle of our _____
Our house, in the middle of our …

Our house, it has a _____
There's always something happening.
And it's usually quite loud.
Our mum, she's so _____.
Nothing ever slows her down, and a _____ is not allowed.

Our house, in the middle of our street. (3x)
(Something tells you that you've got to _____ _____ from it.)
Our house, in the middle of our …

Father _____ _____ late for work.
Mother has to _____ his shirt.
Then she sends the kids to school.
Sees them off with a small _____
She's the one they're going to miss in lots of ways.

Our house, in the middle of our street.
Our house, in the middle of our …

I remember way back then when everything was true.

And when we would have such a very _____ time, such a _____ time, such a _____ time.
And I remember how we'd play simply _____ the day away.
Then we'd say nothing would come between us two _____.

Father _____ his Sunday best.
Mother's tired she needs a _____.
The kids are playing up _____.
Sister's sighing in her sleep.
Brother's got a date to keep, he can't hang around.

Our house, in the middle of our street. (3x)
Our house, in the middle of our …
Our house, was our _____ and our keep.
Our house, in the middle of our street.
Our house, that was where we used to sleep.
Our house, in the middle of our street. (2x)
Our house …

Exercise 6 — Chores

The song you have just heard deals with the, on the one hand idyllic, but on the other hand also limiting picture of a typical family life. When you think of your family, which routines dominate a typical day? Find the correct verbs for describing some of the chores that have to be done in a household.

1. to _____ the lawn
2. to _____ the dishes
3. to _____ the meals
4. to _____ the cat's toilet/the cage
5. to _____ the vacuum cleaning/the hoovering
6. to _____ the garbage out
7. to _____ the dishwasher
8. to _____ the laundry
9. to _____ the ironing
10. to _____ the dog

MUSIC

ADJECTIVES		NOUNS	
aggressive	aggressiv	accompaniment	Begleitung
alternative	alternativ	band	Band
anti-authority	antiautoritär	beat	Takt
arousing	aufwühlend	charts	Hitparade
catchy (tune)	eingängig (Ohrwurm)	chorus/refrain	Refrain
commercial	kommerziell	easy listening	Unterhaltungsmusik
convincing	aussagekräftig, überzeugend	entry/new entry	Einstieg/Neueinstieg
demanding	anspruchsvoll	impact	Einfluss
dreamy	verträumt	melody	Melodie
exciting	aufregend	performance	Aufführung, Vorstellung
explicit	(zu) direkt	release	Neuerscheinung
hard-edged	scharfkantig, „rau"	rhythm	Rhythmus
innocent	unschuldig	scene	Szene
insistent	hartnäckig	songwriter	Liedertexter
jarring	gellend	sound	Sound
latest	am aktuellsten	style	Stil
loud	laut	success	Erfolg
mainstream	durchschnittlich	tune	Melodie
meaningful	sinnvoll, aussagekräftig	vocals	Gesang
melodious	melodiös	voice	Stimme
negative	negativ		
popular	beliebt		
powerful	kraftvoll	VERBS	
provocative	provokant	to admire	bewundern
relaxing	entspannend	to amplify	verstärken
sensitive	einfühlsam	to be on the keys	Keyboard spielen
soft	sanft	to cherish	sehr schätzen
soothing	beruhigend	to develop	(sich) entwickeln
soulful	schwermütig, gefühlvoll	to enter (the charts)	(in die Charts) einsteigen
spoken	gesprochen	to found a band	eine Band gründen
stimulating	anregend	to go into the charts at number 1	auf Platz 1 der Hitliste gelangen
stirring	mitreißend	to go silver/platinum/gold	eine bronzene/... Schallplatte bekommen
strong	stark		
sung	gesungen	to grow on sb.	mehr und mehr gefallen
sweet	lieblich	to hit (the charts)	in die Charts einsteigen
thoughtful	nachdenklich	to jump up places (in the charts)	Plätze in den Charts gutmachen
tremendous	gewaltig	to release	veröffentlichen
tuneful	klangvoll, melodisch	to remind sb. of sth.	jemanden an etwas erinnern
violent	gewalttätig	to reunite	sich wiedervereinigen
vocal	stimmlich	to separate/split up	sich trennen

MEMBERS OF A BAND			
background dancers	Hintergrundtänzer	guitarist	Gitarrist
background singers	Hintergrundsänger	lead guitarist	Frontgitarrist
band leader	1. Mann/1. Frau der Band	lead singer/vocalist	Frontsänger
bassist	Bassist	manager	Manager
drummer	Schlagzeuger	roadie	Bandarbeiter auf Tour
frontman	Frontmann/-frau	vocalist/singer	Sänger

Vocabulary

Exercise 1 Matching

Match the different styles of music with the definitions.

1. Heavy metal _____ a. singer-songwriters, warm sound, catchy tunes, sing-along music
2. Pop _____ b. spoken, rhythmic lyrics, strong beats, often very explicit
3. Techno _____ c. anti-authority, violent, aggressive, negative, hard-edged, political
4. Rap/Hip-hop _____ d. electronic dance music, fast, arousing, strong beat
5. Indie _____ e. sound of the Caribbean, strong rhythm and melodies
6. Punk _____ f. popular music, easy listening, commercial, for young and old
7. Rock _____ g. independent, alternative, often thoughtful lyrics, not mainstream
8. Reggae _____ h. loud, aggressive, fast, thick, massive sound, strong performances
9. Jazz-pop singers _____ i. soulful, calm, "rhythm and blues", sexy
10. R'n'B _____ j. loud, popular music with a strong beat

Exercise 2 Collocations

Find the adjectives that combine with the nouns. The first letters will help you.

1. Now that's a really ca_____ tune.
2. Some people prefer so_____ beats.
3. Eminem sometimes has very pr_____ lyrics.
4. Critics cherish the band's tr_____ power.
5. Stop it! I'm not in the mood for your sw_____ music. Play something more cheerful!
6. I am convinced that me_____ lyrics are as important as a good tune in a song.
7. Phew! I hate that ja_____ sound of that band. It makes me nervous.
8. The band's in_____ beat has made them famous.
9. On their last album, the vo_____ accompaniment was not as good as before.

Exercise 3 Jumbled words

The word "strong" can refer to various nouns. Find the missing ones. (The first letter is written in bold.)

1. fec**p**rreoanm On stage, they always make a strong _____.
2. cy**l**sir Don't you think that "U2" have really strong _____? I know most of them by heart!
3. et**b**a A good band does not only need a strong _____. The looks are also important.
4. c**i**ove Listen! This girl has a very strong _____.
5. oed**m**yl That is a very strong _____. I've been humming it for quite a long time now.
6. y**t**ern Their last album made an extremely strong _____ into the charts.
7. de**l**a ni**s**rge "Franz Ferdinand" have got a very strong _____ _____.
8. c**p**it**a**m The Rolling Stones had a very strong _____ on other bands.

Vocabulary

Exercise 4 Idioms

Match the idioms with the correct meanings.

1.	to make chin music	A	to make the important decisions	1.	
2.	to call the tune	B	to accept the negative consequences	2.	
3.	to face the music	C	in a case of emergency you stop everything you are doing	3.	
4.	for a song	D	all the other things/aspects that are connected to the topic	4.	
5.	You can't unring a bell.	E	you can try it, but you will not make it.	5.	
6.	to march to the beat of your own drum	F	to let no one speak but yourself	6.	
7.	Stop the music!	G	to change your ideas or opinions	7.	
8.	to like the sound of one's own voice	H	to love what you are hearing	8.	
9.	to change your tune	I	to talk a lot	9.	
10.	That's music to my ears.	J	to do things without considering someone else's opinion	10.	
11.	And all that jazz …	K	you buy/sell something too cheap	11.	
12.	Whistle for it!	L	once you have done something you cannot change it anymore	12.	

Exercise 5 Gap filling

Fill in the blanks of this personal review with the words above. Mind the tenses!

success – try – latest – release – to meet – to go – thoughtful – easy listening – to grow – to climb – singles – hit – about – rhythms – tunes – last – to go

I've just bought the _____ CD by Mando Diao "Give me Fire". At first, the CD did not _____ my expectations, but after listening to it for a few times some songs really _____ on me. I remember that two years ago, the _____ album was an immediate _____. It _____ into the charts in the first week of its _____ and it very quickly _____ the charts. Also the new album _____ the charts on place 10, I think, and I am sure it will _____ platinum soon. Some of the _____ have already entered the charts like "Gloria". What I really like _____ Mando Diao is that they have got a blend of stirring _____ and _____ lyrics. It's also that blend of relaxing and arousing _____ that is quite impressive and that really makes you sing along. One might not call this album _____ _____ as the style is sometimes quite demanding, but if you give it a _____ you will surely appreciate it.

ANIMALS

Animal families

ANIMAL	MALE	FEMALE	BABY	GROUP
ape	male	female	baby	shrewdness
bear	boar	sow	cub	sleuth, sloth
bee	drone	queen, worker	larva	hive, swarm (in flight)
bird	cock	hen	hatchling	flock, flight
butterfly	male	female	caterpillar	swarm, army (babies)
cat	tomcat	queen	kitten	clutter, litter (babies)
cattle	bull	cow	calf	drift, herd, mob
cheetah	male	female	cub	coalition
chicken	rooster	hen	chick, pullet	brood
deer	stag	doe	fawn	herd, mob
dog	dog	bitch	pup	litter (babies), pack (wild), kennel
donkey	jack, jackass	jennet, jenny	colt, foal	drove, herd
elephant	bull	cow	calf	herd
fish	–	–	fry, fingerling	school
fly	–	–	maggot	cloud, swarm
guinea pig	boar	sow	pup	group
hamster	buck	doe	pup	horde
horse	stallion, stud	mare	foal	herd
lion	lion	lioness	cub	pride
pig	boar	sow	piglet	drove, herd, litter (babies)
rabbit	buck	doe	bunny	colony, warren
sheep	buck, ram	ewe, dam	lamb	flock
tiger	tiger	tigress	cub, whelp	ambush, streak
wolf	dog	bitch	pup, whelp	pack

Exercise 1 Read the column above and find the right words.

1.	cat: male		12.	rabbit: baby	
2.	fish: group		13.	guinea pig: female	
3.	horse: female		14.	wolves: group	
4.	sheep: group		15.	deer: baby	
5.	cat: baby		16.	fish: baby	
6.	donkey: male		17.	chicken: group	
7.	chicken: female		18.	cattle: baby	
8.	pig: baby		19.	cat: group of small ones	
9.	dog: group of small ones		20.	deer: male	
10.	lion: female		21.	rabbit: male	
11.	fly: group		22.	bee: male	

Vocabulary

Exercise 2 Animal sounds

Which animal makes which sound? Match the numbers with the letters.

1. bee		A	meows, purrs, hisses	1.	
2. bird		B	brays	2.	
3. cat		C	quacks	3.	
4. chicken		D	coos	4.	
5. cow		E	croaks	5.	
6. dog		F	whinnies or neighs	6.	
7. donkey		G	bleats	7.	
8. dove		H	hums and buzzes	8.	
9. duck		I	oinks, snorts, grunts, calls	9.	
10. elephant		J	trumpets	10.	
11. frog		K	chirps, tweets, sings	11.	
12. horse		L	barks, growls, howls, whines, yips, yaps	12.	
13. sheep/lamb		M	clucks	13.	
14. pig		N	sings	14.	
15. whale		O	moos	15.	

Cats and Dogs

Exercise 3 Adjectives for cats and dogs

According to your personal opinion: Which adjectives describe which animal best? Write **C** for cat, **D** for dog.

aggressive	____	cuddly (knuddelig)	____	indifferent	____	playful (verspielt)	____
amiable (liebenswert)	____	cunning (gerissen)	____	intelligent	____	proud	____
arrogant	____	curious	____	jumpy (unruhig)	____	relaxed	____
altruistic	____	cute	____	lazy	____	sassy (keck)	____
bad-tempered	____	delicate (wählerisch)	____	lively (aktiv)	____	self-assured	____
brave (mutig)	____	elegant	____	loveable	____	selfish	____
calm	____	egoistic	____	loyal	____	sensitive (einfühlsam)	____
caring (fürsorglich)	____	energetic	____	malicious (hinterhältig)	____	shy	____
challenging	____	fascinating	____	moody (launisch)	____	sly (listig)	____
cheeky (frech)	____	fearless	____	nos(e)y (neugierig)	____	spoilt (verwöhnt)	____
clever	____	good-natured	____	obedient (gehorsam)	____	stubborn	____
competitive	____	independent	____	picky (wählerisch)	____	sweet-tempered	____

Exercise 4 Pros & Cons: Cats and dogs

Fill the arguments into the correct boxes.

1. annoy neighbours because they are loud
2. are clean
3. are silent and calm
4. are independent
5. are true friends
6. bring home dead mice or birds
7. can be kept in a flat
8. can climb everywhere and damage things
9. can get quite dirty
10. you can take them nearly everywhere
11. you can't leave them alone
12. difficult with children
13. do what they want
14. don't need a lot of space, just some entertainment
15. you have to clean the toilet
16. you have to take them for a walk
17. like children (in general)
18. make you do more exercise
19. need a lot of space to move (garden)
20. their purring makes you feel comfortable
21. can guard the house
22. you can teach them tricks
23. you find hair everywhere (even in hidden places)
24. you have to train them

Vocabulary

CATS		DOGS	
+	−	+	−

Animals: verbs

to abandon	aussetzen	to play with	spielen mit
to care for	sich kümmern um	to praise	loben
to clean (the toilet)	putzen	to put on a lead	eine Leine anlegen
to cry over	weinen um	to romp around	herumtollen
to enjoy	genießen	to scold	schimpfen
to feed	füttern	to spoil	verwöhnen
to fill the bowl	die Schüssel füllen	to take responsibility for	Verantwortung übernehmen
to give a treat	ein Leckerli geben	to take to the vet	zum Tierarzt bringen
to have fun with	Spaß haben mit	to teach tricks	Tricks beibringen
to keep (in)	halten (in)	to train	abrichten/trainieren
to look after	aufpassen	to trim	trimmen
to mistreat	misshandeln	to walk the dog	Gassi gehen
to muzzle	Maulkorb anlegen	to wash	waschen
to neglect	vernachlässigen	to watch	zusehen
to observe	beobachten	to whistle for	pfeifen nach
to pick up the dirt	Kot aufsammeln	to worry about	sich Sorgen machen wegen

Exercise 5

Fill in the missing words. Mind tenses, modes and active or passive forms. The first letters will help you.

1. When you want an animal you have to t_____ r_____ for it.
2. In public areas, you must m_____ your dog and p_____ it on a l_____.
3. When you go on holiday you have to find someone who l_____ a_____ your animal.
4. A snake must be f_____ with living mice.
5. Judy! Don't forget to w_____ the dog! It needs some exercise!
6. We love r_____ a_____ with Biscuit.
7. I once had a very clever dog. I t_____ him loads of tricks.
8. It's horrible to see that so many people a_____ animals in summer.
9. Stop w_____ a_____ Gina. We'll t_____ her to the vet.
10. Don't g_____ her a t_____ again! That dog is way too spoilt.
11. Look at Gin's fur! We must t_____ it.

 Remember: jemandem etwas beibringen: to teach sb. to do sth. / selbst etwas lernen: to learn sth.

Vocabulary

Exercise 6 Different ways of touching an animal

Fill in the missing words.

A:	pat (tätscheln)	D:	stroke (regelmäßig streicheln)	G:	cuddle (knuddeln)
B:	scratch (kraulen: irgendwo)	E:	tickle (kraulen: zwischen den Ohren)	H:	run (laufen lassen)
C:	chuck (kraulen: am Kinn)	F:	hug (umarmen)	I:	carry (tragen)

My dog Fudge really knows how to enjoy life. When I work on the computer, he sits down next to me, looks at me with these big brown dog eyes and off it goes: I must _____ (1) him between the ears and _____ (2) him under the chin. He also loves it when I _____ (3) my fingers over his thick fur. Then he starts grunting like a little piglet and he jumps on my lap. I am glad that Fudge is such a small dog. So I _____ (4) Fudge, but he doesn't want me to _____ (5) him too hard. I think Fudge is a bit delicate with his tummy. He only allows me to _____ (6) it lightly. What he really hates is me trying to _____ (7) him around in my arms. After a while, Fudge calms down a bit and I just _____ (8) him steadily. When Fudge finally jumps down I _____ (9) him once or twice and then he curls up in his basket and starts snoring. And I? I have to go back to work ...

Idioms with animals

Exercise 7 Crossword puzzle

Find the missing animals to complete the idioms.

Across
1. a little _____ told me
3. a _____ nap: a mid-day nap
5. got a bigger _____ to fry
6. _____ party
9. to make a _____ of somebody
10. a memory like an _____
12. to cry _____ tears
14. to have _____ eyes
15. When _____ fly

Down
1. blind as a _____
2. to be _____ hearted
3. _____ feed (*Lappalie*)
4. the black _____ of the family
7. eager _____ (*Arbeitstier*)
8. _____ party (*Junggesellenabschied*)
9. When the cats away, the _____ will play
11. _____ love (young, innocent love)
13. to be _____-tired

Vocabulary

FOOD

Fruit

apple	fig (Feige)	mango	quince (Quitte)
apricot	gooseberry (Stachelbeere)	melon	raspberry (Himbeere)
aubergine	grapefruit	nectarine	red currant (Ribisel)
avocado	grapes (Weintrauben)	orange	squash (Kürbis)
bilberry (Heidelbeere)	guava	papaya	strawberry
blackberry (Brombeere)	kiwi	passion fruit	sweet corn
black currant (schwarze Johannisbeere)	kumquat	peach (Pfirsich)	sweet pepper
blueberry (Heidelbeere)	lemon	pear (Birne)	tangerine
cherry	lime	pineapple (Ananas)	tomato
cucumber	lychee	plum (Zwetschke)	water melon
date (Dattel)	mandarin	pumpkin (Kürbis)	zucchini

 "fruit" has no plural form!

Exercise 1

Match the different types of fruit with the categories.

tree fruit	berries	citrus fruit	1 year fruit

Vegetables

Exercise 2 Jumbled words: Vegetables and cereals

Find the names of the vegetables. The first letter is written in bold and the clues will help you.

icrl**g**a	bulb, family: onion, very spicy, affects your breath
ip**c**ashn	leaves, flowery plant, green, people say that it makes you strong
ke**l**e	family: onion, green stalks, white bulbs, typical in Wales
rat**r**co	root, orange, sweet, rabbits love it
orc**b**lcoi	family: cabbage, green, looks like a tree
e**p**a	small, green seeds in a pod
cletuet	green salad, often used for sandwiches
uw**c**aliflero	family: cabbage, white, has a strong smell when cooked
ab**c**bage	leafy, green vegetable, often used for soups and stews
c**r**ei	small, white cereal grain
n**o**oni	bulb, makes you cry when you cut it
ot**p**toa	tuber, it came from America to Europe, important in the history of Ireland
d**k**inye e**b**na	one of the basic ingredients for chilli, resembles an organ

Vocabulary

What is in your food?

The range of food available is vast, but how healthy are the different products?

chocolate	Schokolade	*game*	Wild	*rice*	Reis
beef	Rindfleisch	*haddock*	Schellfisch	*salmon*	Lachs
biscuits	Kekse	*ice-cream*	Speiseeis	*sardine*	Sardinen
boiled potatoes	Kartoffeln	*lamb*	Lamm	*sausage*	Wurst
bread	Brot	*lobster*	Hummer	*scallop*	Jakobsmuschel
butter	Butter	*marmalade*	Marmelade	*scampi*	Scampi
buttermilk	Buttermilch	*mashed potatoes*	Püree	*shrimps*	Shrimps
cake	Kuchen	*milk*	Milch	*skimmed milk*	Leichtmilch
carp	Karpfen	*mullet*	Meerbarbe	*snapper*	Schnapperfisch
cereal	Müsli	*mussels*	Miesmuscheln	*sole*	Seezunge
cheese	Käse	*mutton*	Schaf	*squid*	Tintenfisch
chicken	Huhn	*olive oil*	Olivenöl	*sunflower oil*	Sonnenblumenöl
chips/fries	Pommes frites	*oysters*	Austern	*toast*	Toast
cream	Rahm	*pasta*	Nudeln	*trout*	Forelle
cod	Dorsch	*pie*	Kuchen	*tuna*	Tunfisch
corn on the cob	Maiskolben	*pork*	Schwein	*turkey*	Truthahn
cottage cheese	Hüttenkäse	*potato wedges*	Wedges	*veal*	Kalb
crab	Krabbe	*poultry*	Geflügel	*whipped cream*	Schlagobers
clam	Venusmuschel	*prawns*	Garnelen	*whole milk*	Vollmilch
crisps	Chips	*pumpkinseed oil*	Kürbiskernöl	*yoghurt*	Jogurt

Exercise 3

Fill in all the words above into the categories. There are 10 words per column.

sugar/fat/oil	proteins				carbohydrates
	meat	fish	seafood	dairy products	

Vocabulary

Adjectives describing food

TASTE	GESCHMACK		
appealing	ansprechend	home-made	hausgemacht
aromatic	aromatisch	iced	geeist
artificial	künstlich	marinated	mariniert
bitter	bitter	pickled	eingelegt
boring	langweilig	poached	pochiert
cheesy	fad	pureed	püriert
delicious	lecker	raw	roh
excellent	ausgezeichnet	roasted	gebraten
disgusting	ekelhaft, widerlich	simmered	geköchelt
fruity	fruchtig	smoked	geräuchert
fresh	frisch	smothered	getränkt/bedeckt
hot/spicy	scharf	steamed	gedünstet
interesting	interessant	stuffed	gefüllt
minty	minzig	toasted	getoastet
mouth watering	besonders gut	topped	verziert
natural	natürlich	whipped	geschlagen (Obers)
organic	biologisch	**TEXTURE**	**BESCHAFFENHEIT**
piquant	pikant	creamy	cremig
pleasant	angenehm	crunchy	knusprig/knackig
pungent	scharf, stechend	crispy	knusprig
rancid	ranzig	crusty	knusprig/krustig
repulsing	abstoßend	doughy	teigig
refreshing	erfrischend	dry	trocken
salty	salzig	fizzy	sprudelig
savoury	geschmackvoll	fluffy	flaumig
soothing	beruhigend	greasy	fettig
sour	sauer	hard	hart
stimulating	anregend	juicy	saftig
sugary	zuckrig	leathery	ledrig (Fleisch)
sweet	süß	mellow	weich
tasteless	geschmacklos	prickly	prickelnd
tasty	geschmackvoll, gut	pulpy	gatschig, matschig
thick	reichhaltig, voll	soft	weich
wonderful	wunderbar	spongy	zu weich, teigig
yummy	lecker	sparkling	spritzig
zesty	pikant	squashy	feucht und weich
		stale	schal
PREPARATION	**ZUBEREITUNG**	sticky	klebrig
baked	gebacken	tender	weich, zart (Fleisch)
blended	gemixt	tough	zäh
boiled	gekocht	treacly	triefend süß
breaded	paniert	**HEAT**	**WÄRME**
burnt	verbrannt	boiling	kochend
buttered	gebuttert	chilled	gekühlt
char-boiled	verkohlt	frozen	gefroren
coated	überzogen	hot	heiß
encrusted	überkrustet	ice-cold	eiskalt
flavoured with	gewürzt mit	lukewarm	lauwarm
fried/deep fried	frittiert	steaming hot	dampfend heiß
GM (genetically modified)	genetisch verändert	warm	warm

Vocabulary

Exercise 4 Opposites

Read through the list of adjectives describing food on the previous page and find the opposites to the following words.

Adjective	Opposite
artificial	
mild	
fresh	
sweet	
cold	
frozen	

Adjective	Opposite
creamy	
soft	
delicious	
fizzy	
tasty	
cooked	

Exercise 5

Find the fitting words.

1. You should avoid eating a_____ flavours.
2. What's that p_____ smell in here? Have you burnt something?
3. If I were you I wouldn't eat the butter. It looks r_____ to me.
4. That's the most r_____ drink I've ever had. Lemon and grapefruit. Great!
5. There is nothing more s_____ than chocolate pudding when you are down.
6. Oh, I love that rich, t_____ taste of your sauce!
7. Y_____! Brownies!
8. That tea is f_____ w_____ vanilla. Interesting!
9. Do you want your hot chocolate t_____ with cream?
10. I can't chew that steak! It's so l_____.

Exercise 6 Word matching

Match the words with the correct explanation or definition. There are more words than meanings. Write the number next to the definition.

1. charred food
2. eating out   _____ a. preventing animal diseases from threatening our health: 'mad cow'
3. organic food   _____ b. the DNA of plants and animals is modified to heighten productivity
4. take-away food   _____ c. food that helps you to lose weight or to decrease cholesterol
5. simmered food   _____ d. put it into the microwave and tuck in – but is it really healthy?
6. food safety   _____ e. food cooked too long so that it is completely burnt
7. lukewarm food   _____ f. natural: no pesticides or additives are used
8. home-made food   _____ g. food stored in vinegar to make it last longer/to preserve it
9. health food   _____ h. going to a restaurant
10. pickled food   _____ i. fetching some food from a (fast food) restaurant to eat it at home
11. ready-made food   _____ j. not hot, not cold
12. GM food

Vocabulary

MOBILE PHONES

Exercise 1 **Ways to communicate**

Fill in "by", "on", "in" or leave a blank.

	TV		sign language		Morse		drum signals
	e-mail		the radio		verbal		texting
	non-verbal		face to face		a mobile phone		online
	gestures		fire signals		a telephone		fax

 Sage niemals „per" wenn du „by" meinst, denn „per" bedeutet „pro": e.g.: per year/pro Jahr

On the phone

to answer the phone	abheben	to keep track of	Übersicht bewahren
to be addicted	süchtig sein	to listen to music	Musik hören
to be available	erreichbar sein	to log on/off (the Internet)	Internet ein-/ausloggen
to be in the loop	auf dem Laufenden sein	to make voice calls	Stimmerkennung benutzen
to charge	aufladen	to navigate via GPS	mit GPS navigieren
to cause cancer	Krebs verursachen	to phone sb.	jemanden anrufen
to chat	tratschen	to pick up	abheben
to check messages	SMS überprüfen	to pimp	„aufmotzen"
to emit radiation	Strahlen aussenden	to replace	ersetzen
to feel safe	sich sicher fühlen	to ring off (BE)	auflegen
to get ...	werden	to ring sb. (up)	jemanden anrufen
to give sb. a ring	jemanden anrufen	to switch on/off	auf-/abdrehen
to hang up	auflegen	to set an alarm	Alarm stellen
to improve	sich verbessern	to take a film/a photo	Film/Foto machen
to keep sb. up-to-date	auf dem Laufenden halten	to text(-message) sb.	SMS schicken
to keep in touch with	in Kontakt bleiben mit	to turn on/off	ein-/ausschalten

Exercise 2

Read through the list of verbs and find the correct expressions.

1.	to send a message via your mobile	
2.	to answer the phone	
3.	to call sb. by saying his/her name	
4.	to phone somebody	
5.	to enter the Internet	
6.	to end a phone call	
7.	to stop a machine or gadget	
8.	to find your way	
9.	to decorate your phone	
10.	to fill empty batteries	

Vocabulary

Exercise 3 Ways of paying for your phone

Match the expressions with the explanations. There are more explanations than expressions.

1. a phone that you share with your colleagues
2. the American word for mobile phone   _____ a. company cell phone
3. a prepaid phone   _____ b. basic charge/line rental
4. a phone you get from your firm   _____ c. contract-based phone
5. monthly note telling you what to pay   _____ d. flat rate
6. fixed amount you must pay   _____ e. phone bill
7. a phone that is tied to a provider   _____ f. pay-as-you-go (payg)
8. a rate allowing you to phone as much as you want _____ g. phone rate/tariff/deal
9. a cheaper rate for your partner   _____ h. cell phone
10. the terms on which you use your phone

Exercise 4 A song

Listen to the song "Ring, Ring" by Mika and fill in the missing words.

Hörübung: CD-Track 14

I was _____ on the fence –
And I thought that I would kiss you –
I never thought I would've _____ you –
But you never let me fall –
Push my _____ against the wall –
Every time you _____ –
You get so emotional –
Oh, I'm freakin' out.
Ring ring
Is that you ____ the _____?
You think you're clever –
But you're never _____ nothing at all.
Hey hey
The way you _____ me around –
You make me _____ when you play me –
Like a kid with a crown.
You got a dangerous _____ –
Now I'm in need of some protection –
That was never my _____ –
Used to love me –
now you _____ me –
See I drove you crazy –
Well if I _____ – You _____ me –

Won't somebody _____ me –
From you now?
Ring _____
Is that you _____ the _____?
You think you're clever –
But you're never _____ nothing at all.
Hey hey
The way you _____ me around –
You make me _____ when you play me –
Like a kid with a crown.
It's _____ I wanted –
Until you lost it –
Why won't you _____ me alone?
_____ _____ the phone –
Just let me go.
Ring _____
Is that you ____ the _____?
You think you're clever –
But you're never _____ nothing at all.
Hey hey
The way you _____ me around –
You make me _____ when you play me
Like a kid with a crown. (2x)

Vocabulary

Exercise 5

The song above illustrates how the phone can interfere with our everyday life and upset our emotions. The following text points out in which way the mobile phone integrates with Janet's life. Fill in the missing verbs, minding the correct forms and tenses. (Re-read the list of verbs on page 99, if necessary.)

The very first thing I do in the morning? That's, of course, having a look at my mobile phone. You know, I have to _____ off the alarm and _____ my messages. Who knows? Perhaps someone has _____ me? I always have to be in the loop. Of course I know that having your phone turned on at night is unhealthy. I have heard that the phone _____ harmful radiation, so I always try to keep it off my head. People say that those rays can affect our health and even _____ cancer. This definitely makes me think about it, but on the other hand, what's life without a mobile phone? I don't want to say that I _____ _____ to my phone, but a day without it? No way. I need my phone to _____ in touch with my friends, to plan my day, to take pictures of the beautiful things I do every day, to listen to music, to _____ _____ the Internet. You see, there are so many functions and features, I can't stop telling you about them. Phones _____ _____ more and more versatile and the individual features _____ constantly. Take for example texting. It's so easy and quick – especially with all these abbreviations. Do you know what that means: RU OK? Don't you think that the mobile is a very effective timesaver? My favourite feature is, however, the camera. _____ a pic and sending it to your friends is such a convenient way of _____ them _____! Another advantage is, of course, that you are always _____. Some people might consider this as a negative aspect. It's definitely quite annoying when the guy sitting next to you on the tube _____ up his phone to discuss his shopping list with his wife. But in other situations the mobile can come in handy. When my mum starts worrying about me, she just has to _____ me a call. And when I am alone I _____ safe because I can call for help in case of an emergency. There are of course people who claim that having a phone can also be dangerous. At some schools, attacks on pupils with mobile phones have increased as some of the brand-new, expensive mobiles are targets for thieves. Anyway, this wouldn't keep me from having a mobile. I can't imagine how people managed to _____ in touch with their friends before mobile phones. Of course, I don't want to say that my mobile kills face-to-face communication. I still love meeting my friends in a café, but there are times when this is not possible. And that's when my mobile comes in. When I feel lonely, I just grab my phone and call Jenny or Mark and then we _____ for hours. This leads me to one of the major drawbacks of mobile phones: the costs. One really has to _____ track of the speaking time, which can be quite annoying. Anyway, I have a 15 € line rental plus 1000 mins and unlimited texts. I think that this contract is quite fair. So, as a conclusion, I want to stress one more time that my mobile phone has become an integral part of my everyday life which, however, will never _____ having a face-to-face chat with my pals.

Vocabulary

INTERNET

Computer

TYPES OF COMPUTERS		INPUT DEVICES	
PC (Personal Computer)	PC	flatbed scanner	Scangerät
tower	Tower	hand scanner	Handscanner
desktop	Desktop/Arbeitsoberfläche	keyboard	Tastatur
laptop	Laptop	mouse	Maus
notebook	Notebook	mouse pad	Mausunterlage
palm top	Palm	wireless (mouse)	drahtlose (Maus)

OUTPUT DEVICES		STORAGE	
CRT monitor	Röhrenbildschirm	CD (Compact Disk)	CD
dot-matrix printer	Nadeldrucker	floppy disk	Diskette
inkjet printer	Tintenstrahldrucker	hard drive	Festplatte
laser printer	Laserprinter	memory stick	Memorystick
LCD flat monitor	LCD-Flachbildschirm	USB flash memory stick	USB-Speicher
speakers	Lautsprecher	zip drive	Zip-Speicher

Exercise 1 Word search

Read the list above and find 14 parts of the computer.

```
P R I N T E R I P S O R T D T K O V U
B I E Y L L T G Q O H U O H F G I I H
P R V H F M H S N U U D I L A F V H P
X I E A X E V Z H R B F M K A Q I O Q
L A M D A Q C J W Y Y S R I D P T Y L
S C A N N E R U Z E U F E H F K T V T
I W T N H V E Q N J D S K H S K R O E
F M P M R Q G B K F E C V E X O L J P
J H W U G L G H S Z I X D L T U Z C R
S G D S O Q I R A T R K R I S I C F D
M P W T T Z E A S R O Z N B Z B Q L J
H E K Z C K N Y X O D O G P Y V L O Y
S D L W A E R E B D M D D Z D A J P H
D J W E A O K E Y B O A R D D D H P K
B Q P H M C T A J R J B I I M R C Y S
P S V E H O X W S K O X N E V O T D H
A R M W N Z U I R R T O W E R E U I N
I H P W L Q N W S O W G N G W F K S B
G Z W P A L M T O P X E R C O E M K E
```

Exercise 2 Jumbled words

Find other parts of a computer. The first letter is written in bold and the clues will help you.

hmotrebodar	basic board in the computer where several components are fixed
mmoed	device to decode transmitted information (e.g.: Internet)
dkis **r**dvei	device to record and retrieve information from a disk
radpate	transforms electric current from high voltage to low voltage (laptop, notebook)
ybatetr	additional power supply for notebooks, laptops, palm tops
BUS fhlas **d**riev	device to record and retrieve information from a "stick"
U**CP**	Central Progressing Unit: executes computer programmes
MRA ki**ds**	Random Access Memory: a form of computer storage

Vocabulary

Internet

Things to do on the Internet:

to add	zufügen	to look up	nachschlagen
to back sth. up	abspeichern	lo load	(auf)laden
to be computer literate	am Computer auskennen	to log on/off	ein-/ausloggen
to bid	mitsteigern	to look for	suchen
to bookmark	markieren	to meet	treffen
to boot	Computer hochfahren	to operate	bedienen
to chat online	chatten	to play	spielen
to check your balance	Konto überprüfen	to post	posten
to copy and paste	kopieren und einfügen	to print	drucken
to crash	abstürzen (Computer)	to process	verarbeiten
to cut and paste	ausschneiden/einfügen	to reboot	neu starten
to do online shopping	online einkaufen	to reset	zurücksetzen
to do research	nachforschen	to save onto	speichern auf
to download	herunterladen	to scroll up and down	scrollen
to drag and drop	ziehen/ablegen	to select	wählen
to enter	eingeben	to send	senden
to gather	sammeln	to set up	konfigurieren
to install	installieren	to socialise	Kontakte knüpfen
to invite sb.	einladen	to surf	surfen
to join	beitreten	to upload	raufladen
to key sth. in	eintippen	to watch	ansehen
to listen to	anhören	to write	schreiben

Exercise 3 Phrases

Match the verbs with the nouns.

1. to add friends	A	information on the Internet		1.	
2. to back up	B	a chatroom		2.	
3. to bid	C	MP3 files		3.	
4. to enter	D	online games		4.	
5. to gather	E	the Internet		5.	
6. to install	F	a homepage		6.	
7. to join	G	an e-mail		7.	
8. to key in	H	to your address book		8.	
9. to listen to	I	a video on YouTube		9.	
10. to log off	J	the computer		10.	
11. to play	K	data onto a CD-ROM		11.	
12. to reboot	L	a programme		12.	
13. to scroll up and down	M	a letter		13.	
14. to send	N	at online auctions		14.	
15. to watch	O	a password		15.	

Exercise 4 Emoticons

If you want to express emotions, you often use special smiley signs. Do you know the missing ones?

happy	:-) :) =) :]	tongue out		annoyed	
sad		love (playful)		confused	
wink		shocked		yelling	
large grin		bored		kissing	

Vocabulary

Exercise 5 e-language

When you write an e-mail to your friends, you often use so-called acronyms. These are capital letters that abbreviate common phrases. Do you know what the following ones mean?

1. AML

| all my life | all my love | |
| all morning long | automated music loading | |

2. A/S/L

| age/sex/location | author/signature/label | |
| artist/song/lyrics | ants/slugs/lizzards | |

3. WWW

| wired world web | world wide web | |
| wireless world web | weird wide world | |

4. LOL

| little old loser | love of life | |
| leaving on light | laugh out loud | |

5. CUL

| cut your laughter | can you listen? | |
| see you later | clean your laptop | |

6. DYK

| do you know? | did you kiss? | |
| don't yell kid! | do you care? | |

7. FAQ

| fine art quality | file at quarantine | |
| fast and quick | frequently asked questions | |

8. GFU

| girlfriend-you? | good friends united | |
| good for you | going for unicorns | |

9. H&K

| hug and kiss | hands and knees | |
| hand kiss | hack and knack | |

Exercise 6 Viruses

Surfing the net is fun, but also bears some risks. The following exercise focuses on terms around major and minor threats you are exposed to when you log on. Match the definitions with the explanations.

1. Trojan horse

2. cookie

3. firewall _____ a. message warning you of inexistent threats

4. hoax _____ b. unwanted mass e-mails that block your e-mail account

5. hacker _____ c. myth or made-up story that circles the net

6. spam _____ d. e-mail asking you to forward it to many different people

7. newbee _____ e. person who gains remote access to your computer

8. urban legend _____ f. allows people remote access to your computer and to perform operations

9. icon _____ g. helps you to protect your computer from attacks

10. chain letter _____ h. stores data about you to identify shopping preferences etc.

11. freeware

12. worm

SCHOOL

Subjects

archaeology	classics	French	philosophy
art and design	computing/IT	games	physical education
arts/fine arts	dance	geography	physics
biology	design and technology	history	PSHE (personal, social and health education)
business and economics	drama	home economics	psychology and sociology
careers	economics	ICT (information and communication technology)	religious education
chemistry	English	mathematics	science (biology, chemistry, geoscience, physics)
citizenship	environmental studies	modern foreign languages	sex education
civics	food technology	music	wood/metalwork

Exercise 1 **Crossword puzzle**

In which courses do you learn

Across
5. how economic systems work?
7. to train your body and to keep fit?
10. how to plan your life?
11. about different religions?

Down
1. about events in the course of societal development?
2. all scientific facts about food.
3. about chemical and physical principles of the world?
4. about the rights and duties as a citizen?
6. about cultural achievements (painting, drawing, ...)?
8. how to act in plays?
9. about the chemical structure of our world?

Vocabulary

What teachers do

to admonish	ermahnen	*to have a good sense of humour*	Humor haben
to argue	argumentieren	*to have favourites*	Lieblinge haben
to assess	beurteilen	*to instruct*	unterrichten
to assign homework	Hausübung geben	*to listen to*	zuhören
to be punctual	pünktlich sein	*to look (attractive)*	(gut) aussehen
to challenge	herausfordern	*to look down on*	herabschauen
to control	kontrollieren	*to motivate*	motivieren
to correct	korrigieren	*to organise*	organisieren
to discourage	entmutigen	*to pay attention (to)*	aufmerksam zuhören
to discuss	diskutieren	*to praise*	loben
to downgrade	abstufen	*to reprimand*	rügen
to educate	erziehen/lehren	*to scold*	schimpfen
to encourage	ermutigen	*to set homework*	Aufgaben geben
to examine	überprüfen	*to show enthusiasm (for)*	Begeisterung zeigen
to favour	bevorzugen	*to supervise*	überwachen
to give advice (singular!)	Ratschlag geben	*to support*	unterstützen
to give deadlines	Abgabetermine setzen	*to talk to*	sprechen mit
to give lessons	Stunden halten	*to teach*	unterrichten
to hand out	austeilen	*to test*	testen/überprüfen
to handle (a situation)	gut umgehen mit	*to upgrade*	aufstufen

Exercise 2 Synonyms

Find words that mean the same.

ORIGINAL	SYNONYM	ORIGINAL	SYNONYM
to admonish		to test	
to assign homework		to compliment	
to teach		to plan	
to encourage		to favour	
to put right		to pay attention	

School discipline

Exercise 3 Crime and punishment

Match the words with the definitions. Some definitions can be used several times.

1. to play truant
2. to get suspended
3. to get detention
4. to be cheeky
5. to prompt
6. to ditch school (AE)
7. to chat
8. to cheat
9. to copy (from)
10. to get grounded
11. to be chucked out of school
12. to skip school

a. to stay at home from school without permission
b. not to be allowed to go to school
c. having to leave school
d. to "steal" your classmate's ideas
e. having to stay behind after school
f. to talk back to your teacher
g. to work with unfair methods
h. to tell your classmate the correct answer
i. to talk to your classmate during the lesson

Vocabulary

The British school system

Exercise 4

Study the chart below and then fill in the missing words from the box.

education – primary – compulsory (verpflichtend) – eleven – sixteen – eighteen – attend – GCSE – secondary – mandatory – Advanced – voluntary

The school _____ system in Britain is divided into three stages:

_____ education – up to age eleven: compulsory

_____ education – up to age sixteen: compulsory

undergraduate (tertiary) education – for those over the age of sixteen: _____

'School education': refers to the _____ phases of education which the law requires children to _____ primary and secondary. These are 11 years of _____ education, comprising children from the age of 5 to the age of 16. In other words, pupils in Britain have to attend school from year 1 to year 11.

Primary schools (5–11-year-olds): In the UK, the first level of education is known as primary education.

Secondary schools (11–16-year-olds): Secondary schools provide compulsory education for children between the ages of _____ and _____. Children may stay at school until the age of _____ in order to pursue further studies. However, this is not compulsory.

From the ages of fourteen to sixteen, pupils study for the **General Certificate of Secondary Education** (_____).

Pupils who stay at school from the ages of sixteen to eighteen in England, may take the _____ **(A)** level examination, which is traditionally required for entry into higher education.

key stage	school year	age	types of schools	
foundation		3–5	nursery school	
1	year 1	5–6	infant school (5–7)	primary schools (5–11)
	year 2	6–7		
2	year 3	7–8	junior school (7–11)	
	year 4	8–9		
	year 5	9–10		
	year 6	10–11		
3	year 7	11–12	grammar school OR comprehensive school compulsory GCSE (11–16)	secondary schools (11–16)
	year 8	12–13		
	year 9	13–14		
4	year 10	14–15		
	year 11	15–16		
5	year 12	16–17	grammar school OR comprehensive high school A-levels (18)	undergraduate (tertiary) level (16–18)
	year 13	17–18		

Vocabulary

Exercise 5

The following exercise lists different concepts of the British education system. Match the definitions with the terms and write the letters next to the numbers.

1.	mandatory education	A	certificate that authorizes you to go to university	1.	
2.	grammar school	B	schools run by the government, non-fee paying	2.	
3.	comprehensive school	C	all fee-paying schools	3.	
4.	GCSE	D	financial support for studying	4.	
5.	A-levels	E	fee paying, preparing for grammar school	5.	
6.	state schools	F	school where pupils live during the term	6.	
7.	public schools (BE)	G	set of courses and contents offered at a school	7.	
8.	Common Entrance Exam	H	secondary ed., fee-paying, limited admission	8.	
9.	independent schools	I	basic secondary school – part of mandatory education	9.	
10.	prep school	J	school that also offers professional education	10.	
11.	curriculum	K	the years you have to go to school	11.	
12.	scholarship	L	school focusing on practical education	12.	
13.	boarding school	M	certificate to end mandatory education	13.	
14.	vocational school	N	test you have to sit for admission to public schools	14.	
15.	secondary modern school	O	academic school preparing students for university	15.	

Exercise 6 Tests

There are many different verbs that collocate with the noun "test". Fill in the correct verbs from the box. The clues on the right side will help you.

to revise – hand in – sit – achieve – retake – fail – pass

1. to _____ an exam   to take or write an exam
2. to _____ an exam paper   to hand the exam paper over to the teacher
3. to _____ an exam   to achieve
4. to _____ an exam   not to achieve
5. to _____ an exam   to do it again
6. to _____ top marks/grades to do very well
7. to _____ for an exam   to study and prepare for an exam

Exercise 7 Adjectives

Which adjectives describe, according to your opinion, teachers (T), pupils (P) or both (B)?

annoying	____	diligent (*eifrig*)	____	interested	____	respectful	____
attentive	____	disrespectful	____	motivating	____	rude	____
brazen (*schamlos*)	____	entertaining	____	neutral	____	smart	____
clever	____	enthusiastic	____	obedient (*folgsam*)	____	strict	____
communicative	____	fair	____	open-minded	____	supportive	____
competent	____	hard working	____	outgoing	____	understanding	____
consistent (*linientreu*)	____	impatient	____	patient	____	unfair	____
cordial (*herzlich*)	____	impertinent	____	reliable (*verlässlich*)	____	warm hearted	____
creative	____	intelligent	____	respectable (*seriös*)	____	well organised	____

GRAMMAR

PRESENT TENSES

Present simple

Statement	I play	we play		
	you play	you play		
	he/she/it play**s**	they play		
Spelling	-y nach Vokal:	-ys: I play – he pla**ys**	Ausnahmen:	I go – he go**es**
	-y nach Konsonant:	-ies: I cry – he cr**ies**		I do – he do**es**
	Zischlaut:	-es: I watch – he watch**es**		I have – he ha**s**
		I push – he push**es**		
		I miss – he miss**es**		
Negation	I do not play		do not = don't	
	you do not play			
	he/she/it **does not** play		does not = doesn't	
Question	Do I play …?		**Question words**	
	Do you play …?		Who, What, Why, When	
	Does he/she/it play …?		Where, Which, How	

Exercise 1 Present simple forms

Find the correct forms of the verbs in brackets. Mind positive sentences, negative sentences and questions.

1. Every Friday, Anne _____ (go) to her favourite club with her best friends.
2. Where _____ (Gill and Pat – live)? They _____ (live) in Vienna.
3. Mona sometimes _____ (watch) her dog playing in the park.
4. Mia and Mike _____ (not play) football in the school team.
5. What colour _____ (be) your new sneakers? They _____ (be) brown.
6. My sister's baby often _____ (cry) at night and it _____ (not want) to sleep.
7. What _____ (Gina-do) at the weekends? She _____ (play) soccer.
8. Pit _____ (be) happy in his new school, but he _____ (not like) the uniforms.
9. My cat often _____ (catch) a mouse and _____ (put) it on my pillow.
10. When _____ (your father – get up) in the morning?
11. Nicholas and Kate _____ (not be) in the garden.
12. Who _____ (play) the lead guitar in your band?

Exercise 2 Read through the sentences in exercise 1 and tick the correct statement.

The present simple tense is used for

a. events happening at the moment. ☐   b. general statements and regular events. ☐

Grammar

Exercises 3 and 4 — Present simple usage – state or activity verbs?

Match the example sentences with the rules **A, B, C, D** or **E**. Write the letter into the box. Then read the sentences again and find out if the underlined verbs are state verbs or activity verbs.

A regular activity   **B** present state   **C** present feeling   **D** opinion   **E** general statement

1. Susan <u>thinks</u> that rabbits are very clever. ☐ _state verb_
2. Bella <u>is</u> not good at playing basketball. ☐ _____
3. I <u>play</u> tennis every Sunday afternoon. ☐ _activity verb_
4. Mr. Thatcher <u>prefers</u> tea to coffee. ☐ _____
5. Gerry <u>lives</u> in Salzburg. ☐ _____
6. This bracelet really <u>costs</u> a fortune. ☐ _____
7. I think Joanna <u>wants</u> some ice-cream. ☐ _____
8. Tony <u>is</u> nervous because of today's Maths test. ☐ _____
9. I don't <u>understand</u> what you want to tell me. ☐ _____
10. Our cat <u>hates</u> being tickled behind her ears. ☐ _____
11. Pete <u>knows</u> a lot about wolves. ☐ _____
12. I <u>need</u> an aspirin. ☐ _____
13. Sorry, I don't <u>remember</u> your name. ☐ _____
14. In the morning, Alexis <u>gets up</u> and <u>has</u> a shower. ☐ _____
15. I <u>believe</u> you! ☐ _____
16. I <u>agree</u> with you. ☐ _____
17. The soup <u>smells</u> great! ☐ _____

Exercise 5 — Tick the correct sentences.

1. Activity verbs in the present simple tense tell about things you do regularly. ❏
2. We use state verbs in present simple tense to make general statements. ❏
3. Activity verbs in present simple express that you are doing something at the moment. ❏
4. State verbs in present simple express a state you are in, your feelings or opinions at the moment. ❏

Exercise 6 — Adverbs of frequency

Underline the adverbs of frequency and match the example sentences with the rules.

1. full verbs: adverb comes between subject and verb
2. modal verbs: adverb comes after the modal verb
3. two-part verbs: adverb comes between the parts

A I can never remember her name.
B Sue doesn't usually smoke.
C I often eat ice-cream.
D Joe is usually late.
E We have often got pizza.
F You might never see her again.

A	
B	
C	
D	
E	
F	

Grammar

Present progressive / Present continuous

Statement	I	am	playing	we	are	playing	
am/is/are + verb-ing	you	are	playing	you	are	playing	
	he/she/it	is	playing	they	are	playing	
Negation	I	am not	playing	we	are not	playing	I am not = I'm not
	you	are not	playing	you	are not	playing	you are not = you aren't
	he/she/it	is not	playing	they	are not	playing	he is not = he isn't
Question	Am	I	playing?	Are	we	playing?	
	Are	you	playing?	Are	you	playing?	
	Is	he/she/it	playing?	Are	they	playing?	
Spelling	swim – swimming: double consonant when the preceding vowel is short!						
	write – writing: final -e is dropped						
	lie – lying: final -ie turns into -ying						
	panic – panicking: final -c turns into -cking						
	!be – being						

Exercise 1 — Present progressive forms

Find the correct forms of the verbs in brackets. Mind positive sentences, negative sentences and questions.

1. My budgie _____ (not sit) in its cage! Look, it _____ (fly) out of the room.
2. What _____ (you – do)? I _____ (do) my homework.
3. Because of the climatic change, more and more species _____ (die) out.
4. Why _____ (the alarm clock – beep)? Is it already time to get up?
5. Currently, my grandparents _____ (not travel) around the world.
6. The sea level of the Pacific Ocean _____ (rise) at a dramatic speed.
7. Look at Sue! She _____ (get) nervous. She is going to see Mike today, isn't she?
8. Hi Tina! Thanks for calling. _____ (you – have) a good time in Australia?
9. No, Jonathan _____ (not ride) his bike at the moment.
10. _____ (Max and Fran – dance) over there?
11. Pam _____ (have) a party today.
12. _____ (your father – write) an e-mail to his boss?

Exercise 2 — Present progressive usage

Match the example sentences with the different meanings this tense can convey.

1. activity happening at the moment, people are in the middle of doing it

    _____ Currently we are living in a small apartment.
    _____ Mo tells Pia, "I'm reading a great book at the moment."
    _____ Susan? She is checking her e-mails in her room.

2. activity happening for a limited period of time, not necessarily now

    _____ Oh no! Ruff is running after a squirrel!
    _____ I am doing a Pilates course this semester.

Grammar

Exercise 3 — Present progressive usage

Read the text. Then tick the correct meaning of the sentences below.

> Alan is a senior at Springfield High. This semester, he has chosen English II and Science I as main courses. Next semester, he will add Trigonometry II and Basketball. He normally lives with his parents, but as their house is being refurnished at the moment, he is staying with his best friend, Colin. Currently, Alan is studying in the library, when he is interrupted by Gina, a girl he fancies a lot. They are talking about their plans for the weekend. Alan tells Gina that he is writing an important paper for English II. So he probably won't be able to stay out long at the weekend.

1. *Alan is studying at the library.*
   - a He studies a lot at the library.
   - b He is sitting at the library now.

2. *Alan is staying with Colin.*
   - a He is staying with Colin at the moment.
   - b He lives at Colin's place for a while.

3. *Alan is studying English II and Science I.*
   - a Alan is sitting in the library, studying.
   - b This semester, Alan has chosen these courses.

4. *Alan is writing an important paper.*
   - a He is sitting in front of his computer, typing.
   - b He is busy with his paper most days of the week.

Exercise 4 — State and activity verbs: present continuous

Normally, state verbs do not take the progressive aspect. Here is a list of the most common state verbs.

be	adore	agree	assume	believe	belong to	consider	contain
cost	disagree	feel	hate	have	hope	know	look
love	own	prefer	realise	regret	resemble	smell	taste

However, there are certain special cases where these verbs take the progressive aspect. Then, the meaning of the sentence changes.
Find a state verb from the box for each pair and fill in the present simple or the progressive form so that it matches the meanings.

1. a   You <u>are being</u> rude today!   annoying behaviour
   b   I <u>am</u> fine, thanks.   factual statement

2. a   With growing gas prizes, people _____ public transport.   current trend
   b   Do you _____ milk or lemon for your tea?   general info

3. a   Why _____ (you) the soup so carefully?   current action
   b   Wow, that cake _____ great!   passive state

4. a   Sue, you _____ tired. Go to bed.   passive state
   b   Why _____ (she) at me so angrily?   current action

5. a   My cat really _____ sleeping in my lap.   general statement
   b   Look! The children _____ themselves a lot.   temporary situation

6. a   Sparky _____ running along the shore.   general statement
   b   Look! Sparky _____ running along the shore.   temporary situation

7. a   The Smiths _____ a party at the moment.   current action
   b   My best friend _____ the biggest house I've ever seen.   general statement

Grammar

Present simple or present progressive?

Present simple	Present progressive
general activities	activities happening now
repeated actions	activities happening at a limited period around now
present and general state	temporary situation
feelings and opinions	current, limited feelings and opinions

Exercise 1 Present simple or present progressive?

Circle the correct form.

1. We *are being/am/are* cold. Could you please close the window?

2. Can I call you back? I *have/am having/has* a meeting at the moment.

3. Watch Peter! He *look/looks/is looking* out of the window again.

4. My sister *not like/doesn't like/don't like* lemon ice-cream, but she *is hating/hate/hates* walnut.

5. *Is/Do/Does* Stephen do ice-skating? Yes, but at the moment he *have/is having/has* a cold.

6. How often *does/is/do* Jeff and Peter *play/playing/plays* tennis?

7. That shirt *is looking/look/looks* boring. This one *am/are/is* much better.

8. What *are/do/does* you normally *doing/do/does* at the weekend, Tina? I *am relaxing/do relax/relax*.

Exercise 2 Present simple or present progressive?

Tick the correct sentences and correct the wrong ones.

1. I am thinking of moving into another city. _____

2. I am thinking that this is a very cute dress. You should buy it. _____

3. Look at Stephen! What does he do? _____

4. Where do Alan plays tennis? In a club or just with friends? _____

5. Why do you taste the soup so carefully? Is it too hot? _____

6. Oh no! The teacher looks at me angrily. What have I done? _____

7. You can't go in now! They have a meeting. _____

8. Stephen doesn't likes swimming in cold water. _____

Exercise 3 Present simple or present progressive?

Read the pairs of sentences below. Decide who of the two people could say each of the sentences. Then write the capital letters on the lines provided.

1.	a	I don't play the piano.	A	A professional pianist.	1a:	_B_
	b	I'm not playing the piano.	B	A person not interested in music.	1b:	_A_
2.	a	I am living in different hotels.	A	A tourist on a world trip.	2a:	____
	b	I live in different hotels.	B	A rock star without a permanent home.	2b:	____
3.	a	I don't eat meat.	A	Someone on a special diet to lose weight.	3a:	____
	b	I'm not eating meat.	B	A vegetarian.	3b:	____
4.	a	I don't play computer games.	A	A person without a computer.	4a:	____
	b	I'm not playing computer games.	B	A pupil studying for a test.	4b:	____

Grammar

Exercise 4 Present simple or present progressive?

Fill in the correct forms of the verbs in brackets. Mind statements, questions and negations.

Julie: Hi Terry. Could you help me with my homework please? I _____ (try) to do this exercise, but I _____ (not have) a clue how to start.

Terry: No problem. What _____ (you – do)?

Julie: I _____ (struggle) with today's Maths homework. Normally, I always _____ (find) the answers immediately, but this exercise _____ (be) too hard for me, I'm afraid.

Terry: I see. You _____ (do) Maths with Mr. Jenkins this semester, right? _____ (you – like) his course?

Julie: It _____ (be) okay. Which courses _____ (attend) this semester?

Terry: English III, French II and Trigonometry II. You know, I _____ (prefer) languages to science. Julie, tell me, do you know the girl that _____ (sit) over there?

Julie: Sure. That's Mona. She _____ (not be) in any of my courses this semester, but I _____ (know) her from last semester's volleyball. Mona _____ (adore) languages too.

Terry: Great. You see – I _____ (think) of asking her for a date, but I simply _____ (not dare) asking her out of the blue ... What _____ (you – think)? Could you help me?

Julie: Okay, okay. I will ask her for you ... if you don't mind helping me. I _____ (guess) that this should be okay for you?

Terry: 'Course. So, let's see ...

Exercise 5 Present simple or present progressive?

Write sentences with the following words. Mind the tense as well as the word order.

1. usually/cook/my father/dinner/on Sunday

   _____

2. Tina/mind/never/help/with the homework/her brother

   _____

3. Jonathan/take part in/this year/a Salsa course

   _____

4. buy/cat/I/think of/a

   _____

PRESENT PERFECT TENSES

Present perfect simple

Statement	I	have	played	we	have	played	
have/has + 3rd form	you	have	played	you	have	played	
	he/she/it	has	played	they	have	played	
Negation	I	have not	played	we	have not	played	I have not = I haven't
	you	have not	played	you	have not	played	you have not = you haven't
	he/she/it	has not	played	they	have not	played	they have not = they haven't
Question	Have	I	played?	Have	we	played?	
	Have	you	played?	Have	you	played?	
	Has	he/she/it	played?	Have	they	played?	
! 3rd form/ past participle	base form + -ed e.g.: play – played; cry – cried; stop – stopped irregular forms e.g.: be – been; go – gone; fly – flown (see page 133, 134)						

Exercise 1 Present perfect simple forms

Fill in the correct forms of the verbs. Mind statements, negations and questions.

1. I _____ (be) in Rome twice, but I _____ (not be) in Paris yet.
2. Susan cannot open her car because she _____ (lose) her key.
3. _____ (you – ever – go) on a hiking tour in the Alps?
4. How often _____ (Doug and Carrie – have) a fight over Doug's weight?
5. It's quite cold in here. Someone _____ (forget) to close the window over night.
6. When Bella meets the Cullens, they _____ (not live) in Forks for a very long time.
7. We _____ (always – want) to fly to Hawaii to celebrate our tenth anniversary.
8. Wow, your room looks great! _____ (you – paint) it recently?
9. This year, five thunderstorms _____ (hit) the Caribbean Sea so far.
10. My left foot hurts terribly because I _____ (stumble) over a step.

Exercise 2 Present perfect simple usage

Match the example sentences with the meanings they convey.

1. an event happening in the past that has its result in the present

2. an event happening at an unspecific moment in a time period covering the past up to now

3. a situation lasting from a moment in the past up to now

4. an event having happened so recently that it still is relevant now

____ Don't worry. I have just sent you an e-mail.
____ I am tired because I haven't slept well.
____ Jenna has already been to Singapore and Manila.
____ Pamela has had her turtle for three years now.
____ Mum is angry because I have broken her favourite vase.
____ It has just stopped raining. We can go now.
____ This year, my team has already won seven matches.
____ I have been to Ferro High School for seven years now.
____ Have you ever seen a more gorgeous man?

Grammar

Present perfect progressive

Statement							
have/has + been + verb-ing	I	have	been	playing	we	have	been playing
	you	have	been	playing	you	have	been playing
	he/she/it	has	been	playing	they	have	been playing
Negation	I	have not	been	playing	we	have not	been playing
	you	have not	been	playing	you	have not	been playing
	he/she/it	has not	been	playing	they	have not	been playing
Question	Have	I	been	playing ...?	Have we		been playing ...?
	Have	you	been	playing ...?	Have you		been playing ...?
	Has	he/she/it	been	playing ...?	Have they		been playing ...?

Exercise 1 **Present perfect progressive forms**

Fill in the correct forms of the verbs. Mind statements, negations and questions.

1. What _____ (you – do)? You look exhausted.
2. What's the matter with you? I _____ (wait) for you for three hours!
3. Jacob and Joy _____ (live) together for five years now.
4. Infant mortality _____ (get) worse in some 3rd world countries.
5. How long _____ (Hugh – work) on his car?

Present perfect simple or present perfect progressive?

Exercise 1 **Read the example sentences and then match the definitions with the example sentences (A–H).**

	Present perfect simple		Present perfect progressive
A	■ I have painted my room. It looks great now.	E	■ I have been painting my room all day long. I'm completely exhausted.
B	■ I have completely forgotten about our date. Sorry for being late.	F	■ I have been waiting for you for two hours!
C	■ Prices have increased by 3 %.	G	■ Prices have been increasing for a while.
D	■ Today, my family has dropped in three times to see our first baby.	H	■ Since the early afternoon my whole family has been dropping in to see our first baby.

 We use present perfect tense when there is a connection between an action in the past and the present!

	Present perfect simple
A, B	We use present perfect simple tense to emphasize the **result** a past action has on the present.
	When we talk about **repeated actions** and mention the number of times the action has been repeated, we use present perfect simple.
	When we talk about a **changing situation** over a period of time up to now, we use present perfect simple.
	Present perfect progressive
	We use present perfect progressive to emphasize the **action** itself, rather than the result.
	We use present perfect progressive to emphasize the **durational** aspect of the action.
	When we talk about **repeated actions** from the past up to now without mentioning the number of times the action has been repeated, we prefer present perfect progressive.
	When we talk about a **changing situation** without mentionining specific facts, we prefer present perfect progressive.

Grammar

Exercise 2 Present perfect simple or present perfect progressive?

Fill in the verb written in *italics* on the right side in the correct form.

1. a Jane _____ for her cat all afternoon long.

   b _____ (you – already) my missing scarf? *look for*

2. a Today Luke _____ better than ever before.

   b Michelle _____ for two hours. Now she's exhausted. *run*

3. a Oh no! My piece of cake _____. Bacon – you sly dog!

   b Various socks _____ from my drawer since we got Bacon. *disappear*

4. a Christian _____ London three times so far.

   b We _____ London since 1998 and we've always liked it. *visit*

5. a My daughter _____ this boy for two months now!

   b Sarah? Oh, I _____ (not) her today. *see*

Present perfect or present simple?

You might have realized that present perfect simple tense does not have a corresponding tense in German. It may be claimed that the so-called German „Perfekt" is an equivalent to the English present perfect, but this assumption only refers to „Perfekt" forms, not to its usage. The English present perfect is a special time concept on its own that may not be compared to any German time scheme.

Exercise 1

Read the example sentences and complete the summary with the words from the box.

We have lived in Austria since my birth.
I love talking on my mobile phone.
My bag is gone. Someone has stolen it.
Joanne has been dating Alan for a while now.

It's snowing! Let's go sleigh riding down the hill.
My mum always does yoga in the evening.
Max has been walking for eight hours. He's tired.
Sylvia and Nadine are quarelling.

present perfect progressive	present progressive	present perfect simple	present simple

1. We use _____ to talk about **general** statements and **regular** activities.

2. We use _____ to talk about activities happening **now**, at the moment.

3. We use _____ to talk about **past** events having a connection to **now**.

4. We use _____ to stress the **duration** or **repetition** of events **up to now**.

Exercise 2

Translate the following sentences. Mind the tenses.

1. Wir haben unseren Hund seit drei Jahren. _____

2. Jill geht oft mit ihren Freunden tanzen. _____

3. Wie oft war Yves schon in Schottland? _____

4. Edward hat sein Auto seit 2 Jahren. _____

5. Mary hat ihre Maus noch nicht gefüttert. _____

6. Wie lange wohnst du schon in New York? _____

Grammar

PAST TENSES

Past simple

Statement	I	played	we	played	
past form/2nd form	you	played	you	played	
	he/she/it	played	they	played	
Negation	I did not play		we did not play		
	you did not play		you did not play		!did not = didn't
	he/she/it did not play		they did not play		
Question	Did I play …?		Did we play …?		
	Did you play …?		Did you play …?		
	Did he/she/it play …?		Did they play …?		
past form/2nd form	base form + -ed		e.g.: play – played; cry – cried		
	irregular forms! (see page 133, 134)		e.g.: be – was, were; have – had; go – went		
!to be:	negation: I wasn't – you weren't		question: Was I …? Were you …? Was he …? Were we/you/they …?		

Exercise 1 Past simple forms

Find the mistakes and correct them.

1. Kate didn't won the first price in the Maths competition. _____
2. Who did play tennis with you? _____
3. Did you be at the club last weekend? _____
4. I buyed this dress last week in a new boutique in town. _____
5. Yesterday Janet didn't wrote an e-mail to her friend Sienna. _____
6. When went you to the dentist? _____
7. I weren't at the cinema with Michael. _____
8. Jonathan didn't his French homework. He simply forgot. _____

Exercise 2

Find the correct forms of the verbs in brackets. Mind statements, negations and questions.

1. Maggie _____ *(catch)* a bad cold yesterday. So she _____ *(go)* to the doctor.
2. Andrea _____ *(not fly)* to Paris because she _____ *(not have)* enough money.
3. Jake! You _____ *(not do)* me a favour when you _____ *(try)* to help me.
4. When _____ *(Steve – leave)* yesterday? I _____ *(want)* to say bye.
5. _____ *(be – Caroline)* at school last Monday? I _____ *(not – see)* her.
6. Last week, the sun _____ *(rise)* much earlier. And when _____ *(it – set)*?
7. What has happened to your hair? It _____ *(not be)* that red I last saw you.
8. Sorry. I _____ *(not be)* able to see you yesterday. I _____ *(feel)* horrible.
9. Who _____ *(drive)* my car yesterday? What exactly _____ *(you – do)* with it?

Grammar

Past progressive/Past continuous

Statement	I	was	playing	we	were	playing	
was/were + verb-ing	you	were	playing	you	were	playing	
	he/she/it	was	playing	they	were	playing	
Negation	I	was not	playing	we	were not	playing	I was not = I wasn't
	you	were not	playing	you	were not	playing	you were not = you weren't
	he/she/it	was not	playing	they	were not	playing	he was not = he wasn't
Question	Was	I	playing?	Were	we	playing?	
	Were	you	playing?	Were	you	playing?	
	Was	he/she/it	playing?	Were	they	playing?	

!Remember that most state verbs do not take the progressive aspect. (See page 112)

Exercise 1 Past progressive forms

Fill in the correct forms of the verbs in brackets. Mind statements, negations and questions.

1. This morning, the sun _____ (shine) and the birds _____ (sing).

2. While Bree _____ (cook) her husband _____ (watch) TV.

3. What _____ (you – do) at 7 p.m.? I _____ (have) dinner.

4. _____ (Sue – have) a shower when the telephone rang?

5. When I looked out of the window I saw that it _____ (get) dark outside.

6. Last Saturday at three I _____ (play) tennis with my girlfriend.

7. I _____ (stay) in Paris when my best friend _____ (live) in Nice.

8. Josephine _____ (not wait) in front of her phone when Pacey finally called.

Exercise 2 Past progressive usage

Read through the different meanings the past progressive can convey. Then match the example sentences in exercise 1 with the correct definition.

A It is used for unfinished actions in the past. They were in the middle of happening. _____

B It is used for actions happening around a certain time in the past. _____

C It is used to compare parallel actions in the past. _____

D It is used for background descriptions of a story set in the past. /_____

Exercise 3 Find the mistakes and correct them.

1. What did you do last Friday at ten o'clock? _____

2. Who were Jody waiting for when you met her yesterday? _____

3. Did the sun shone when you went into the mountains? _____

4. I watched TV when suddenly the doorbell rang. _____

5. Phil wasn't do the washing-up when his mum called him. _____

6. P.J. entered the room when suddenly her cat was jumping out. _____

Grammar

Past simple or past progressive?

Exercise 1 **Past simple or past progressive?**

Read the definitions. Then write the numbers of the fitting examples in the boxes provided.

Past simple		Past progressive	
	■ finished actions in the past single events happening in the past		■ unfinished actions in the past that were in the middle of taking place
	■ one event happening after the other		■ comparing parallel actions
			■ actions happening around a certain time
			■ background information

1	I got up, brushed my teeth and dressed.	4	Last year we travelled around the world.
2	While Sue was cutting the grass Marcus was watering the flowers.	5	I was brushing my teeth when my sister came in and wanted to take a shower.
3	When we arrived it was raining heavily.	6	At ten? Oh, I was cleaning the kitchen.

Exercise 2 **Past simple or past progressive?**

Match the example sentences (A or B) with the meanings.

A When I came into the kitchen my mum made breakfast.   ___ She was in the middle of making breakfast.

B When I came into the kitchen my mum was making breakfast.   ___ She started making breakfast when she saw me.

Exercise 3 **Past simple or past progressive?**

Fill in the correct forms of the verbs in brackets. Mind statements, negations and questions.

1. What _____ (you – do) last Monday at ten? I _____ (want) to see you.

2. I haven't talked to my best friend Marla for a while. When I last _____ (see) her she _____ (look for) another job.

3. What _____ (Peter – think) about your idea of buying a dog?

4. Our dog _____ (steal) the cake while I _____ (not look).

5. _____ (I – disturb) you when I _____ (call) you yesterday? No, I _____ (not do) anything special.

6. Yesterday, I _____ (hear) a strange noise. Someone _____ (try) to get into our house. I _____ (not know) what to do.

7. We _____ (meet) Gina at the bus station last Friday. She _____ (go) to Brighton. We _____ (not have) much time, but while we _____ (wait) for our buses we _____ (have) a little chat.

8. What _____ (Jake – want) to be when he was a child? A rock star.

9. The car _____ (drive) too fast when the accident _____ (happen).

10. My mum _____ (drive) me to the party yesterday. So I _____ (not have) to wait for the bus in the rain.

Grammar

Past simple or present perfect?

Exercise 1 **Signal words**

Match the words in the box with the example sentences.

ever – last year – for – in 1492 – so far – already – since – yesterday – never – yet – in 2006 – last week – yet – an hour ago – this week

Past simple	Present perfect
_____ we travelled to San Francisco.	I have _____ been to San Francisco.
I saw *Dr. House* _____ evening.	Have you _____ seen *Dr. House*?
Columbus discovered America _____.	Has Rory discovered her present _____?
I tried to call you _____.	My boyfriend hasn't called me _____.
Stephanie Mayer wrote *New Moon* _____.	We have _____ read *New Moon*.
_____ was the best week in my life.	_____ has been the best week ever.
William Shakespeare wrote many plays.	J.K. Rowling has written seven books _____.
We moved into this house in 2001.	We have lived here _____ 2001.
We lived here for ten years, but then we moved to a bigger house.	We have lived here _____ eight years and we are still very happy.

Exercise 2 **Past simple or present perfect?**

Complete the definitions with the words in the box.

present – past – have – unfinished – finished – do not have any – result

The **past simple** is a _____ tense. It refers to actions that are _____ from today's

perspective. They _____ connection to the present.

The **present perfect** is a _____ tense. It refers to actions that _____ a connection to the

present. Either, the action is _____, or it has a _____ in the present.

Exercise 3 **Past simple or present perfect?**

Fill in the correct forms of the verbs in brackets. Mind statements, negations and questions.

1. Heidi _____ *(be)* my best friend since kindergarten. We _____ *(go)* to school

    together and then we both _____ *(study)* medicine. After university, we _____

    (not start) working at the same hospital, but we still meet regularly.

2. _____ *(you – see)* Tim yesterday? No, but I _____ *(just – call)* him.

3. Ina _____ *(not feel)* very well last Monday, but she _____ *(recover)* quickly.

    She _____ *(already – be)* to work today.

Grammar

Past perfect simple

Statement	I	had	played	we	had	played	
had + 3rd form	you	had	played	you	had	played	
	he/she/it	had	played	they	had	played	
Negation	I	had not	played	we	had not	played	I had not = I hadn't
	you	had not	played	you	had not	played	
	he/she/it	had not	played	they	had not	played	
Question	Had	I	played?	Had	we	played?	
	Had	you	played?	Had	you	played?	
	Had	he/she/it	played?	Had	they	played?	

Exercise 1

Read the example sentences and fill in the words from the box.

past perfect – past – present tense – past tense – present – present perfect

_____	_____
Why are you tired? Because I haven't slept well.	I was tired yesterday because I hadn't slept well.
Your boyfriend is looking angrily at you. What have you said to him?	Yesterday at the party, your boyfriend was looking angrily at you. What had you said to him?
The school bell is ringing. Have you all finished?	I had finished my paper just before the bell rang.
Ausgangszeit: _____	*Ausgangszeit:* _____
This tense is used for events happening before the _____.	This tense is used for events happening before the _____.

Exercise 2 Past simple/past progressive or past perfect?

Fill in the correct forms of the verbs in brackets. Mind statements, negations and questions.

1. I was driving to work when I realised that I _____ *(forget)* to feed my cat.

2. When Elias _____ *(come)* into the kitchen he saw that he _____ *(not turn off)* the oven. There _____ *(be)* smoke everwhere.

3. We _____ *(have)* a lot of fun, dancing to great music, when suddenly the doorbell _____ *(ring)*. Our neighbours _____ *(call)* the police!

4. Before Suzanna _____ *(start)* to bake her favourite cookies, she _____ *(think)* of buying all the important ingredients. She _____ *(cut)* the nuts when she realized that she _____ *(not buy)* enough eggs.

5. When I came home I saw that my whole family _____ *(eat)* without me.

6. After Emma _____ *(hear)* the news she _____ *(start)* to sing, dance and laugh.

Grammar

Past perfect progressive/Past perfect continuous

Statement	I	had	been	playing	we	had	been	playing
had + been + verb-ing	you	had	been	playing	you	had	been	playing
	he/she/it	had	been	playing	they	had	been	playing
Negation	I	had not	been	playing	we	had not	been	playing
	you	had not	been	playing	you	had not	been	playing
	he/she/it	had not	been	playing	they	had not	been	playing
Question	Had	I	been	playing …?	Had	we	been	playing …?
	Had	you	been	playing …?	Had	you	been	playing …?
	Had	he/she/it	been	playing …?	Had	they	been	playing …?

Exercise 1 Past perfect progressive forms

Fill in the correct forms of the verbs. Mind statements, negations and questions.

1. It _____ (snow) for two weeks before the ski lifts opened.

2. How long _____ (Jody – practice) before she won the championship?

3. They _____ (work) on their project for months, but they couldn't present any good ideas at last week's presentation.

4. Although Jenna _____ (listen) hard to her teacher, she was not able to answer the questions in the test.

5. It _____ (rain) for days when the dike broke and the town was flooded.

6. How long _____ (your father – ask) your mother to go out with him before she finally said yes?

7. The sun _____ (not shine) for three months when the fog finally lifted and the whole world brightened up.

Present perfect progressive or past perfect progressive?

Exercise 1

Read the example sentences. Then complete the definitions.

Present perfect progressive	Past perfect progressive
■ Sue has been trying to explain the problem again and again, but Pete still doesn't understand her.	■ Sue had been trying to explain the problem again and again but Pete simply didn't understand her.
■ We have been sitting on this plane for twenty minutes now, waiting to take off. There must be some problem.	■ We had been sitting on the plane for twenty minutes, waiting to take off. Later we found out that there had been a problem with the engine.
■ **Time basis: Present**	■ **Time basis:** _____
■ The present perfect progressive is used to stress the duration of actions taking place from the past up to _____.	■ The past perfect progressive is used to stress the duration of actions taking place before the _____.

Grammar

Exercise 2 Present perfect progressive or past perfect progressive?

1. Please, take Ruff for a walk. He _____ (sit) in his basket all morning long.

2. We _____ (discuss) our plans for the summer holidays for two hours, when mum finally said that she was tired of listening to our complaints.

3. How long _____ (sit) in front of your computer? Your eyes are red and you look quite exhausted. Turn it off and go to bed!

4. When Sienna was told that she wouldn't get the job, she first couldn't believe her ears because she _____ (work) so hard for it.

5. The war between England and France _____ (go on) for more than one hundred years when England was finally defeated in 1453.

6. Phoebe! You _____ (occupy) the bathroom for nearly two hours! Get out and let me have a shower.

7. Look at Tamara! She _____ (sing and dance) all night long, but she still looks great.

Past perfect simple or past perfect progressive?

Before you do the exercise, read the information on present perfect tenses on page 115 ff again. You can easily transfer the rules for present perfect tenses to past perfect tenses. Then do the following exercise.

Exercise 1 Past perfect simple or past perfect progressive?

1. Conner was really sorry that he _____ (break) his promise to help his girlfriend with the Maths homework. He couldn't go to her place to help her because he _____ (try) to fix his car all afternoon long, without success.

2. Robby _____ (ask) Jackie fifteen times to go out with him when she finally gave in and said yes.

3. Joy _____ (think of) apologizing to her best friend the whole afternoon long when she finally called Michaela. Joy told her that she was very sorry and that she _____ (make) a big mistake.

4. Last Sunday, my parents and I wanted to go to our favourite restaurant. When we arrived there, we had to find out that the restaurant _____ (close) two weeks ago.

5. When the teacher asked Patricia a question about the film they _____ (just – see), Patricia couldn't give the correct answer. She _____ (talk) to her best friend during the whole lesson.

6. When I wanted to get the cake from the kitchen, I saw that it was gone. I was quite sure that my dog _____ (steal) it.

Grammar
FUTURE TENSES

Will-future	Going-to-future	Present progressive	Present simple
will/won't + base form	be + going to + base form	be + verb-ing	present simple forms
Perhaps I **will see** the film with Eric.	I am definitely **going to see** the film with Eric.	Tonight I **am seeing** this film with Eric.	The film **starts** at nine.
spontaneous, not sure	personal plan, intention	fixed arrangement	fixed dates (timetables)

Will-future

Exercise 1 Will-future forms

Fill in the correct forms of the verbs in brackets. Mind statements, negations and questions.

1. _____ (you – close) the door after me, please?

2. I don't think that Jeannine _____ (stay) long. She looks tired.

3. You seem to have problems with your homework. I _____ (help) you.

4. Do you want to go jogging with me? Sure. I _____ (join) you after work.

5. I'm afraid I _____ (not to be able to) see you tomorrow. I'm sorry.

6. Jenna hopes that her boyfriend _____ (call) her in the afternoon.

Exercise 2 Will-future usage

Match the meanings with the example sentences in exercise 1.

Offering to do something. Spontaneous decision out of the moment. _____

Agreeing to do something. Spontaneous decision out of the moment. _____

Promising to do something. Spontaneous decision out of the moment. _____

Asking somebody to do something. Spontaneous decision out of the moment. _____

Predicting events that are not sure to happen. (probably, I expect, I'm not sure, I (don't) think) _____

Going-to-future

Exercise 1 Going-to-future forms

Fill in the correct forms of the verbs in brackets. Mind statements, negations and questions.

1. A: Tony is in town. B: I know. I _____ (visit) him this evening.

2. I know that Phil _____ (marry) Annie. She accepted his proposal last week.

3. There are yellow clouds in the sky. It _____ (hail) soon.

Exercise 2 Going-to-future usage

Match the meanings with the example sentences in exercise 1.

Personal decisions that have already been planned. ____

Future predictions based on present observations. ____

Something is sure to happen. ____

Grammar

Exercise 3 Will-future or going-to-future?

1. "Have you heard that Mo has got a new job?" "No. I _____ (call) him later."

2. "Fin has found a new apartment." "I know. I _____ (see) it next Monday."

3. "This bridge doesn't look very safe!" "No, it _____ (break) down soon."

4. "Why is Bernie putting on his shoes?" "He _____ (meet) his girlfriend."

5. "I'm afraid I _____ (not have) time to have dinner with you. I'm sorry."

Present progressive and present simple with future meaning

Exercise 1 Present progressive or present simple?

Read the example sentences. Then complete the definitions at the bottom.

Present progressive	Present simple
We are seeing each other on Monday.	My plane leaves on Monday at seven.
Lenny is having a great party this Friday.	When does the party start?
Shelley and Rick are getting married this June.	Where does the ceremony take place?
What time are you meeting Andrea tomorrow?	The film begins at nine.

We use the _____ for future activities that are already arranged. These are personal arrangements with fixed dates.

We use the _____ for official future activities. They may be fixed on timetables or programmes. (e.g.: public transport, cinema, invitations)

Mixed future tenses

Exercise 1

Fill in the correct forms of the verbs in brackets. Mind statements, negations and questions.

Robin: What _____ (do) this weekend? Have you already made any plans?

Spence: I'm not sure. I think I _____ (spend) some time with Mona. Why?

Robin: 'Cause Jake and I _____ (have) a great party Friday night. If you change your mind, you can come, of course.

Spence: Good idea. I _____ (ask) Mona. Where _____ (party – take place)?

Robin: At *Paddy's*. I'm sure that there _____ (be) loads of people.

Spence: Sounds great. If we come, we _____ (take) some crisps with us. Is that okay?

Robin: Sure! We _____ (serve) sandwiches, chips and brownies. Crisps would be great.

Spence: Fine. So I _____ (ask) Mona, but I am quite optimistic that she _____ (say) yes. Bye Robin.

Robin: Bye.

Grammar

MODAL VERBS

Modalverben haben eine ganz besondere Stellung im grammatikalischen Zeitengefüge.
- Sie bilden Verneinung und Frage ohne „do/does/did".
- Sie behalten in allen Personen ihre Form. (Kein *3rd person „s"*)
- Sie können nicht in allen Zeiten verwendet werden: Man muss sie umschreiben.

Die folgende Liste zeigt dir die wichtigsten Modalverben und ihre Umschreibungen (*multi-part verbs*):

	Present tense	**Past tense**	**Future tense**
können	I can sing.	I could sing.	(I can sing.)
can/to be able to	I am able to sing.	I was able to sing.	I will be able to sing.
nicht können	I can't sing	I couldn't sing.	(I can't sing.)
can't/not to be able to	I am not able to sing.	I wasn't able to sing.	I won't be able to sing.
könnte	I might help you.	----------	I might help you.
might/could	I could help you.	----------	I could help you.
müssen	I must sing.	----------	----------
must/have to	I have to sing.	I had to sing.	I will have to sing.
nicht müssen	I don't have to sing.	I didn't have to sing.	I won't have to sing.
don't have to/needn't	I needn't sing.	I didn't need to sing.	I won't need to sing.
dürfen	I may sing.	----------	----------
may/to be allowed to	I am allowed to sing.	I was allowed to sing.	I will be allowed to sing.
nicht dürfen	I may not sing.	----------	----------
may not/must not	I must not sing.	----------	----------
not to be allowed to	I'm not allowed to sing.	I wasn't allowed to sing.	I won't be allowed to sing.
sollen	I should sing.	----------	----------
should/to be supposed to	I am supposed to sing.	I was supposed to sing.	I will be supposed to sing.
nicht sollen	I shouldn't sing.	----------	----------
	I'm not supposed to …	I wasn't supposed to …	I won't be supposed to …
eigentlich sollen	I ought to sing.	----------	----------

Exercise 1 Modal verbs

Paraphrase the sentence either with a modal or a multi-part verb.

1. Our cat can climb trees faster than squirrels. _____

2. We may go to the cinema. _____

3. We shouldn't eat the cake. _____

4. I wasn't able to fix the blender. _____

5. You are not allowed to leave now. _____

6. Sue needn't worry about it. _____

7. I can't see you tomorrow. _____

8. Paul might forget about it. _____

Grammar

Exercise 2 Modal verbs

Fill in the correct form of the modal verbs. Mind the tenses.

1. You really _____ (eigentlich sollen – besuchen) your granny these days.

2. Lilly _____ (nicht dürfen – einkaufen gehen) with her friends yesterday.

3. _____ (können – der Mechaniker – reparieren) your car until next week?

4. Jeannie _____ (sollen – lernen) more for her test. If not, she will fail.

5. You _____ (sollen – kaufen) some toffees for mum when you go shopping.

6. I think Alison _____ (nicht müssen – machen) anything for her wedding.
   All her family members are going to help her. She _____ (könnte) as well relax a bit.

7. Emma _____ (nicht müssen – aufpassen) her little brother last weekend.
   So she _____ (dürfen – ausgehen) with me. We had a great evening.

8. I'm sorry! I _____ (nicht können – lesen) your essay so far.

9. Tim! You know that you _____ (nicht dürfen – tragen) shoes in here!

10. _____ (du – müssen – fragen) your parents if you are allowed to go skiing with us?

Exercise 3 Modal verbs

Find the mistakes and correct them.

1. Joey hasn't to do much homework today.   _____
2. In Austria, children mustn't go to school on Sunday. _____
3. Mary weren't able to do her homework.   _____
4. We didn't must help in the garden yesterday.   _____
5. Jake not allowed to stay up late on schooldays.   _____
6. Chris hadn't to help his father in the garden last weekend. _____

Exercise 4 Modal verbs: Translations

1. Peter darf seine Freundin nach zehn nicht anrufen.

   _____

2. Wir werden morgen nicht zu deinem Konzert kommen können.

   _____

3. Dürfen wir euer Auto ausborgen, um in das Einkaufszentrum zu fahren?

   _____

4. Ich musste noch nie in meinem Leben so eine blöde Aufgabe machen.

   _____

5. Wir konnten den Gipfel am letzten Sonntag nicht erreichen, weil das Wetter schlecht war.

   _____

Grammar

Perfect modal verbs

Wenn du über Modalitäten in der Vergangenheit berichten willst, musst du die Modalverben in die *perfect*-Formen setzen. Die folgende Tabelle zeigt dir die wichtigsten *perfect modal verbs*.

Modal verb	Perfect modal verb	Examples
can't	can't have had	They can't have had a great holiday. *Sie können keinen schönen Urlaub gehabt haben.*
could	could have studied	I could have studied more, but I didn't. *Ich hätte mehr lernen können.*
must	must have lost	You must have lost your umbrella on the train. *Du musst deinen Schirm in der Bahn verloren haben.*
should	should have called	You should have called Marge two hours ago. *Du hättest Marge vor zwei Stunden anrufen sollen.*
should not	should not have left	Petra should not have left so early yesterday evening. *Petra hätte nicht so früh gehen sollen.*
may	may have left	Where is Bruce? He may have already left the party. *Bruce hat die Party vielleicht schon verlassen.*
might	might have hurt	Why did you do that? You might have hurt yourself! *Du hättest dich verletzen können.*

Exercise 1 Perfect modal verbs

Read the sentences above again and complete the rule.

Perfect modal verbs express modalities happening in the _____.

They are built with: _____ + have + _____

Exercise 2 Modal verbs

Fill in the verbs in brackets in the correct form.

1. You really _____ (should – ask) Tonia to go to Prom night with you.
2. Chris _____ (might – help) you if you had asked him.
3. He _____ (can't – break) the vase. He wasn't in the room when it happened.
4. I _____ (could – buy) more eggs if you had told me to do so.
5. Frank _____ (must – study) hard because he knew all the answers.
6. Liza _____ (may – invite) you if you hadn't talked bad about her.
7. We _____ (should not – touch) that dog. It looks dangerous.
8. Nora _____ (must – buy) new eggs because hers were rotten.
9. George _____ (cannot – do) his homework tomorrow.
10. They _____ (must – spend) a great week in Rome. They look so happy!
11. My cat _____ (must – sleep) in my bed. There is cat hair everywhere.
12. You _____ (could – help) me! I know you had time.

Grammar

Mixed tenses: Full verbs and modal verbs

Fill in the correct form of the verbs. Mind the tenses.

Nina: Hi Sue! Nice to see you! How _____ (be) you? I _____ (not see) you for quite a while.

Sue: Hello Nina! I'm okay, but I _____ (be) a bit stressed at the moment.

Nina: Really? Why?

Sue: Well, yesterday we _____ (must) write a Maths test and the day before our English teacher _____ (want) us to hand in our book reports.

Nina: Oh, poor you! That _____ (not sound) good! But I'm sure that you _____ (get) an A or a B on your Maths test.

Sue: Well I hope so. Because if I _____ (not pass) it, I _____ (may not) to go to the cinema at the weekend. And I really _____ (want) to go because Jason, this cute guy from class 5B, _____ (ask) me to go out with him.

Nina: Wow! That's great! Tell me all about it. How _____ (that – happen)?

Sue: Well, last Friday after we _____ (come) back from the Physics lesson, Jason _____ (wait) in front of our classroom. I _____ (wonder) what he _____ (do) there but I would have never thought that it _____ (be) because of me.

Nina: I can imagine. Because if you _____ (know) that he was waiting for you, you _____ (be) excited, I guess.

Sue: That's absolutely true! Let me go on! I _____ (go) into the classroom and he _____ (follow) me. At first I _____ (not see) that he _____ (stand) behind me, but suddenly he _____ (call) my name and so I _____ (turn) around.

Nina: _____ (he – look) good?

Sue: Oh yes, he did! He _____ (wear) his blue polo shirt, the one that perfectly _____ (match) his eyes.

Nina: Gorgeous! But hang on for a minute because my mobile phone _____ (ring). ... (on the phone) "Hello Peter! ... Well I _____ (not – can) talk to you right now because I _____ (chat) with Sue at the moment. ... Alright – I _____ (call) you in the evening, I promise. Bye ..."

Sue: _____ (be) that Peter?

Grammar

Nina: Yes. He just _____ (want) to know if I _____ (already – do) my German homework. But never mind. Just go on telling me about Jason and you!

Sue: Well ... there isn't much more to say. He _____ (ask) me if I _____ (want) to see the new James Bond film on Friday and I _____ (say) yes. So if I _____ (pass) that stupid Maths test, Jason and I _____ (have) a date at the weekend.

Nina: That's so romantic! When do you think _____ (you – get) back the test? Before the weekend?

Sue: Yes, I'm sure that Mrs Jackson _____ (give back) the tests by Thursday because she _____ (travel) to Ireland with class 6C on Friday.

Nina: I cross my fingers for you and Jason! Call me as soon as you _____ (know) the result and _____ (give) my love to your sister!

Sue: I will! Oh by the way – _____ (you – hear) about Eric and Meredith?

Nina: No! What _____ (you – talk) about?

Sue: I'm not sure, but some people _____ (say) that they _____ (split up). It's not sure, but I _____ (see) Meredith with another guy in yesterday's dancing class.

Nina: That _____ (not can) be true! Eric and Meredith _____ (start) dating three years ago and from that moment on they _____ (spend) every single minute together, as far as I know.

Sue: Sure. I know what you mean. Before Meredith _____ (meet) Eric we _____ (be) best friends. But then she _____ (stop) seeing me. I _____ (feel) quite unhappy back then, you know.

Nina: Yeah – I can imagine. Do you think this _____ (change) now that Meredith and Eric _____ (split up)?

Sue: I _____ (doubt) it. You see – we _____ (not have) much contact in the last years. So, our interests _____ (may change) a lot. I _____ (must – admit) that I _____ (not know) much about Meredith.

Nina: I see. Sorry Sue, but my bus _____ (leave) in a minute and I _____ (not must) miss it. See you tomorrow?

Sue: Sure! See you!

Grammar

IRREGULAR VERBS

base form	past form	past participle	
awake	awoke	awoken	*aufwachen*
be	was/were	been	*sein*
beat	beat	beaten	*schlagen*
become	became	become	*werden*
begin	began	begun	*beginnen*
bet	bet	bet	*wetten*
bite	bit	bitten	*beißen*
bleed	bled	bled	*bluten*
blow	blew	blown	*blasen*
break	broke	broken	*(zer)brechen*
bring	brought	brought	*bringen*
build	built	built	*bauen*
burn	burnt (burned)	burnt (burned)	*verbrennen*
buy	bought	bought	*kaufen*
can/to be able to	could/was able to	–/have been able to	*können*
come	came	come	*kommen*
choose	chose	chosen	*wählen*
cost	cost	cost	*kosten (Geld)*
creep	crept	crept	*kriechen*
cut	cut	cut	*schneiden*
do	did	done	*tun, machen*
deal	dealt	dealt	*handeln/beschäftigen*
dig	dug	dug	*graben*
draw	drew	drawn	*zeichnen*
dream	dreamt (dreamed)	dreamt (dreamed)	*träumen*
drink	drank	drunk	*trinken*
drive	drove	driven	*fahren, lenken*
eat	ate	eaten	*essen, fressen*
fall	fell	fallen	*(nieder)fallen*
feed	fed	fed	*füttern*
feel	felt	felt	*fühlen*
fight	fought	fought	*kämpfen*
find	found	found	*finden*
flee	fled	fled	*flüchten*
fly	flew	flown	*fliegen*
forbid	forbade	forbidden	*verbieten*
forget	forgot	forgotten	*vergessen*
forgive	forgave	forgiven	*vergeben*
freeze	froze	frozen	*(er)/(ein)frieren*
get	got	got	*bekommen, werden*
give	gave	given	*geben*
go	went	gone	*gehen, fahren (by ...)*
grow	grew	grown	*wachsen*
hang	hung	hung	*hängen*
have	had	had	*haben*
hear	heard	heard	*hören*
hide	hid	hidden	*vestecken*
hit	hit	hit	*schlagen*
hold	held	held	*halten*
hurt	hurt	hurt	*verletzen*
keep	kept	kept	*behalten, aufbewahren*
know	knew	known	*kennen, wissen*
lay	laid	laid	*legen*
lead	led	led	*führen*

Grammar

IRREGULAR VERBS

base form	past form	past participle	
learn	learnt (learned)	learnt (learned)	*lernen*
leave	left	left	*verlassen, lassen*
let	let	let	*lassen*
lie	lay	lain	*liegen*
light	lit	lit	*anzünden, erleuchten*
lose	lost	lost	*verlieren*
make	made	made	*machen*
may/to be allowed to	–/was allowed to	–/has been allowed to	*dürfen*
mean	meant	meant	*meinen, bedeuten*
meet	met	met	*sich treffen*
must/have to	–/had to	–/have had to	*müssen*
must not/not be allowed to	–/was not allowed to	–/haven't been allowed to	*nicht dürfen*
pay	paid	paid	*(be)zahlen*
put	put	put	*setzen, legen, stellen*
read	read	read	*lesen*
ride	rode	ridden	*reiten, (mit)fahren*
ring	rang	rung	*läuten*
rise	rose	risen	*erheben, aufgehen*
run	ran	run	*laufen*
say	said	said	*sagen*
see	saw	seen	*sehen*
sell	sold	sold	*verkaufen*
send	sent	sent	*(ab)schicken*
set	set	set	*setzen, einstellen*
shake	shook	shaken	*schütteln, beben*
shine	shone	shone	*scheinen, glänzen*
shoot	shot	shot	*schießen*
show	showed	shown (showed)	*zeigen*
shut	shut	shut	*schließen*
sing	sang	sung	*singen*
sit	sat	sat	*sitzen*
sleep	slept	slept	*schlafen*
smell	smelt (smelled)	smelt (smelled)	*riechen*
speak	spoke	spoken	*sprechen*
spell	spelt	spelt	*buchstabieren*
spend	spent	spent	*verbringen, ausgeben*
spring	sprang	sprung	*springen, hüpfen*
stand	stood	stood	*stehen*
steal	stole	stolen	*stehlen*
stick	stuck	stuck	*stecken, kleben*
sting	stung	stung	*stechen*
strike	struck	struck	*schlagen*
swear	swore	sworn	*schwören*
sweat	sweat	sweat	*schwitzen*
swim	swam	swum	*schwimmen*
swing	swung	swung	*schwingen*
take	took	taken	*nehmen, bringen*
teach	taught	taught	*lehren, unterrichten*
tell	told	told	*erzählen*
think	thought	thought	*denken*
throw	threw	thrown	*werfen*
understand	understood	understood	*verstehen*
wake	woke	woken	*wecken*
wear	wore	worn	*tragen*
win	won	won	*gewinnen*
write	wrote	written	*schreiben*

LANGUAGE IN USE

WHAT IS IT ALL ABOUT? – EINLEITUNG

Neben der *Listening Comprehension (LC)*, der *Reading Comprehension (RC)* und dem Schreiben eigener Texte ist *Language/English in Use* ein weiterer, wichtiger Teilaspekt bei der Zentralmatura. Hier geht es darum zu zeigen, dass du die englische Sprache sicher und fehlerfrei anwenden kannst. Je flexibler du im Umgang mit dem Englischen bist, desto leichter werden dir die Übungen fallen. Achte beim Lernen (vor allem beim Vokabellernen) stets darauf, dass du dir Wortgruppen und Wortfamilien einprägst, also zum Beispiel nicht nur das Verb *to improve* (verbessern), sondern auch gleich das Nomen *(improvement)* und im Idealfall auch das Gegenteil *(deterioration)*. Dadurch erreichst du mit der Zeit eine unglaubliche Ausdehnung deines Wortschatzes und du wirst sehen, dass das Verfassen von Texten und Aufsätzen wesentlich einfacher wird.

False friends

Auch die sogenannten *false friends* sind ein Thema in diesem Zusammenhang. Es handelt sich hierbei um Paare von Wörtern oder Ausdrücken aus zwei Sprachen (in unserem Fall Englisch und Deutsch), die orthografisch (also von der Art, wie man sie schreibt) oder phonetisch (die Art, wie man sie ausspricht) ähnlich sind, jedoch unterschiedliche Bedeutungen haben. Hier findest du nun eine Liste der gängigsten *false friends*. Präge sie dir gut ein, denn so kannst du unnötige Vokabelfehler bei den Schularbeiten vermeiden!

FALSE FRIENDS			
ENGLISCH ▶ DEUTSCH		**DEUTSCH ▶ ENGLISCH**	
ENGLISH WORD	**DEUTSCHE ÜBERSETZUNG**	**DEUTSCHES WORT**	**ENGLISH EXPRESSION**
actual	wirklich, tatsächlich	aktuell	topical, current
also	auch	also	so
arm	Arm	arm	poor
art	Kunst	Art	way, sort, kind
biro	Kugelschreiber	Büro	office
brave	mutig	brav	good, well-behaved
brief	kurz	Brief	letter
chef	Küchenchef	Chef	boss
college	Hochschule	Kollege	colleague
concern	Anliegen, Angelegenheit	Konzern, Firma	affiliated group
concurrence	Einverständnis, Mitwirkung	Konkurrenz	competition
consequent	daraus folgend	konsequent	consistent
desert	Wüste	Dessert, Nachspeise	dessert
eagle	Adler	Igel	hedgehog
eventually	schließlich	eventuell	possibly, maybe
fabric	Stoff	Fabrik	factory
fast	schnell	fast, beinahe	almost
for 10 years	seit 10 Jahren	seit 2010	since 2010
gift	Geschenk	Gift	poison
handy	handlich, praktisch	Handy	mobile, cell phone
herd	Herde	Herd	cooker, stove

Language in Use

FALSE FRIENDS

ENGLISH ▶ DEUTSCH		DEUTSCH ▶ ENGLISCH	
ENGLISH WORD	DEUTSCHE ÜBERSETZUNG	DEUTSCHES WORT	ENGLISH EXPRESSION
housework	Hausarbeit	Hausaufgaben	homework
lake	See	Lake (= Salzlösung)	brine
map	Landkarte	Mappe (Hefter)	folder
mark	Note (Zensur)	Marke	brand
murder	Mord	Mörder	murderer
novel	Roman	Novelle	novella
rock	Stein, Fels	Rock	skirt
roman	römisch	Roman	novel
sensible	vernünftig	sensibel	sensitive
snake	Schlange	Schnecke	snail, slug
still	(immer) noch	still	silent, quiet
strong	stark	streng	strict
to become	werden	bekommen	get
to overtake	überholen	übernehmen	to take over
sea	Meer	See	lake
to spare	verschonen, übrig haben	sparen	to save
to spend	ausgeben, verbringen	spenden	to donate
where	wo	wer	who
I will	ich werde (Zukunft!)	ich will	I want (I would like)

Testformate von *Language in Use*

Wir wollen dir nun die Testformate von *Language in Use* ein wenig näherbringen, damit du schon jetzt weißt, worauf du dich bei der Matura einstellen musst. Folgende Arten von Übungen (meist sind verschiedene Testformate miteinander kombiniert) gibt es:

■ **MULTIPLE GAP TEXT**

Bei dieser Art der Aufgabenstellung geht es darum, einen Lückentext zu bearbeiten. Du hast pro Lücke vier Möglichkeiten vorgegeben und musst die richtige herausfinden (also zum Beispiel ähnliche Nomen, verschiedene Präpositionen, Bindewörter, Zeiten oder Ähnliches).

■ **GAPPED TEXT**

Auch hier soll ein Lückentext mit vorgegebenen Wörtern vervollständigt werden. Es gibt mehr Wörter als Lücken (meist sind es zwei mehr) und die Übung zielt auf dein Verständnis für den Text als Gesamtes und dein Vokabelwissen ab.

■ **ERROR CORRECTION**

In einem gegebenen Text musst du erkennen, wo sich einzelne Worte eingeschlichen haben, die nicht dorthin gehören. Schreibe das „überflüssige" (falsche) Wort auf die dafür vorgesehene Linie neben der jeweiligen Zeile. Aber Achtung: Nicht in jedem Satz befindet sich ein Fehler!

■ **WORD (TRANS)FORMATION**

Diesmal hast du bei einem Lückentext die Wörter zwar vorgegeben, allerdings musst du diese in die richtige Form umwandeln (ein Nomen beispielsweise in ein Adjektiv oder eine Nennform in das *gerund*, also die *-ing*-Form). Hier brauchst du viel Flexibilität in der englischen Sprache.

Language in Use

Task 1 Multiple gap text

You are going to read a text about the influences of the economic and financial crisis. Some words are missing from the text. Choose the correct answer (A, B, C or D) for each gap (1–10) in the text. Write your answers in the boxes provided. The first one (0) has been done for you.

Economic crisis influencing families' eating behaviour

These days reports and news about the (0) ... financial and economic crisis are flooding the media. Reducing salaries here, cutting payments there – keeping together one's money has become more important in the last few months. But which (1) ... does this crisis have, especially (2) ... people's eating behaviour?

A survey, published by Oxford academics at the beginning of this year, (3) ... that as a result of the current recession more and more families tend to eat at home. Furthermore, 45% of the parents questioned said that they are trying hard to (4) ... that everyone in the family eats the same meal to keep the costs down. This is sometimes annoying for the family's children, but that's the way life develops at the moment.

Another side effect of the crises is the fact that less families go out to restaurants. (5) ... in earlier times the average English family went to a restaurant twice a week, this has now been reduced to once a week at a maximum. Family dinners at home have become more popular again and this not only (6) ... money but also ties the family together.

An absolute no-go during family dinners is watching TV. Almost 85% of those people (7) ... in the survey stated that the TV is turned off during meal times and the family comes together sitting (8) ... the table. In this context it might also be worth mentioning that nearly everybody (97%) said table manners are important. For sure, they have changed in the last few decades but still remain essential, surprisingly also for young people.

Last but not least, also the shopping habits (9) ... food have changed due to the recession. More people have bought frozen food in the last eight to twelve months, justifying their shopping behaviour with a significant reduction in their (10) ... . These days frozen food – especially frozen vegetables – are as popular as never before. Families also appreciate the fact that cooking with deep frozen products has stopped them wasting food. So why not using a sensible alternative?

0	A: actual	**B: current**	C: up to date	D: common
1	A: effects	B: reasons	C: origins	D: affects
2	A: at	B: in	C: about	D: on
3	A: revealed	B: surprised	C: confessed	D: demanded
4	A: making sure	B: become sure	C: endure	D: make sure
5	A: whereabouts	B: when	C: whereas	D: as
6	A: spared	B: saves	C: safes	D: spares
7	A: parting	B: participation	C: participated	D: participating
8	A: at	B: on	C: by	D: for
9	A: confessing	B: concerned	C: concerning	D: considering
10	A: extinctions	B: expenses	C: extensions	D: expressions

0	1	2	3	4	5	6	7	8	9	10
B										

Language in Use

Task 2 Gapped text

You are going to read a text about English universities and their graduates. Some words are missing from the text. Choose from the list (A–P) the correct part for each gap (1–13) in the text. There are two extra words that you should not use. Write your answers in the boxes provided. The first one (0) has been done for you.

Women less likely to gain university place

In our modern world, in which (0) ... against racism, poor education and stereotypes are fought, one should think that also (1) ... between the sexes is no longer an aspect (2) ... considering and discussing. Surprisingly, this is not the case. (3) ... least not at Britain's top universities. Checking out last year's applicants at Oxford university, we'll soon realise that the number of women applying and (4) ... really studying at Oxford, is significantly lower than that of their male colleagues.

But what's the reason for this fact? That's (5) ... to explain as social circumstances rather make us think that women are the precursors at the universities. Why? Well, on (6) ... women have better grades at their GCSE and A-level, they (7) ... to work harder for school and university, read more books, have a slightly better overall knowledge and are more open-minded towards new ways of learning. In short, their basic conditions seem to be better. Well yes, *seem* is the important word here because, as mentioned before, there are in fact more male students at Oxford university.

A study published in 2009, (8) ... on educational analysis, demonstrates that fact with the following figures: some 87% of women had been (9) ... straight As at A-level, compared with 82% of the men. Nevertheless, 35% of the women were offered places at Oxford, against 40% of the men. Incredible, isn't is?

Let's finally give away (10) ... explanations for this phenomenon. One of these is undoubtedly the fact that more than three-quarters of the academic staff at Oxford are male and white. Not surprisingly, they tend to recruit according to their own image, prefering male over female students. Another reason is related to the fact that women might get pregnant and are therefore seen as a risk-group being (11) ... to dropout. Last but not least, the rather old-fashioned concept of the man nourishing the family is still nowadays in people's minds. Consequently it's also this (male) head of the family who should (12) ... the best possible education.

All that might not only sound unfair but it probably also is. But (13) ... that has been the case for the last few decades and it's surely not going to change soon.

A: get	E: predicted	I: focusing	M: at
B: worth	F: positively	J: average	**N: prejudices**
C: tend	G: prone	K: then	O: possible
D: difficult	H: whereas	L: unfortunately	P: equality

0	1	2	3	4	5	6	7	8	9	10	11	12	13
N													

Language in Use

Task 3 Error correction

You are going to read a text about stewardesses and their job routine. In most lines of the text there is an unnecessary word that should not be there. Find it and write it down in the space provided after each line. Some lines are correct. Indicate these with an OK. The first two lines have been done for you.

Up, up and away – what a stewardess' life is really like

The number of **the** young girls dreaming about becoming a stewardess once being	_the_	1
grown up, is countless. Their dream includes leading a life full of suspension,	_OK_	2
regularly flying to all top destinations in the world and visiting the worlds'	_____	3
metropolises. They always imagine to fly to New York on one day and to Paris on	_____	4
the other, having enough time for sightseeing, shopping and going out. Sounds	_____	5
like the perfect life, doesn't it?	_____	6
But the world has strictly changed. On the one hand because change constantly	_____	7
happens and on the other hand because of the world's financial crisis. So	_____	8
nowadays airlines struggle with the bankrupcy and are forced to agree to mergers.	_____	9
Consequently the hard reality also catches up with the stewardesses as sooner	_____	10
than they can say "Welcome on Board". Longer flight times, more shorter relaxing	_____	11
times and most probably also less wages characterise the life of an average	_____	12
stewardess these days. In most cases they don't even have the chance to change	_____	13
anything because once they complain, they are told about to leave the company	_____	14
which would, of course, result in unemployment. Something none of us risks in	_____	15
times like these. Patricia Westhagen, stewardess at one of the most important	_____	16
British airlines, summarizes the problem in her own words: "I've been working as	_____	17
stewardess for almost eleven years up now and I've always liked my job. But	_____	18
things have changed, not to the better if I may say. There's a much more	_____	19
competition nowadays, not only among the colleagues, and there's simply more	_____	20
of pressure. This can also be felt during the flights. The passengers are less likely	_____	21
to understand and accept saving measures such like paying extra for a warm meal.	_____	22
They don't want to understand that and start an arguing on board. Very often they	_____	23
leave the airplane being rather frustrated. That's not as easy for me too because	_____	24
I try to give my best which has become more and more difficult in the last few	_____	25
years. I cannot deny that there is a tendency towards more unfriendly, impatient	_____	26
and impolite passengers but they must also be handled."	_____	27
However, "making all the best out of everything" is the motto. Not only for	_____	28
stewardesses but also for everybody. "As long as there are still no fun parts in my	_____	29
job, I go on doing it", says Patricia Westhagen smiling so cheerfully. And by doing	_____	30
so she also tries to motivate her colleagues.	_____	31

Language in Use

Task 4 Word formation

You are going to read a text about the consequences of environmental pollution. Some words are missing from the text. Use the words in brackets to complete each gap (1–12) in the text. Write your answers in the spaces provided at the end of the text. The first one (**0**) has been done for you.

Global warming and other disasters

Today's climate is changing, that's a fact that cannot be (**0**) … (**denial**). Just think about the never-ending hot summers that already start in late March or the relatively warm winters with some 13 degrees Celsius in the middle of December. Overall, the temperatures are rising and the climate is changing with a common trend towards global warming.

The reasons for this (**1**) … (**develop**) can (**2**) … (**easy**) be (**3**) … (**explanation**), the key-word in this context is greenhouse effect. Gases (the most common one of these is the so-called Carbon dioxide) trap heat and consequently lead to the earth's warming. It goes without saying that this phenomenon also effects the fauna (animals) and flora (plants) and numerous species either change or (**4**) … (**disappearance**) completely. It's again needless to say that such (**5**) … (**develop**) might imbalance our relatively fragile ecosystem.

So there's no doubt about the earth's temperatures rising and mankind has (**6**) … (**knowledge**) about this problem for quite some time. But no one knows (not even scientists) with any (**7**) … (**precise**) how fast the earth will get warmer or whether this increase will make a significant change in people's lives. When talking about our environment we surely deal with a very complex system. Slight changes can have an enormous impact and make a big (**8**) … (**different**) with regard to the overall system. According to experts the earth's temperature will rise between one and three centigrades by the year 2025 but in the end we will have to wait and see what will really happen.

In the meantime, however, (**9**) … (**change**) our lifestyles, developing new ways of saving energy and various other projects that help to (**10**) … (**protection**) the nature will have to take place. And they should be given priority because otherwise we will (**11**) … (**destruction**) our own planet and our own living space. Only if everybody works hard to (**12**) … (**achievement**) the same goal, we might have a chance to change something and save our planet as well as our own lives.

Write your answers here:

0 _____*denied*_____

1 _____

2 _____

3 _____

4 _____

5 _____

6 _____

7 _____

8 _____

9 _____

10 _____

11 _____

12 _____

Language in Use

Task 5 Multiple gap text

You are going to read a text written by an Indian immigrant. Some words are missing from the text. Choose the correct answer (A, B, C or D) for each gap (1–10) in the text. Write your answers in the boxes provided. The first one (0) has been done for you.

A question of identity

Marithim Sualek moved from India to England when he was five years old. He (0) ... in Cardiff for the last 43 years and has (1) ... English citizenship. In his autobiography "My Quest for Identity" he expressed his feelings and sorrows with regard to his life between two cultures.

"Being about five years old when I came to England, I only had (2) ... memories related to India and I had not formed my Indian identity yet. So when I started to (3) ... elementary school I realized for the first time that things like racism, cultural differences and (4) ... exist. For sure, at that time I didn't fully understand what that would mean for the rest of my life. High school was the toughest time for me as gangs of white youths used to go around Paki-bashing.

After having (5) ... my school-leaving exam I went to university and from then on things improved slowly and I became well integrated into the white culture. It was about (6) ... that age that I realized I was leading two lives. Two lives that could not be more different from each other. Whenever I was at home and together with my family I was Marithim the guy from India. But outside, at university, at the cinema, in restaurants I was Marty the guy from next door. I soon started to experience culture conflicts and I had difficulties identifying with either the one or the other culture.

Moreover I had to deal with two cultures that had virtually nothing in common. While the belief of "individualism" is (7) ... in the white society, Indian culture is characterized by a general sense of "collectivism". This means that white youngsters are expected to drink, smoke, go out and have girlfriends while Indian teens are tied to their families and relatives, forming a community and a unit with them.

It's needless to say that (8) ... circumstance has presented a real problem for me. Because on the one hand I was expected to (9) ... with my white friends and their culture and on the other hand with my family and the Indian community. For me the problem itself has not changed but I (10) ... how to handle it."

0	A: has lived	B: lives	**C: has been living**	D: lived
1	A: affirmed	B: arranged	C: accepted	D: acquired
2	A: few	B: little	C: many	D: lots of
3	A: visit	B: join	C: participate in	D: attend
4	A: hopelessness	B: honesty	C: hostility	D: hospitality
5	A: taken	B: made	C: done	D: failed
6	A: from	B: on	C: in	D: at
7	A: professional	B: productive	C: prominent	D: provocative
8	A: these	B: this	C: those	D: that
9	A: convince	B: confront	C: conform	D: confess
10	A: had learned	B: have learned	C: learned	D: learn

0	1	2	3	4	5	6	7	8	9	10
C										

Language in Use

Task 6 Gapped text

You are going to read a text about school life in Victorian times. Some words are missing from the text. Choose from the list (A–P) the correct part for each gap (1–13) in the text. There are two extra words that you should not use. Write your answers in the boxes provided. The first one (0) has been done for you.

Hard times in Victorian schools

The 19th century, the so-called Victorian Age, was not only (0) ... by the industrial revolution but also by an obligation for all children up to the age of eleven to go to school. But schools (1) ... that time differed a lot from nowaday's schools.

To begin with, school buildings were usually big and (2) ... and renovation work was not carried out. This means that once the building itself was too shabby to go on teaching there, it was simply abandoned. (3) ... were rather big, too and the number of students sitting (4) ... one classroom was up to almost one hundred. Incredible, isn't it? There were no separated classrooms, only loose (5) ... were used to section the single rooms. It goes without saying that the noise level was very high and that it was (6) ... possible to concentrate in a surrounding like that. If there were windows, they were so high that the pupils couldn't look out. The reason for this is easy to explain: it should (7) ... distraction and ensure that the kids concentrate (8) ... the lessons.

Present day school kids would probably describe Victorian lessons as boring and uninteresting. Why? Well, on the one hand because there were no group activities, no pair work or any kind of fun in the way teachers taught. The only thing they did was writing on the blackboard and the pupils had to copy the information. Everybody had his/her own slate and a litte (9) ... to clean it when necessary. On the other hand the reader was very tedious, too. It was the Bible and for most kids (10) ... that age, reading the Bible was simply far too difficult. They didn't properly understand the meaning of the long and complicated sentences and consequently they soon lost their interest. Only at the end of the Victorian Age books of moral were introduced.

But also after having left school life didn't really improve for the children. Most of them had to start working in factories and they often had to work non-stop for 16 hours a day. Because of their small and slim bodies they were used to clean and repair machines and quite frequently (11) ... happened which left them being handicapped for the rest of their lives. But there was no alternative, at least not for the children coming from (12) ... families. They had to contribute to the family's income because otherwise they would not have survived. Only those children coming from a (13) ... background were lucky enough to continue school and find a good job.

A: classes	E: avoid	I: accidents	M: on
B: hardly	F: from	J: at	N: shabby
C: sponge	**G: marked**	K: in	O: of
D: rich	H: curtains	L: carpets	P: poor

0	1	2	3	4	5	6	7	8	9	10	11	12	13
G													

Language in Use

Task 7 — Error correction

You are going to read a text about Mount St. Elias. In most lines of the text there is an unnecessary word that should not be there. Find it and write it down in the space provided after each line. Some lines are correct. Indicate these with an OK. The first two lines have been done for you.

Mount St. Elias – defeating the longest ski-descend

When talking about **the** Mount St. Elias, we're not talking about any unimportant	_the_	1
mountain. We're talking about the second highest peak in the United States	_OK_	2
(behind Mount McKinley with 20.322 feet). It's located in Alaska (Youkon Ranges)		3
and having the shape of a huge, beautiful pyramid, Mount St. Elias has a hight of		4
18.008 feet (5.489 meters). It was the first of the more giant Alaskan mountains		5
to be discovered there and the first to be climbed (after eight attempts) and		6
was long ago believed to be the least highest mountain in North America. When		7
seen from the deep south, Mount St. Elias is a truly spectacular mountain with an		8
awesome vertical relief. It also sometimes produces the largest single ice field in		9
Alaska, called the Malaspina.		10
It is exactly that ice field that has been attracting less ski alpinists for years.		11
Climbing up to the top of that impressive but also more difficult mountain, then		12
getting your skis ready and going down the so seemingly endless mountain. Of		13
course that's a risky and dangerous business because first of all it's very steep.		14
You mustn't make a single mistake because it's not very likely that it was your		15
last mistake. More than a dozen people have partly lost their lives on Mount St.		16
Elias so far. So a good concentration is needed. Furthermore you never really know		17
about the dangers of avalanches. If the snow is very loose and at the conditions		18
not ideal, it might be the case that you activate an avalanche while skiing down.		19
It's obvious that alpinists pay with their lives in such situations.		20
But it's not only the way all down from the top of the mountain that can turn into		21
a life-threatening affair. Also climbing up is the hard work, requires an excellent		22
physical condition, emotional strength and the will to carry on even if you think		23
you cannot move any further more. People who plan to climb to the top are usually		24
taken to Haydon Shoulder by a small propeller-driven aircraft. That's the place		25
where they start their tour. Depending on the weather and the fact how fast they		26
move upwards, they make one or two stops at base camps they set up themselves.		27
This means that the alpinists who have to carry a lot of heavy equipment.		28
By now there's only one question left: why do the people do that? Well, most		29
probably because of they get a kick out of it, they want to push themselves and		30
find out their personal limits. Doing something that only very few people do is		31
definitely less interesting, exciting and thrilling for them.		32

Language in Use

Task 8 Word formation

You are going to read a text about burnout and its dangers. Some words are missing from the text. Use the words in brackets to complete each gap (1–12) in the text. Write your answers in the spaces provided at the end of the text. The first one (**0**) has been done for you.

Burnout: When stress starts to make you ill

Burnout is a phenomenon more and more people suffer from these days. Times have become more (**0**) ... (**stress**), people are supposed to work more and often household duties, sports or free time activities rob the rest of our energy. But what exactly is burnout, how should we deal with it and, most important, what can we do to prevent ourselves from running into it?

To begin with, burnout is a psychological term for the experience of long-term (**1**) ... (**exhausted**) and limited interest in your own surrounding. Eventhough it is no recognized disorder, its (**2**) ... (**appear**) must be taken serious and it should be (**3**) ... (**treatment**). It's interesting to (**4**) ... (**observation**) that people who suffer from burnout, follow a certain pattern which can be (**5**) ... (**description**) as follows: at first there's usually a special (**6**) ... (**necessary**) to prove oneself, followed by working harder and consequently neglecting one's own needs. At that point people affected (**7**) ... (**denial**) the fact that there is a problem. What is happening instead is a reorganisation of one's own values, meaning that one's hobbies, friends and family might be completely dismissed. Those aspects don't seem to be (**8**) ... (**importance**) any longer. Of course, people feel unhappy and unsatisfied with their lives but they don't see any (**9**) ... (**possible**) to leave this vicious circle. So their reaction is quite (**10**) ... (**understand**): they become frustrated, cynical and aggressive and reduce their social contacts to a minimum. By now the behavioural change also becomes apparent to others but there is little they can do. The person who suffers from burnout feels an inner (**11**) ... (**empty**) and becomes depressive. In the worst case they try to compensate this emptiness with drugs like alcohol. They might also start to eat excessively or go shopping all the time.

But what can people do not to suffer from burnout? Well, first of all it's essential to understand that your job is not the most important part in your life. It should be fun and you should like going there every morning. But you should also like leaving it in the afternoon and you must learn to also leave the problems behind because otherwise you can't (**12**) ... (**relaxation**). Try not to work at the weekend, it's reserved for you and your interests and it's supposed to refill your "inner batteries".

Write your answers here:

0 _stressful_
1 _____
2 _____
3 _____
4 _____
5 _____
6 _____
7 _____
8 _____
9 _____
10 _____
11 _____
12 _____

TESTING SECTION

TEST 1

RC: The cool school

Read the article about Canada's only school for creative teenagers, then do the task below.

Spotting the difference
Do you sometimes feel like you are much more creative than your classmates? Do you often have the impression that the things you learn at school are not the things you really need in life? Do you permanently think that your teachers don't understand you, your talents and your needs? It might be the case that you belong to the gifted group of creative teenagers and long for an academic education that fits your personality. 1 _____ Well, you are wrong because there is an alternative.

Discover the CCS, the Canadian Creative School
The CCS was founded in the late 80s and this type of school is unique in Canada. 2 _____ This might sound unconventional but it means studying dancing, singing, acting, music, theatre and TV/film production. Students enter at the age of 14 and they have to take a rather difficult test (in theory and in practice) in order to be allowed to study there. 3 _____ The annual number of students who pass the test (and can start their studies) is about one third of the number mentioned above. The school lasts for five years and finishes with an A-level exam.

The curriculum
Profound academic studies have a high value at the CCS. That's why students have to take subjects like Maths, English, Science and at least one foreign language at an obligatory basis. 4 _____ These might for example be radio production, theatre- and video production, recording and many more. That's also the reason why an average school day lasts up to eight hours a day, usually six days a week. Besides, the number of holidays is significantly shorter than in any other school.

Speaking for itself
Despite all these "disadvantages", the enthusiasm among the students is enormous. 5 _____ When walking through the school building one has the impression that every single student likes attending this school and is grateful for the chance to get a good education there. "It's simply a creative environment for creative people", says 17-year old Gil. 6 _____ "And unlike in other schools, you don't stand out when you are creative and therefore different. That's simply fantastic."

Task Fill in the sentences.

Its focus is on studying arts.	**A**
They don't even seem to mind their stressful school routine.	**B**
The number of creative subjects is unbelievable.	**C**
Additionally they have their "creative" subjects.	**D**
The annual number of students who take this exam is about 1.450.	**E**
Useless to mention that she was smiling brightly while talking with us.	**F**
You believe that "conventional" High Schools are your only option?	**G**
"It's extremely difficult to pass this type of test. I've taken it twice and failed both times", says a 14-year old girl.	**H**

3 Punkte pro richtiger Antwort: ☐ / 18

Testing section

Language in Use: multiple gap text

You are going to read a text about the importance of having breakfast. Some words are missing from the text. Choose the correct answer (A, B, C or D) for each gap (1–10) in the text. Write your answers in the boxes provided. The first one (0) has been done for you.

Discovering British Breakfast

It's something everybody knows about and nobody (0) ... does: having breakfast and knowing how important that is. (1) ... ages doctors and nutritionists have been telling us how essential it is to start your day with a (2) ... breakfast because that might energise you for the rest of the day. Fact is, (3) ..., that nine million Britons breakfast on nothing but a hot or cold drink.

Especially pupils and students are said to show a weaker (4) ... without breakfast but a study which has recently been published revealed that this is not the case. Children aged between ten and fifteen were tested using short-term memory tests and the results of these tests didn't show any difference between (5) ... children and full ones. So it doesn't really matter if you have breakfast or not. What matters, however, is whether you feel the need for having breakfast. If yes then you should have breakfast and if no it's absolutely okay to eat later. It's no good forcing somebody to eat something just because you are told to do so.

If you feel like having breakfast you should take care to eat the right things. Don't have a full English breakfast with bacon, eggs, sausages and tomatoes because that's way too much and might only make you (6) ... . Rather take care to eat (7) ... things that give you energy like cereals, wholemeal bread, nuts and fruit. Get (8) ... a hot cup of tea maybe with some honey in it. Drink a glass of fresh orange juice but take care not to take in too much sugar.

There's one last positive aspect about having breakfast: It helps you to keep the right diet. If you have cereals or muesli in the morning, your (9) ... of fat during the rest of the day will be lower. Having breakfast also means that you avoid having ravenous appetite and therefore you are more likely to eat (10) ... .

0	A: originally	B: surprisingly	**C: actually**	D: currently
1	A: since	B: for	C: many	D: about
2	A: wealth	B: wealthy	C: health	D: healthy
3	A: however	B: well	C: anyway	D: consequently
4	A: performance	B: endurance	C: reluctance	D: maintenance
5	A: starving	B: starved	C: hunger	D: starvation
6	A: dreamy	B: excited	C: tired	D: funny
7	A: this	B: these	C: that	D: those
8	A: yourself	B: yourselves	C: oneself	D: ourselves
9	A: instead	B: intake	C: interest	D: intent
10	A: few	B: fewer	C: little	D: less

0	1	2	3	4	5	6	7	8	9	10
C										

2 Punkte pro richtiger Antwort: ☐ / 20

Testing section

Tenses

Fill in the words in brackets in the correct tense. Mind statements, negations and questions.

Karen: Hi Donna! Why _____ (be) you so late? I _____ (sit) here for an hour and I even _____ (call) you half an hour ago, but you _____ (not answer) your phone. You seem to be quite upset. _____ (anything – happen) to you or your family?

Donna: Sorry, Karen. I _____ (know) that I'm too late, but you _____ (not can) imagine the hell I _____ (must) go through this afternoon. This _____ (be) the most horrible day in my life.

Karen: Oh no, Donna! Tell me all about it.

Donna: Okay. When I _____ (come) home from school today, my parents _____ (wait) for me at the kitchen table. After I _____ (take off) my shoes I _____ (sit) down next to my mother. I _____ (can) see that there _____ (be) tears in her eyes. So I _____ (ask) her what _____ (happen).

Karen: Oh my dear – what _____ (she – tell) you?

Donna: She _____ (grab) my hand and I _____ (realize) that she was very upset. Then she _____ (point) at Cinnamon's basket …

Karen: Your dog's basket?

Donna: Yeah. Cinnamon _____ (not be) in it. That _____ (be) strange because my dog _____ (usually – sleep) in his basket in the afternoon.

Karen: That moment must _____ (be) horrible for you. I know how much Cinnamon _____ (mean) to you. _____ (you – have got) a clue what might _____ (happen) to your dog?

Donna: That's the problem. I _____ (not have) any idea. According to my mum, Cinnamon _____ (play) in the garden all morning long. At eleven, mum _____ (want) to call him in, but Cinnamon _____ (not come). We _____ (spend) all afternoon looking for him, without success.

Karen: Oh Donna. I _____ (be) so sorry for you.

Donna: Thanks, Karen. Oh – wait a second, please. My mum _____ (call) me on my mobile. *(Two minutes later.)* Oh Karen! I _____ (must) leave you now. Cinnamon _____ (wait) for me at our neighbour's place. They _____ (just – find) him in their garden.

Karen: Oh, great! Tell me when you have found out what exactly _____ (happen).

0,5 Punkte pro richtiger Antwort: ☐ / 19,5

Testing section

LC: Seattle Program claims to treat Internet addiction

Hörübung: CD-Track 15

Multiple matching

Find out who said which things.

- **A** for Noah Adams, the presenter of the show
- **K** for Martin Kaste, the interviewer
- **B** for Ben Alexander, the internet addict
- **C** for Dr. Hilarie Cash
- **G** for Dr. John Grohol

Complete the chart by writing the correct letter next to the number of the sentence. The phrases are not written in the order of their appearance.

1.	People can waste a lot of time on the Internet.	1.
2.	This country's first Internet detox program is just ouside Seattle.	2.
3.	When Ben Alexander entered college he started playing World of Warcraft.	3.
4.	Ben Alexander spent entire days gaming on the Internet.	4.
5.	When the situation got worse he asked his parents for help.	5.
6.	Ben Alexander is the first client of the program.	6.
7.	The Internet detox program is called reSTART.	7.
8.	The detox program offers contact with animals like goats and chickens.	8.
9.	Ben Alexander has never built anything before the camp.	9.
10.	People get addicted to rewarding things. The Internet works on that principle.	10.
11.	Being addicted means doing something out of habit, ignoring the negative sides.	11.
12.	John Grohol is the founder of an online mental health site.	12.
13.	Not everything people like doing is an addiction.	13.
14.	Ben Alexander does not mind being interviewed.	14.
15.	Hilarie Cash is working hard on finding more clients for the detox camp.	15.

1 Punkte pro richtiger Antwort: ☐ / 15

Gesamtpunkte:	☐ / 72,5	
Notenschlüssel:	66–72,5 Punkte	Sehr gut
	58–65 Punkte	Gut
	48–57 Punkte	Befriedigend
	36–47 Punkte	Genügend
	0–35 Punkte	Nicht genügend

TEST 2

RC: My life in a flat-sharing community

Read the following text and first decide whether the statements are true (T) or false (F) and put a cross in the correct box. Then identify the sentence in the text which supports your decision (justification). Write the first four words of this sentence in the space provided.

Hi, I'm Martin! I'm 22 years old and currently I study Science and Microbiology at the University of Dublin. When I started to study, about two years ago, I decided to move to Dublin because living close to university saves a lot of time. My parents' house is in the countryside and going to Dublin takes almost one hour. This means that on average I lost two hours per day just by travelling. So the decision to move to the city was quite an easy one.

Of course my parents support me financially but I also have to earn my own money so that I am able to pay my rent. About one year ago a friend of mine brought an interesting idea to my mind. He asked me why I didn't take in a flat mate to keep the costs low. At first I completely dismissed this thought but the longer I thought about it, the more I liked it. Sharing my flat with somebody could be great fun and it would save me a lot of money.

But where do you find the perfect fellow lodger? I started to ask friends and colleagues who I knew from my courses whether they were looking for an apartment. Regrettably nobody was. Therefore I decided to place an advertisement in the local newspaper, searching for a student who would be interested in a flat-sharing community. I soon got to know Bob. He's great and he has turned out to be the greatest buddy ever. We immediately became best friends and sharing my flat with him is the best decision I've ever made.

So what does our life look like? Well, most people say that our apartment is pure chaos. I wouldn't say it's chaos but rather creativity, you know what I mean. Of course we've got lots of stuff lying around but then who hasn't? We tidy up from time to time, mostly after having celebrated unforgettable parties. And it's simply a great feeling not to be alone and to always have somebody around who you can talk to if you like. I wouldn't want to live alone any longer.

Task Tick the following statements true (T) or false (F) and write the justification.

	T	F	JUSTIFICATION
1. Living close to Dublin saves a lot of money for Irish students.			
2. Martin didn't mind spending so much time in public transport.			
3. Martin's parents give him some money so to help him afford his apartment.			
4. The idea of sharing his flat with a colleague has occured to Martin.			
5. At first Martin couldn't really imagine what it would be like to share his flat.			
6. It wasn't an easy task to find a flat mate.			
7. Accepting a flat mate has turned out to be one of the best things in Martin's life.			
8. The guys don't like living in an untidy apartment.			

2 Punkte pro richtiger Antwort: ☐ / 16

Language in Use: gapped text

You are going to read a text about the NRJ Music Awards. Some words are missing from the text. Choose from the list (A–P) the correct part for each gap (1–13) in the text. There are two extra words that you should not use. Write your answers in the boxes provided. The first one (0) has been done for you.

NRJ Music Awards 2010

Every year the so-called NRJ Music Awards take (0) ... in Cannes, France. As the name already (1) ..., it is an award show in which the winners of the different (2) ... are identified by the listeners. They can vote online and, of course, the winner is the one who has got most (3) ... . The different categories are as follows: album of the year, male artist of the year, song of the year, female artist of the year, band or duet of the year and newcomer of the year.

This musical (4) ... usually takes place at the weekend and thousands of people (5) ... to the Côte d'Azur, spend two wonderful days there, try to see some stars and (6) ... the awards show. Surely lots of young people celebrate at the aftershow party, (7) ... themselves and have a good time. But things are not always (8) ... because sometimes people drink too much alcohol and start getting problems. They might become aggressive and consequently get in touch with the police. In that case an (9) ... nice weekend could turn into a nightmare.

In the course of the last years the NRJ Music Awards have (10) ... more popular and this awards show has been taking place for ten years now. Lots of international stars come to the show and make party. For the year 2010 the stars walking along the red (11) ... were Kelly Rowland, Beyoncé, Jay-Z and of course many more. Radio NRJ Vienna normally raffles off (*verlosen*) some tickets for the aftershow party and it goes without saying that these ticktes are very (12) ... among the listeners. But how do they get these tickets? First they have to vote for their favourite stars. By doing so they register themselves. If they are (13) ..., Radio NRJ phones them and plays a game with them in which they have to answer three questions related to music. They can score points with their correct answers. The one who scores most points is then sent to the awards show including the aftershow party and possibly a meet and greet with one of the stars.

The winners' names for the NRJ Music Awards 2010 are: album of the year – David Guetta: One Love, male artist of the year – Robbie Williams, song of the year – Black Eyed Peas: I Gotta Feeling, female artist of the year – Rihanna, band of the year – Tokio Hotel and newcomer of the year – Lady Gaga.

A: categories	E: travel	I: become	M: happy
B: enjoy	F: originally	J: funny	N: popular
C: place	G: carpet	K: go to	O: votes
D: singer	H: event	L: lucky	P: says

0	1	2	3	4	5	6	7	8	9	10	11	12	13
C													

1 Punkte pro richtiger Antwort: ☐ / 13

Testing section

Tenses

Fill in the words in brackets in the correct tense. Mind statements, negations and questions.

Lauren: Hi Jake! You _____ (look) tired. What _____ (do) all afternoon long?

Jake: Oh, hi Lauren. I'm sorry for _____ (look) so horrible, but I _____ (work) in the garden for five hours. My mum _____ (alread – ask) me weeks ago to help her, so I _____ (must) go through with it, you see?

Lauren: Yeah, I know what you mean. By the way, Sophie _____ (call) me half an hour ago. You should _____ (be) at her place about an hour ago, she said. _____ (you – forget) to tell her that you were busy?

Jake: Of course not! I _____ (leave) a message on her mobile as soon as I _____ (be) sure that I would not _____ (can) see her today.

Lauren: That's too bad. She must _____ (miss) your message.

Jake: Seems so. I _____ (call) her now because I _____ (not want) her to be too angry with me. *(Two minutes later.)* She _____ (cannot) talk to me because she _____ (stir) some soup in the kitchen. I _____ (must) apologize later, I'm afraid.

Lauren: Good idea. Sounds like she _____ (not forgive – you – yet). Anyway, what _____ (you – do) at the weekend?

Jake: I'm not sure. Perhaps, I _____ (stay) at home and relax.

Lauren: I _____ (have got) a better idea. I _____ (go) to this great party at Monika's place. Why _____ (you – not come) with me? Sophie can join us too.

Jake: I'm not sure. Sophie _____ (not like) parties too much.

Lauren: That's a pity. Ah, what I wanted to ask: What _____ (you – do) yesterday evening at ten? I _____ (try) to phone you, but you _____ (not answer). _____ (you – may) go to the cinema with Jim? I thought that your mum _____ (not want) you to see Jim yesterday.

Jake: You are right. I _____ (not be) at the cinema. I _____ (write) my paper for German all evening long. I _____ (work) really hard and I _____ (turn off) my phone before I started.

Lauren: I see. No problem. It was great to talk to you. See you tomorrow!

0,5 Punkte pro richtiger Antwort: ☐ / 17

Testing section

LC: Airline going to the dogs ... and cats too

Hörübung: CD-Track 16

Multiple choice

Find the best answers to the questions.

a. Why do passengers on the new airline normally do not take much luggage with them?
   - A Because the airline only flies short distances, like Washington – Chicago.
   - B Because the passengers are not allowed to take too much luggage with them.
   - C Because the passengers normally do not need much luggage.
   - D Because it costs too much to take luggage on board.

b. Who or what does Pet Airways fly?
   - A Pet parents with their pets on a neighbouring seat.
   - B Pets only fly in cargo.
   - C Pet parents with their pets in an extra cabin.
   - D Only pets in the main cabin.

c. Who is Alysa Binder?
   - A The founder of Pet Airways.
   - B One of the pet attendants working for Pet Airways.
   - C A specialist on pet transport systems.
   - D One of the two founders of Pet Airways.

d. Which of the following rules applies to normal planes?
   - A No pets are allowed to travel by plane.
   - B Pets smaller than 15 pounds have to take an extra seat.
   - C Pets bigger than 15 pounds have to travel in cargo or luggage.
   - D Pets that do not fit under the seat are not admitted to planes.

e. How are "pawsengers" looked after during the flight?
   - A They are monitored via video.
   - B Flight attendants for pets take care of them.
   - C Special trained vets calm them down.
   - D Pet parents can check on their pets during the flight.

f. What happens after a pet is dropped at the airport?
   - A It is taken to one of the Beechcraft 1900 planes.
   - B It is fed, given water and walked before taken to the plane.
   - C It is taken to the pet lounge where its state of health is checked.
   - D A pet attendant talks to the pet parent about the pet's special needs.

g. How is the pet's safety guaranteed during the flight?
   - A There are special pet boxes with belts.
   - B Pet attendants keep the pets on their laps.
   - C Tranquilizers are used to keep the animals calm.
   - D Other passengers take care of the pets.

2 Punkte pro richtiger Antwort: ⬜ / 14

Gesamtpunkte:	⬜ / 60	
Notenschlüssel:	54–60 Punkte	Sehr gut
	48–53 Punkte	Gut
	40–47 Punkte	Befriedigend
	30–39 Punkte	Genügend
	0–29 Punkte	Nicht genügend

Testing section

TEST 3

RC: Saving money – the "cheapest family" shows how

Read the article about how to save money, then do the task below.

It's clear to everybody: In times of economic crises, money must be saved as food prices constantly rise, energy costs have increased and interest rates are hardly payable any longer. While most families (not only in America by the way) do not know how to pay for these things, America's "cheapest family" is not affected by the current problems and worries. They go on living comfortably, not suffering from any cutbacks. But how is that done? Let's take a look at the details.

The "cheapest family" is a family of seven coming from Minnesota. Father Joseph is a worker in a coalmine (with an average income), mother Lauren cares for the household and the kids. The five children are aged between 9 and 21 years, all of them attend school or do an additional education. The amount of money the family spends on food every month is $370, compared to about $710 for a family of four. You ask yourself how this can work? Well, here's the answer.

Saving money is a full time job for the family. They only go shopping once a month and then they buy everything they are going to need in the course of the next four weeks. This means that mother Lauren first thinks about the meals of the next weeks, writes a list and then off they go. The whole family is involved in the shopping trip and they set out with walkie-talkies so that they can compare different bargains in different supermarkets and stores. They watch out for special sales or "buy two for the price of one" offers. Once they have found something that is cheap, they buy a big amount of it and freeze the stuff they don't need immediately. They even freeze fresh vegetables, dairy products and bread.

But that's not enough. The family also buys fresh fruit one month ahead, which – for sure – leads to some changes in the diet. "We have to eat the stuff that does not keep well for long first. These are usually bananas and grapes. The things that keep well for longer, like pears, apples and oranges, can wait", says father Joseph. The family does not consider their diet poor or imbalanced. Rather the contrary is the case.

In times of financial crisis and difficulties, America's "cheapest family" is more satisfied than ever. While – as mentioned above – other families no longer know how to finance their lives and how to pay back the mortgages, the "cheapest family" has managed to repay the credit for their house in only nine short years. And they do know that this is just because of their frugal lifestyle.

Task Note taking

Answer the questions in <u>not more than four words</u> (key words are enough).

A	Why is it so important in times of financial crisis to save money?	
B	Why has the life of the "cheapest family" not changed during the crisis?	
C	Why does only the father contribute to the family income?	
D	Why is it necessary that all members of the family go shopping?	
E	When shopping fruit just once a month, why's that problematic?	
F	What was the biggest financial success of the family?	

2 Punkte pro richtiger Antwort: ☐ / 12

Testing section

Language in Use: error correction

You are going to read a text about Christina Stürmer's career. In most lines of the text there is an unnecessary word that should not be there. Find it and write it down in the space provided after each line. Some lines are correct. Indicate these with an OK. The first two lines have been done for you.

Turning into a star: Christina Stürmer

You surely have already heard about her as she is one of Austria's most famous	OK	1
pop stars: Christina Stürmer. She was **been** born on the 9th of July 1982 in the	been	2
north of Upper Austria and from all early childhood onwards she has had a special	_____	3
love for music. Of course her parents were soon realized how fond Christina was of	_____	4
music and so she attended a choir session every week. Already as a grown child she	_____	5
was supported by her parents who enabled her to learn the German flute and the	_____	6
saxophone. Christina further of developed her talent and so she founded a cover	_____	7
rock band called *Scotty*. At that a time she switched to singing which is obviously	_____	8
still today her most great passion.	_____	9
As far as her global education is concerned Christina was an apprentice in a	_____	10
bookshop and worked there full hours. This is still today the reason for why	_____	11
she loves books a lot and is very keen on them. After having been finished her	_____	12
apprenticeship in 2002 she participated in an Austrian casting show which was	_____	13
called *Starmania*. Several young singers who took part in this show and tried to	_____	14
become a star and be successful. The show which was presented by Austrian host	_____	15
star Arabella Kiesbauer and took place once in a week. Surprisingly Christina was	_____	16
not the winner of this casting show (it was a singer called Michael Tschuggnall)	_____	17
but she ranked second. Shortly afterwards she published her first song *Ich lebe*	_____	18
which was in the Austrian charts for few nine weeks. By and large she also became	_____	19
popular in Germany and her single *Vorbei* that was released in September 2004.	_____	20
At that time her former producer Alexander Kahr did supported her a lot.	_____	21
Among other aspects, the lyrics of Christina's songs deal with topics like love,	_____	22
alcohol, drugs, authorities, violence, war and some peace. Her music can now be	_____	23
considered as the milestone in Austrian rock and pop music and *Christina*	_____	24
Stürmer & Band have acquired international reputation. The band is currently (in	_____	25
2010) consists of the following members: Oliver Varga coming from Austria and	_____	26
playing the guitar, Gwenael Damman comes from France and is responsible for	_____	27
the e-bass, Klaus Pérez-Salado is a Spanish and plays the drums and last but not	_____	28
least Matthias Simoner who plays accordion, the guitar and keyboard.	_____	29
According to all her homepage (www.christinaonline.at) Christina's favourite films	_____	30
are *X-Men*, *Blow*, *Spaceballs* and *Hinter dem Horizont*.	_____	31

0,5 Punkte pro richtiger Antwort: ☐ / 14,5

Testing section

Tenses

Fill in the words in brackets in the correct tense. Mind statements, negations and questions.

Tristan: Hey Luke! I _____ (not see) you for ages! _____ (you – enjoy) your skiing holiday last week?

Luke: Yeah, Tristan, I really _____ (do). Before we _____ (arrive) it _____ (snow) a lot. So the snow _____ (be) perfect. You know that I _____ (adore) skiing. I _____ (be) really looking forward to racing down the slopes. Of course, I _____ (want) to be early, but on the first day it _____ (take) Tony ages to get started.

Tristan: I see. When _____ (get) to the gondola, then?

Luke: At eleven! When we _____ (arrive) a big crowd _____ (wait) to be taken to the mountain top. We _____ (must) queue up for forty-five minutes.

Tristan: That must _____ (be) hard for you!

Luke: Sure it was. But then we _____ (finally – can) put on our skis and to enjoy the perfect weather and the great snow.

Tristan: Oh, that _____ (sound) fantastic.

Luke: Absolutely. On the third day, however, something unexpected happened. We _____ (sit) on a chair lift, laughing and joking, when it suddenly _____ (come) to a halt. We _____ (not bother) much because we _____ (get) stuck on that lift before. After fifteen minutes, however, Joey _____ (start) panicking. It _____ (begin) to snow shortly before the lift stopped and it _____ (get) worse from minute to minute. We _____ (not can) see much, but we _____ (guess) that we _____ (be) the only people on the lift! Then Mike _____ (have) an idea. He _____ (take) his mobile phone and phoned Mike and Tessa, who _____ (wait) for us at the bottom of the mountain. Five minutes later, the lift went on. Imagine! The lift staff _____ (turn off) the lift as they thought that it was empty because of the bad weather.

Tristan: That's horrible. However, you can't say that your holiday was boring. So, _____ (you – do) that trip again next year?

Luke: I'm not sure. Perhaps, I _____ (go) somewhere warm next year.

Tristan: I see. So, tell me about Mike and Tessa …

0,5 Punkte pro richtiger Antwort: ☐ / 16,5

Testing section

LC: The modern vampire: Bloodthirsty, but chivalrous

Note form
Answer the questions in key words.

a. What are the titles of the two most popular vampire series on the current book market?
   1. _____
   2. _____

b. What does the vampire in the 1931 film do with women he wants?
   _____

c. What does Nuzum, author of the book *The Dead Travel Fast,* say about vampires and culture?
   _____

d. In the past, how were vampires, according to Eric Nuzum, presented? Name three adjectives.
   _____

e. Which new characteristics do the current vampire heroes have?
   _____

f. In the TV series *True Blood,* which fact attracts Sookie even more to Bill?
   _____

g. What does Bill, the hero of *True Blood*, try to do to Sookie?
   _____

h. According to Charlaine Harris, what makes Bill even more alluring?
   _____

i. What are the names of the main characters of the *Twilight* series?
   _____

j. Which choice makes the *Twilight* hero, according to the author Stephenie Meyer, so popular?
   _____

k. According to Meyer, what is the message of the *Twilight* books that appeals to teenagers?
   _____

l. What does Nina Auerbach say about the vampires presented in the 1960s and 1970s?
   _____

m. How does Nina Auerbach consider the new vampires?
   _____

n. What is her idea of a love relationship?
   _____

1 Punkte pro richtiger Antwort: ☐ /15

Gesamtpunkte:	☐ /58	
Notenschlüssel:	53–58 Punkte	Sehr gut
	46–52 Punkte	Gut
	38–45 Punkte	Befriedigend
	29–37 Punkte	Genügend
	0–28 Punkte	Nicht genügend

TEST 4

RC: A completely different sort of hero

Read the article, then do the task below.

Have you ever tried to define the word *hero*? What is a hero? What do people have to do in order to be called hero? And what are their characteristics? The word *hero* (the female form is *heroine*) derives from Greek mythology and originally described a demigod. But what about the modern use of this word?

Nowadays heroes are mostly people who have done something important and/or unbelievable. They might have saved somebody else's life or they might have done something nobody has ever dared doing before. Usually they are very brave, courageous and lion-heared. This, however, does not always have to be the case.

Moira is 15 years old and attends Uttah Junior High School. Many people consider her to be a heroine. Why? Well, here comes why: when Moira was eleven years old she suffered bad injuries in a car accident. Both her parents died in the crash and Moira was left alone in an orphanage. Even though she's a very witty and clever girl, she hasn't been able to articulate herself since this accident. A blockade in her brain is responsible for that circumstance.

Most of us would have been put off by bad experiences like these, but not Moira. Eversince she's been determined to stand up again and fight for her right to live a normal life. She's never accepted attending a special school and she's never accepted her faith. So, can we call a brave little girl like her a heroine because she has never given up? Is that a characteristic that would be valid for a hero? I'd say yes it is because whenever there's somebody who stands up for his/her own or another person's right for life and freedom can be called a hero.

Task — Multiple choice

Choose the answer (a, b, c or d) which you think fits best according to the text:

1. What is the original meaning of the word *hero* and where does this word come from?
   a. It was used in the Stone Age and it means "halfgod".
   b. It was used in ancient English myths and it means "being God".
   c. It was used in Greece myths and it means "godlike".
   d. It was used in Greece myths and it means "halfgod".

2. What happened when Moira was 15 years old?
   a. Her parents were involved in a small car accident.
   b. Her parents suffered from a terrible illness.
   c. Her parents had a lethal car accident.
   d. Her parents died in a plane crash.

3. How has the accident changed Moira's life and her lifestyle?
   a. The girl hasn't been able to speak since then.
   b. She wasn't able to speak shortly after the accident.
   c. Moira hasn't spoken to the doctors since the accident.
   d. The young girl hasn't been able to say certain words since then.

4. What has Moira been determined to do since the accident?
   a. She's been determined to never speak a word again.
   b. She's been determined to live the life of a handicapped teenager.
   c. She's been determined to change her whole life.
   d. She's been determined to live a normal life again.

3 Punkte pro richtiger Antwort: ☐ / 12

Testing section

Language in Use: word formation

You are going to read a text about child labour in India. Some words are missing from the text. Use the words in brackets to complete each gap (1–12) in the text. Write your answers in the spaces provided at the end of the text. The first one (**0**) has been done for you.

Child labour in India: Facing the truth

With its culture full of (**0**) … (**excitement**) folk stories, India has always been an interesting and fascinating country. Its history dates back to the 16th century when the (**1**) … (**Portugal**) first started trading there. By 1760, however, Britain was the most important European power in India. Within the next century India became even more (**2**) … (**significance**) for Great Britain as the British industry got its raw materials there and India was a huge market for British goods. For sure, a lot has changed in India and the Indian culture, society and government. There is, however, one problem that is still today a hot spot: child labour. Very often children have to work for very little money and in most cases the work is also dangerous. One of the typical jobs Indian children have to carry out is for example a bidi roller. Many young children sit together in a dark and small room and have to roll cigarettes. They do that all day long and roll about 500–600 bidis. On average they get 15 rupees a day and their only (**3**) … (**entertain**) is listening to the radio. Quite often children also work as brass workers in factories and (**4**) … (**do**) a job like that presents an enormous health risk as the kids are (**5**) … (**exposure**) to chemical fumes and are covered in dust from head to toe. Being a shopkeeper is another typical job for a child. The shops usually don't consist of more than a (**6**) … (**wood**) matchbox on four legs and the kids have to try hard to find a good place where to set up their shop. Traditionally anything that can be turned into money is (**7**) … (**sale**) there. Match-packing is also popular among children. In that case they have to fill matchsticks into boxes and then pack dozens of boxes into big packages. In a day hundreds of boxes are filled and it's useless to say that this sort of job is extremely (**8**) … (**tired**). Finally, many kids work as whistlemakers and (**9**) … (**production**) up to 4,000 whistles a day. In a job like that the children really have to hurry up because fewer whistles mean less money.

Sadly the majority of Indian kids doesn't have the chance to go to school and be taught how to read and write. They have to support their families (**10**) … (**finance**) in order to be able to (**11**) … (**survival**) and by doing so they are forced to work from an early age onwards. They don't know what it (**12**) … (**meaning**) to live a life without worries, sorrows and the fear not to have enough to eat.

Write your answers here:

0 _____ *exciting* _____
1 _____
2 _____
3 _____
4 _____
5 _____
6 _____
7 _____
8 _____
9 _____
10 _____
11 _____
12 _____

1 Punkte pro richtiger Antwort: ☐ / 12

Testing section

Tenses

Fill in the words in brackets in the correct tense. Mind statements, negations and questions.

Claire: Danny, listen! I _____ (just – win) four tickets for the *Green Day* concert next March. _____ (you – come) with me?

Danny: Sure! But tell me when and how _____ (you – get) the tickets?

Claire: Last week, there _____ (be) a quiz show on Radio W. I _____ (call) them, I was put through, and then I _____ (must) answer some questions about *Green Day*. Of course, I _____ (can) to give all the correct answers. And then they called me back today, telling me that I had won.

Danny: Cool! But you _____ (win) four tickets. What _____ (you – do) with the other ones?

Claire: I think that I _____ (ask) Julie and Tim to join us.

Danny: So you _____ (not hear) the news? Julie _____ (stay) in Canada for a semester. You _____ (must) ask someone else, I'm afraid.

Claire: Wow, thank you for telling me. I _____ (look forward) to going to the concert with you, Julie and Tim. _____ (you – remember) the last time we _____ (go) to a *Green Day* concert?

Danny: Definitely. We _____ (wait) for Julie and Tim at the back of the concert hall when the backstage door _____ (open).

Claire: Yeah, you and I _____ (be) in the middle of a discussion about our favourite songs, when – BANG – Billy Joe _____ (appear). I _____ (not can) believe my eyes and ears. He _____ (invite) us in and _____ (give) us a backstage tour!

Danny: We _____ (talk) to the rest of the band when we _____ (remember) Julie and Tim!

Claire: As far as I remember, they _____ (be) quite angry. When we _____ (call) Tim, he even _____ (shout) at me, "What's the matter with you? Julie and I _____ (stand) here in the cold for half an hour."

Danny: They sure _____ (be) upset, but when they _____ (hear) what _____ (happen), they _____ (get) excited. And when they _____ (allow) to come backstage too, they _____ (not blame) us anymore.

Claire: Oh, I _____ (never forget) that day …

0,5 Punkte pro richtiger Antwort: ☐/18

Testing section

LC: What's wrong with this snowflake?

Hörübung: CD-Track 18

1. True or false?

   a. The radio show is about extravagant Christmas decoration. _____
   b. Scientists complain about the unnatural images of flying reindeer. _____
   c. Jon Hamilton is a chemist. _____
   d. Before Christmas, a lot of scientifically wrong images of snowflakes are displayed. _____
   e. Thomas Koop admires the natural beauty of ice crystals. _____
   f. He says that artists sometimes harm the beauty of ice crystals. _____
   g. Thomas Koop is a professor at a British university. _____
   h. He complains that artists show snowflakes with five or eight sides. _____
   i. Sometimes, the crystal structure of ice allows octagonal shapes. _____
   j. Natural snowflakes can take various kinds of shapes, but usually with five sides. _____

2. Answer the questions (key words).

   a. What are the molecular building blocks of ice crystals?
   _____

   b. How many sides do ice crystals normally have?
   _____

   c. How many sides do ice crystals occasionally have?
   _____

   d. How many sides do ice crystals never take?
   _____

   e. Why did Koop finally complain about the wrong images of snowflakes?
   _____

   f. What did Koop's letter to the journal call for?
   _____

   g. According to Koop, what should people discuss in their holidays?
   _____

   h. Where does Koop's manifesto on snowflakes appear?
   _____

1 Punkte pro richtiger Antwort: ☐ / 18

Gesamtpunkte:	☐ / 60	
Notenschlüssel:	54–60 Punkte	Sehr gut
	48–53 Punkte	Gut
	40–47 Punkte	Befriedigend
	30–39 Punkte	Genügend
	0–29 Punkte	Nicht genügend

Titelverzeichnis Audio-CD

Titelnummer auf der CD	Zeit	Buch Seite	Titel
1	4:11	7	Spotting lies: Listen, don't look
2	3:57	8	Meet Snuppy, the world's first cloned dog
3	4:43	10	The PS 22 Chorus: Fifth-grade chorus becomes a YouTube hit
4	7:31	12	A Facebook tale: Founder unfriends pals on way up
5	3:59	14	Doctors urge research on cell phone-cancer issue
6	3:07	16	Study may tie food additives to hyperactivity
7	3:28	17	Homework: When dangerous animals attack
8	3:01	19	Teen T-shirt entrepreneur wins $ 10, 000
9	6:06	20	Using music to mentor venezuela's poorest youth
10	7:05	22	A real-life school of rock
11	4:55	24	New Hampshire split over high school cheating
12	4:56	26	Some spend thousands to save pets
13	3:13	87	Madness, Our house. CD Madness: The Rise and Fall. Virgin, 2000
14	2:52	100	Mika, Ring, Ring, CD Mika: Life in Cartoon Motion (Extended). Universal Records, 2007
15	3:12	147	Seattle Program claims to treat Internet addiction
16	2:41	151	Airline going to the dogs ... and cats too
17	4:18	155	The modern vampire: Bloodthirsty, but chivalrous
18	2:17	159	What's wrong with this snowflake?

DURCHSTARTEN

ENGLISCH
GYMNASIUM

Übungsbuch Lösungsheft

inkl. HÖRÜBUNGEN AUF CD UND TESTS

9 — 5. Klasse AHS

VER1TAS
Gemeinsam besser lernen

LÖSUNGEN ZU DEN BUCHSEITEN 7 UND 8

LC 1: SPOTTING LIES: LISTEN, DON'T LOOK

1.
a. a person who is not a member of the police or army
b. to move nervously
c. act of questioning a suspect
d. another word for fear
e. act of tricking or misleading someone
f. to force sb. to do sth.
g. an imprisoned person

2.
a. T **b.** F **c.** T **d.** F **e.** T

3.
a. making eye contact
b. sweat
c. innocent

4.
a. C **b.** B **c.** D

5.
a. R **b.** T **c.** H **d.** T **e.** H

6.
a. offers baseline of detail
b. the event being investigated
c. they compare them
d. 1: number of descriptive phrases
   2: the level of detail
e. tell the story backwards
f. 30 percent
g. do more training

LC 1 – TRANSCRIPT: SPOTTING LIES: LISTEN, DON'T LOOK (CD-TRACK 01)

STEVE INSKEEP, host: It's MORNING EDITION from NPR News. Good morning. I'm Steve Inskeep.
LINDA WERTHEIMER, host: And I'm Linda Wertheimer.
Researchers are taking a closer look at a common encounter that changes the direction of many lives. It's what happens when a police officer questions a civilian.
INSKEEP: At some point, the cop may have to make a hard judgment about whether a suspect is being truthful. The wrong call can wreck an investigation, let a guilty person go free, or send an innocent person into a nightmare. Now, experts are looking for ways to make that decision a little more scientific. NPR's Dina Temple-Raston reports.
DINA TEMPLE-RASTON: Forget what you've learned from cops on TV. Liars do not necessarily have trouble making eye contact. The guilty don't fidget or sweat more. In fact, research shows that innocent people can be just as nervous.
(Soundbite of TV clip)
Unidentified Man: Where were you Tuesday night between 09:00 and 03:00 the next morning?
TEMPLE-RASTON: That's the TV version of the way we think most interrogations start, with the suspect on the defensive.
(Soundbite of TV clip)
Unidentified Woman: You didn't get to where you are today by being the type of person who makes mistakes. It would be a mistake not to tell me what happened.
Mr. KEVIN COLWELL (Forensic Scientist, Southern Connecticut State University): A lot of different signs of anxiety are mistaken for signs of deception.
TEMPLE-RASTON: Kevin Colwell is a forensic scientist at Southern Connecticut State University in New Haven.
Mr. COLWELL: Interrogation, the whole goal is to convince somebody, or trick them or coerce them, whatever it takes, to get them to confess to the crime.
TEMPLE-RASTON: Colwell has been trying to get interrogators to change that mindset, to see these encounters as opportunities to get information that might solve the crime, rather than an occasion to elicit a confession.
Mr. COLWELL: The idea is you are convinced that that's the person who did it, and so you are no longer searching for other answers.
TEMPLE-RASTON: Colwell and a forensic psychologist named Cheryl Hiscock-Anisman are at the forefront of this kind of interview research. And they have been taking their theories out into the field. A few weeks ago, they sat down with the San Diego Police Department. Sergeant Romeo De Los Reyes was part of that group.
Sergeant ROMEO DE LOS REYES (San Diego Police Department): We've always learned that communication is 60 to 90 percent nonverbal. So this was a different approach to dealing with deception.
TEMPLE-RASTON: Here's how it works: Hiscock-Anisman, who is at National University in California, suggests interviewers begin with a non-threatening question.
Dr. CHERYL HISCOCK-ANISMAN (National University, California): When I was living in Texas, and I was running inmates for one of my studies, we asked them: What was the first day like for you in prison?
TEMPLE-RASTON: She says she chose that question for two reasons. The first was that it was a vivid memory; the second was that it was a very likely to get a truthful answer.
Dr. HISCOCK-ANISMAN: There's no need to lie about your first day in prison, even if you're an inmate.

LÖSUNGEN ZU DEN BUCHSEITEN 8 UND 9

TEMPLE-RASTON: That first question gives interviewers a baseline. It tells them how much detail someone provides when they are telling a story truthfully. Next, they ask a person to tell them about the event being investigated. Interviewers then compare the two stories. Do they use the same number of descriptive phrases? Do they remember the same level of detail? Then comes the harder question.
Dr. HISCOCK-ANISMAN: Then I'd say, now what I want you to do is, I want you to go back to that time, and I want you to describe every single thing that happened, but this time I want you to tell me what happened last and work all the way backwards.
TEMPLE-RASTON: And can they usually do that or do they stumble?
Dr. HISCOCK-ANISMAN: Well, a liar is going to have a hell of a time.
(Soundbite of laughter)
TEMPLE-RASTON: Try this on your teenager next time they come home late. The point is an honest person can pass this test. In fact, Hiscock-Anisman says she's found they tend to add about 30 percent more detail than people who are lying. That said, there are still practical questions on how law enforcement might use this research. Sergeant De Los Reyes of San Diego says he can see how the system might work with someone who has decided to talk, but what about someone who doesn't want to cooperate? Even so, the San Diego Police Department has asked the researchers back. They want to do more training.
Dina Temple-Raston, NPR News.

LC 2: MEET SNUPPY, THE WORLD'S FIRST CLONED DOG

1.
embryo, cell, surrogate mother, offspring, gene

2.
a. ☐   b. ☑   c. ☐   d. ☑   e. ☐   f. ☑

3.
a. 2   b. 3   c. 1

4.
a. 2 000   b. 123   c. 3   d. 1   e. 2   f. 22

5.
a. Seoul National University puppy
b. to avoid accidental pregnancies
c. 1. make transplant research easier
   2. to study diseases

6.
Palca: Kraemer's team has abandoned a **large-scale** program to clone dogs, in part because **success** proved so difficult. Dogs have a unique physiology that makes their eggs hard to work with. But reproductive **scientist** Calvin Simerly of the University of Pittsburgh School of Medicine says even though the principles of cloning have been worked out, each species presents its own **challenges**.
Simerly: You have to learn the uniqueness about that model and then design research around those unique properties. So it's just not **one size fits all**.
Palca: Simerly knows that too well. He's spent years trying to **clone** a monkey, so far without success.

LC 2 – TRANSCRIPT: MEET SNUPPY, THE WORLD'S FIRST CLONED DOG (CD-TRACK 02)

MELISSA BLOCK, host: From NPR News, this is ALL THINGS CONSIDERED. I'm Melissa Block.
MICHELE NORRIS, host: And I'm Michele Norris.
First, there was Snoopy. Now there's Snuppy. Unlike Charlie Brown's beagle, Snuppy is an Afghan hound. Snuppy's claim to fame is that he's a clone, the first cloned dog ever created. NPR's Joe Palca has more.
JOE PALCA reporting:
It's been eight years since Dolly, the cloned sheep, started a cloning craze. So far scientists have successfully cloned mice, goats, pigs, rabbits – yes, rabbits – cats, rats, mules and horses. But the dog turned out to be difficult. Three years ago a team of Korean scientists decided to give the dog a try. It's the same team that successfully cloned a human embryo.
To make the dog clone, the Korean scientists started with skin cells from an adult Afghan hound. They then inserted a skin cell's DNA into a dog egg from which the DNA had been removed. Once the egg starts dividing, you have a cloned embryo. Dr. B.C. Lee of Seoul National University says they used nearly 2,000 eggs to make their cloned embryos.
Dr. B.C. LEE (Seoul National University): We make 1,095 cloned embryo and transport to 123 dogs.
PALCA: The 123 dogs served as surrogate mothers. As they report in tomorrow's issue of the journal Nature, for all those embryos, the team only got three pregnancies. One fetus miscarried. Two carried to term. One of the puppies died of pneumonia at 22 days, but the other is now three and a half months old and apparently fine. That's the one called Snuppy, named for Seoul National University.
Dr. LEE: Seoul National University puppy, S-N-U-P-P-Y.
PALCA: (Laughs) I like that.
Lee says they chose an Afghan hound to clone because they wanted to make it easy to make sure they really had a clone and not an accidental normal pregnancy. Snuppy's surrogate mother was a Golden Retriever. And you know when an Afghan hound comes out of a Golden Retriever, someone is tinkering with Mother Nature. Lee says his team did not undertake its cloning work to help out pet owners anxious to replicate prized animals.
Dr. LEE: Absolutely not. We just doing it for the scientific procedure and the scientific knowledge.

PALCA: There are several reasons scientists would like to clone dogs. The dog is used in many types of medical research. Duane Kraemer works on animal cloning at Texas A&M University. Kraemer says, for one thing, cloning makes transplant research easier. A pair of cloned animals will have nearly identical immune systems, so transplanted organs and tissue won't be rejected.
Mr. DUANE KRAEMER (Texas A&M University): Also, of course, to study the genetic component of diseases, it's nice to have identical animals so that one can determine which genes more readily are responsible for the various traits or diseases that they might have.
PALCA: Kraemer and his colleagues nearly took the prize for creating the world's first cloned dog.
Mr. KRAEMER: We had produced a pregnancy that went 38 days, and then another one that went to term, but the offspring was stillborn.
PALCA: Kraemer's team has abandoned a large-scale program to clone dogs, in part because success proved so difficult. Dogs have a unique physiology that makes their eggs hard to work with. But reproductive scientist Calvin Simerly of the University of Pittsburgh School of Medicine says even though the principles of cloning have been worked out, each species presents its own challenges.
Mr. CALVIN SIMERLY (University of Pittsburgh School of Medicine): You have to learn the uniqueness about that model and then design research around those unique properties. So it's just not one size fits all.
PALCA: Simerly knows that only too well. He's spent years trying to clone a monkey, so far without success. Joe Palca, NPR News, Washington.
NORRIS: You can see a family photo of Snuppy, his dad and surrogate mother at our Web site, npr.org.

LC 3: FIFTH-GRADE CHORUS BECOMES A YOUTUBE HIT

1.
1. F **2.** E **3.** D **4.** B **5.** A **6.** C

2.
a. F **b.** T **c.** T **d.** F **e.** T

3.
a. C **b.** B **c.** D

4.
a. is unlike other teachers **b.** really works with them
c. helps get it right **d.** doesn't yell at them / is really nice

5.
a. B **b.** B **c.** B **d.** B **e.** A **f.** A **g.** B **h.** A **i.** A

6.
a. ☑ **b.** ☑ **c.** ☑ **d.** ☐ **e.** ☑ **f.** ☐ **g.** ☑ **h.** ☐

7.
B: There is something just magical about their **performances**. I think it's their selections. I think they sing **selections** people don't expect. I try to teach them that there's more to music than what they're hearing necessarily on the **radio** and to be open. And they bring their own thing to it. They have a **sound**. And when you bring something unique to the table, yeah, that **catches** people's interest.
A: Despite success, Breinberg says the future of the chorus is **uncertain**. He's still waiting to hear if, given education budget cuts in New York City, his chorus will be fully **funded** this year.

LC 3 – TRANSCRIPT: FIFTH-GRADE CHORUS BECOMES A YOUTUBE HIT (CD-TRACK 03)

ROBERT SIEGEL, host: They are an Internet sensation with more than 40 YouTube videos. They are adored by big name artists, including Tori Amos and Stevie Nicks, whose songs they've performed. They've been on MTV and "Nightline," and they are only 10 and 11 years old. I'm talking about the fifth-grade chorus from Public School 22 in Staten Island, New York.
And as NPR's Margot Adler reports, their singing has captivated millions.
MARGOT ADLER: It's still summer, and school is out, but Gregg Breinberg, the choral director of the PS22 Chorus, is rehearsing with the group in Central Park for a performance. They start by warming up.
Mr. GREGG BREINBERG (Choral Director, PS22 Chorus): Cool. One more, really high if you can.
PS22 CHORUS (Musical Group): (Singing) (Unintelligible).
ADLER: Since it's summer, only half of the chorus is here, and it's bittersweet because all these children will be leaving for sixth-grade and different middle schools, many of which may not even have a music program, given budget cuts. But even at half their numbers, and having not practiced together for months, you can feel their magic immediately. Here they are learning a new song, "The World," by Empire of the Sun.
(Soundbite of song, "The World")
PS22 CHORUS: (Singing) I asked the world a question: When did you begin? I asked him of his problems: Where did you go wrong?
Mr. BREINBERG: Good. We're going to do that again, and I want a little more power. And, guys, there's no feeling. You know, it's like a question. Like, you're questioning the world. Like, how did – did you ever wonder, like, how did all this happen? You know, it's amazing. So you've got to just look around at the beauty around you. You've got to feel it.
ADLER: PS22 has its share of troubled kids and poor kids. Seventy-five percent of the students qualify for free lunch. And for many, English is a second language. But the fifth-graders say Gregg Breinberg, who they call Mr. B, has brought life to their school.
Ms. MAIMOUNA FAYE (Member, PS22 Chorus): He's not like any other music teacher.
ADLER: Maimouna Faye is sad to be moving on.
Ms. FAYE: He really works with us. He, like, helps us get it right. He doesn't yell at us. He is really nice.
Mr. BREINBERG: I think I'm a little bit nontraditional. I mean, I'm intense. You know, I'm very passionate about the music. And if I don't feel like they're giving 100 percent, yeah, I will get intense with them and say, come on, guys, this isn't fair. I'm working so hard for you. I'm trying to do my best for you. You have to come through for me. You have to give 100 percent.

ADLER: But Breinberg says he's also a goofball. He's eccentric and emotional. He will weep at performances and says he's a role model, one that says it's okay for boys to cry.
Mr. BREINBERG: But I also want to bring to them that it's okay to be yourself. And what's so wonderful about these kids is they're in this environment that we've created together that allows them to express themselves and totally be wacky and silly.
ADLER: And be willing to make mistakes. Gabriel Vasquez and Maimouna Faye say being in the chorus allowed them to do something that they often don't have a place for.
Mr. GABRIEL VASQUEZ (Member, PS22 Chorus): Letting out your emotions, showing your feelings.
Ms. FAYE: If I was mad one day, I could go to chorus and just let it all out without, like, yelling at somebody or getting mad or pouting or something like that.
ADLER: They've only begun to professionally record their performances. Here they are singing Lady Gaga's "Just Dance."
(Soundbite of song, "Just Dance")
PS22 CHORUS: (Singing) How does he twist the dance? Can't find a drink, oh, man. Where are my keys? I lost my phone. What's going on on the floor? I love this record, baby, but I can't see straight anymore. Keep it cool, what's the name of this club? I can't remember, but it's all right, all right. Just dance, gonna be okay, da da doo. Just dance, spin that record, babe, da da doo-doo. Just dance, gonna be okay, da da doo-doo. Just dance. Dance, dance. Just, just dance.
ADLER: Breinberg says there are many factors as to why they have become such a sensation.
Mr. BREINBERG: There is something just magical about their performances. I think it's their selections. I think they sing selections people don't expect. I try to teach them that there's more to music than what they're hearing necessarily on the radio and to be open. And they bring their own thing to it. They have a sound. And when you bring something unique to the table, yeah, that catches people's interest.
ADLER: Despite success, Breinberg says the future of the chorus is uncertain. He's still waiting to hear if, given education budget cuts in New York City, his chorus will be fully funded this year.
Margot Adler, NPR News, New York.
SIEGEL: And you can see the PS22 Chorus perform at the new npr.org.
You're listening to ALL THINGS CONSIDERED from NPR News

LC 4: A FACEBOOK TALE: FOUNDER UNFRIENDS PALS ON WAY UP

1.
a. prank	**b.** sophomore	**c.** launch	**d.** semisecret	**e.** upset	**f.** investor
g. froze	**h.** salacious	**i.** geek	**j.** dorm	**k.** shed	**l.** malicious

2.
a. F	**b.** F	**c.** F	**d.** T	**e.** T	**f.** F
g. T	**h.** F	**i.** T	**j.** T	**k.** T	**l.** F

3.
a. Mark's good friend   **b.** exclusive, semisecret Harvard societies
c. only cool people   **d.** starting own finals club

4.
a. M	**b.** M	**c.** E	**d.** M	**e.** M
f. S	**g.** S	**h.** E	**i.** E	**j.** E

5.
a. C   **b.** B   **c.** B

6.
a. C   **b.** B   **c.** A/D   **d.** A

LC 4 – TRANSCRIPT: A FACEBOOK TALE: FOUNDER UNFRIENDS PALS ON WAY UP (CD-TRACK 04)

GUY RAZ, host: Welcome back to ALL THINGS CONSIDERED from NPR News. I'm Guy Raz.
Facebook reached another milestone this past week: the social networking site said it signed up its 250 millionth user on Tuesday.
Just five and a half years ago, Mark Zuckerberg invented the program in his Harvard University dorm room. Within months, he became the youngest self-made billionaire in history.
Zuckerberg's rise to Internet royalty is dramatized in a new book, "The Accidental Billionaires." In that book, Mark Zuckerberg goes from Harvard miscreant to Silicon Valley playboy, all the while callously shedding himself of the little people who helped him on his way up.
Ben Mezrich wrote that book, something he calls a dramatic narrative account. Mezrich is best known for chronicling an MIT blackjack ring in the book "Bringing Down the House."
He describes how Facebook was started as a prank in the fall of 2003 – actually a malicious prank, called facemash.
Mr. BEN MEZRICH (Author, "The Accidental Billionaires"): Mark Zuckerberg, after a particularly bad date, was home in his dorm room. He was a sophomore, and he was drinking some beers, and he hacked into all of the computer systems at Harvard, and he pulled pictures of all the girls on campus up, and he created a hot-or-not Web site where you could vote on who the hottest girl at Harvard was.
And this ended up crashing all the servers at Harvard as everyone tried to log on at the same time, and Mark almost got kicked out of school. So he decided to launch Facebook, originally called The Facebook. Instead of voting on who the hottest girl was, everyone put their own pictures up, and you could all meet each other, and it would be like your own, actual social network put onto the Web.
RAZ: And this originally was designed just for Harvard students. It was exclusively for Harvard students.

Mr. MEZRICH: I believe part of that was that Mark and Eduardo, who was his good friend at the time, were both trying to get into one of the finals clubs at Harvard, which are the semisecret societies. They're kind of like fraternities. But the idea was if you get into one of these clubs, they're very exclusive, you get to be one of the cool people on campus. And I think Mark started Facebook as an exclusive site to be his own finals club.
RAZ: You mention Eduardo – Eduardo Saverin. He was also very much tied to the founding of Facebook.
Mr. MEZRICH: Right. Well, he was the really the one in there – he was there in the beginning. I mean, he was Mark's best friend, and when Mark came up with the idea of Facebook, he came to Eduardo and said, I want to do this site. I need some money.
Eduardo had money. So he offered to put up $1,000, and Mark said, you get 30 percent of the company, and I get 70 percent.
RAZ: How did Mark Zuckerberg end up in California in the summer of 2004?
Mr. MEZRICH: He met this kid, Sean Parker, the bad boy of Silicon Valley. Sean Parker was the kid who co-founded Napster with Shawn Fanning. He saw Facebook on someone's computer and then met with Mark.
RAZ: So Mark goes to California. Eduardo doesn't. He stays behind on the East Coast, and that's really where their falling out begins, right?
Mr. MEZRICH: Right. These are two best friends, but when Mark starts building this company, Eduardo goes to New York. He's trying to sell advertising for their Web site but really, he goes and finishes school, and that's the beginning of the separation.
RAZ: So what eventually happened between Mark Zuckerberg and Eduardo Saverin?
Mr. MEZRICH: Well, what's interesting is, you know, you have a bunch of points of view what really happened. Eduardo was, you know, finishing school and realized that Mark was moving on without him, and he got very upset, and one of the things that he did is he froze the bank accounts, and this was a signal to Mark that something had to be done about Eduardo.
Mark and Sean Parker then went and found their first angel investor, Peter Thiel, who put $500,000 into the company.
RAZ: And eventually, they freeze Eduardo out, and then Sean Parker, who helps introduce Mark Zuckerberg around Silicon Valley, is also sort of shut out. Do you believe that Mark Zuckerberg betrayed these friends? I mean, even in your account in the book, it's clear that this is Mark Zuckerberg's brainchild. I mean, he essentially comes up with everything.
Mr. MEZRICH: Right. I think it's more than Mark doesn't think like other people do. He's socially different, and it seems that he sheds a lot of friends along the way because he's so focused on building this company.
I completely understand his point of view. From his point of view, he built Facebook. From Eduardo's point of view, we were two best friends in a dorm room who built Facebook.
I do think that Mark has a way of sort of losing the people that he's been with all along, but it may just be his focus is so intense that everything else kind of just turns gray.
RAZ: Now, much of your book is based on interviews with Eduardo Saverin and others who are unnamed. You didn't interview Mark Zuckerberg for this book. Why not?
Mr. MEZRICH: No, Mark opted out of talking to me. I spent a year attempting to talk to him. It was kind of like waiting for Godot. It was a continuous process of almost, almost, almost getting to talk to him. And in the end, he and Facebook are somewhat terrified of what I was going to write. They didn't want me writing the story of their sophomore year, you know?
RAZ: He has agreed to cooperate with another writer.
Mr. MEZRICH: Right. He's – yes, he's cooperating with, I think, one or two writers, I'm not sure, and they'll write a very different book than what I wrote. My feeling is that what I'm doing is very true, and in truth, any of the characters in the book who are sitting in their room reading my book, they won't hate it because I'm the biggest proponent of Facebook. But, you know, there's some salacious stuff in there, and Mark didn't want to talk to me, and it's understandable.
RAZ: Salacious, you say, Mr. Mezrich. As you know, a lot of people have criticized your book – reviewers, and people who know the story of Facebook's founding. BusinessWeek actually calls this a fictionalized account.
Mr. MEZRICH: Right.
RAZ: You argue that it's not.
Mr. MEZRICH: Well, listen. There are a lot of journalists out there who don't quite get what I do or are frustrated by the way that I write. I write these narrative nonfiction stories. They're true stories but written in an exciting, entertaining way. They're written almost like a movie.
Everything in that book is based on sources – and numerous ones, not just Eduardo – many, many thousands of pages of court documents and lots of different articles. And then I take that information and turn it into scenes that are active and visual, and I'm extremely clear about what I'm doing. There are certain scenes in the book where I say, this is what probably happened, because I have a lot of information about what happened there, but I can't say for sure. So I say this scene is how I believe it took place.
RAZ: I mean, some scenes, as you've admitted, are actually invented.
Mr. MEZRICH: Well, I mean, you know, I'm very open about my process, much as anybody who's trying to speculate, based on facts, what happened in a place. There are certain chapters where I can only speculate based on the facts. I don't have Mark Zuckerberg telling me. And even if I did, whether he was telling me the truth or not is something I wouldn't know.
RAZ: And do you know whether Eduardo or Mark Zuckerberg have read this book?
Mr. MEZRICH: I don't know. I think that Mark really, if he sat down and read the book, he would actually like it because I feel like he and I have a lot of things in common, this sort of geek bond and this view of the world. But, you know, I don't know what Mark will really think of it.
RAZ: Ben Mezrich is the author of "The Accidental Billionaires: The Founding of Facebook." It's published by Doubleday.
Mr. Mezrich, thanks so much.
Mr. MEZRICH: Thank you very much.
RAZ: We contacted Facebook for its take on the book. No one would talk to us but Elliot Schrage, Facebook's vice president of global communications, sent this email reply. Quote: Ben Mezrich clearly aspires to be the Jackie Collins or the Danielle Steel of Silicon Valley. In fact, his own publisher put it best: The book isn't reportage, it's big, juicy fun. We particularly agree with the first part of that, and think any readers will concur.
You can read an excerpt from "The Accidental Billionaires" on our Web site, npr.org.

LC 5: DOCTORS URGE RESEARCH ON CELL PHONE-CANCER ISSUE

1.
short-term exposure, increase, panel, radiation, urge, reiterate, volunteer, gab

2.

a. F	b. F	c. T	d. T	e. T	f. F
g. T	h. T	i. F	j. F	k. T	l. F

LÖSUNGEN ZU DEN BUCHSEITEN 14–16

3.
a. only a low number
b. due to chance
c. to text message, use headsets or earpieces, limit use of mobiles, to use landlines
d. discourage children from cellphoning / restrict children's cellphone use / to be cautious

4.
a. During a hearing in the **American** parliament, the importance of restricting children's use of cell phones was repeated.
b. Ronald Herberman urged his **faculty and staff** to limit cell phone use.
c. Ronald Herberman **cannot prove** that cell phones are dangerous.

5.

A Herberman and his colleagues are asking **for help** in their efforts to get cell phone companies to release billing **records** for future studies. This is the strategy already under way in a **long-term** European study. Lawrence Challis says it includes about 200,000 cell phone using **volunteers** and loads of documentation from their cell phone bills. This way, researchers won't have to **rely on** people's faulty memories about how much they **gabbed** five years ago.

C Most of these volunteers will have used their phones for about five to ten years previously. So you've then got a much better calibration of how much they used.

A If lots of gabbing over time is predictive of any **increased** risk of **disease**, in five years or so this study will show it. Allison Aubrey, NPR News.

LC 5 – TRANSCRIPT: DOCTORS URGE RESEARCH ON CELL PHONE-CANCER ISSUE (CD-TRACK 05)

MICHELE NORRIS, host: From NPR News, this is All Things Considered. I'm Michele Norris.
MELISSA BLOCK, host: And I'm Melissa Block. The suspicion that cell phones may be linked to brain cancer has percolated for years, but the vast majority of scientific studies have shown no association between the two. NPR's Allison Aubrey reports on why the question isn't settled and why a few doctors went to Capitol Hill today to push for long-term research.
ALLISON AUBREY: There are a lot of studies on short-term exposure to cell phones. The National Cancer Institute has reviewed more than a dozen of them looking for a possible link to brain cancer. They found little or no increased risk within the first 10 years of use. On top of that, at the very time when cell phone usage increased dramatically and phones became more powerful, from 1987 to 2005, there was no upturn in the incidence of brain cancers in the United States. Dr. Dimitrios Trichopoulos is a professor of cancer prevention at the Harvard School of Public Health. He says when you combine everything we know so far, there's no cause for alarm.
Dr. DIMITRIOS TRICHOPOULOS (Professor of Cancer Prevention, Harvard School of Public Health): It seems convincing that there is definitely no important increase, nothing that would make us very much worried.
AUBREY: British scientists have weighed in as well. Dr. Lawrence Challis headed up a government panel in England last year that reviewed 23 studies on cell phone use and health effects. Just like the National Cancer Institute, the panel concluded that radio-frequency radiation from cell phones poses no short-term health risk. They say the amount of radiation is just too low to cause harm. But Challis says among the few studies that included people who had been using cell phones for a longer time, more than a decade, there is uncertainty. Some studies identified a very low number of brain cancers among cell phone users, but it's just as likely those were due to chance as it is that cell phones played a role.
Professor LAWRENCE CHALLIS (Chairman, Mobile Telecommunications Health Research Programme): If you look at all the work that's been done, there are slight hints of something for people who use them for more than 10 years and some of the brain cancers, but they are not totally convincing hints. All they are is suggestions that we can't be sure there isn't something there.
AUBREY: Despite this uncertainty about long-term exposure, the British panel did not urge people to give up cell phones. Challis says people who are concerned have several options. They can text message, use headsets or earpieces, and they can limit use of their mobile phones by using landlines. The panel recommendations were stronger when it comes to children. The group, which called itself the Stewart Committee, advised parents to err on the side of caution.
Dr. CHALLIS: Children may be appreciably more sensitive to radio frequency, so I think the advice given by the Stewart Committee was that children really should be discouraged from using phones.
AUBREY: This advice to restrict children's use of cell phones was reiterated today during a hearing on Capitol Hill. Physician Ronald Herberman, who heads the University of Pittsburgh's Cancer Institute, made headlines last summer when he urged his faculty and staff to limit cell phone use. In testimony today, Herberman said he's not an expert on the risks of cell phones, but he said it's his opinion that they pose a larger risk for everyone than the current science sheds light on.
Dr. RONALD HERBERMAN (Director, University of Pittsburgh Cancer Institute): I cannot tell this committee that cell phones are definitely dangerous, but I certainly cannot tell you that they are safe.
AUBREY: Herberman and his colleagues are asking for help in their efforts to get cell phone companies to release billing records for future studies. This is the strategy already under way in a long-term European study. Lawrence Challis says it includes about 200,000 cell phone using volunteers and loads of documentation from their cell phone bills. This way, researchers won't have to rely on people's faulty memories about how much they gabbed five years ago.
Dr. CHALLIS: Most of these volunteers will have used their phones for about five to ten years previously. So you've then got a much better calibration of how much they used.
AUBREY: If lots of gabbing over time is predictive of any increased risk of disease, in five years or so this study will show it.
Allison Aubrey, NPR News.

LC 6: STUDY MAY TIE FOOD ADDITIVES TO HYPERACTIVITY

1.
2: substance added to colour edible products
6: incapacity of concentrating, heightened need to move
1: chemical substance added to conserve food
3: mixture of substances
4: any chemical substance added to (edible) products
5: complete removal

LÖSUNGEN ZU DEN BUCHSEITEN 16–18

2.
a. B   b. D   c. C   d. A

3.
a. to follow instructions
b. to finish a task
c. to respond when addressed
d. to control impulses

4.
a. ☑   b. ☑   c. ☐   d. ☐   e. ☐   f. ☐   g. ☑   h. ☑

5.
a. Children who stop consuming food additives will **not necessarily** get rid of hyperkinetic behaviour.
b. Some studies testing small amounts of dyes and preservatives have found there are **no** harmful effects.
c. The remaining question is what **combinations** of additives at which doses may be worth worrying about.

LC 6 – TRANSCRIPT: STUDY MAY TIE FOOD ADDITIVES TO HYPERACTIVITY (CD-TRACK 06)

MICHELE NORRIS, host: What do you get when you combine fruit juice with a food dye called Sunset Yellow and the preservative called sodium benzoate? Some researchers in England say you may get more hyperactive behavior in young children. A new study in the British medical journal Lancet tested the effects of these food additives on groups of 3-year-olds and 8-year-olds.
NPR's Allison Aubrey reports.
ALLISON AUBREY: Researchers at the University of Southampton mixed four types of food dyes with juice and served the concoctions to children multiple times over the course of six weeks. The drinks were mixed to look and taste the same as a juice drink that contained no dyes or preservatives. Neither the children nor their parents were told which drink they were given. Throughout the study, teachers and parents were asked to observe the children's behavior to look for things such as...
Dr. GENE ARNOLD (Professor Emeritus of Psychiatry, Ohio State University) The ability to follow instructions, to finish a task, to respond when spoken to, and to control impulses.
AUBREY: Gene Arnold is a child psychiatrist at Ohio State.
He says the researchers found that some children who drank the juice spiked with additives did act somewhat more inattentive and impulsive than kids who drank the additive-free drinks.
Dr. ARNOLD: There does seem to be some sensitivity to some common food additives, mainly colorings, and then also sodium benzoate – a preservative.
AUBREY: But how strong was the effect? Child psychiatrist Shashank Joshi of Stanford University says the effect was quite small. He says after reviewing the findings, he takes issue with the press release written to promote the study. It read: Food additives increase levels of hyperactivity in children.
Dr. SHASHANK JOSHI (Assistant Professor, Psychiatry and Behavioral Science – Child Psychiatry, Stanford University): I would probably rephrase that and say, some food additives may increase levels of hyperactivity in some children.
AUBREY: Joshi explains that previous studies have shown that kids who are already impulsive and inattentive who may or may not have an attention deficit disorder but do have behavior problems are more likely to be sensitive to food additives. Other children without behavior problems may be less sensitive, and any effect of food dyes and preservatives on their lives wouldn't be noticeable.
Joshi says the new study finds the difference in hyperactive behavior between the kids who drank the juice with additives compared to those who didn't get the additives is only about 10 percent.
Dr. JOSHI: Parents might say, hey, a 10 percent reduction? They'll say, I'll take it. But I think it's important to not take this away and go, you know, if I eliminate all the additives from my kid's diet, it's going to get rid of their hyperkinetic behavior.
AUBREY: Joshi says the study adds to a growing knowledge about the effects of additives and the diet. Some studies testing small amounts of dyes and preservatives have found there are no harmful effects. What's left to be untangled is what combinations of additives at which doses may be worth worrying about.
Allison Aubrey, NPR News, Washington.

LC 7: HOMEWORK: WHEN DANGEROUS ANIMALS ATTACK

1.
a. encounter   b. rear end   c. entanglements   d. chomp   e. trough   f. wheelbarrow

2.
a. F   b. F   c. T   d. F   e. T   f. F   g. F

3.
SUSIE: So I **was snorkelling** in the Dry Tortugas off of the tip of Florida and I was with a man and a teenage boy. And the man suddenly **dove** down and **picked** up a three-foot-long nurse shark.
And the shark was **furious** and it wanted to attack the first thing that it could see. And unfortunately, I was the first thing that it **saw**. And so the shark is coming at me and I was whirling side-to-side trying to get away from it. And suddenly I feel this chomp and the nurse shark **bit** very hard into my rear end. The shark bite **left** a perfectly round scar that lasted for many years.

4.
a. everyday problems at home
b. loading the dishwasher, setting the thermostat
c. 202-408-5183
d. to leave a number

LÖSUNGEN ZU DEN BUCHSEITEN 17–20

LC 7 – TRANSCRIPT: HOMEWORK: WHEN DANGEROUS ANIMALS ATTACK (CD TRACK-07)

ANDREA SEABROOK, host:

Now for your homework. This week we asked for your stories of animal encounters. This came in from Avner Ussan(ph). He once worked as a zookeeper at the Tel-Aviv Zoo.

Mr. AVNER USSAN: One of my duties was to feed the small monkeys. There was a trough in front of their cage and we would simply dump the food into the trough. They would reach through the cage bars and grab whatever they felt like. Well, on this particular day, as I was turning the wheelbarrow over, I leaned towards the cage and there happened to be a small monkey on one of the shelves. He grabbed my hair and basically yanked and pinned me to the bars. So I was basically flailing.

There were people watching, laughing, having a good time. And you could tell the monkeys were enjoying themselves. They were just rolling and jumping and really enjoying the scene. I grabbed a tomato from the trough and flung it at the cage, flung it at him, and instead of it fitting between the bars, it actually hit the bar and splashed back at me, which was much to the delight of all the onlookers and the monkeys.

(Soundbite of music)

SEABROOK: Enough monkeying around. Susie Shane(ph) sent in this cinematic story of man versus beast.

Ms. SUSIE SHANE: So I was snorkelling in the Dry Tortugas off of the tip of Florida and I was with a man and a teenage boy. And the man suddenly dove down and picked up a three-foot-long nurse shark.

(Soundbite of music)

Ms. SHANE: And the shark was furious and it wanted to attack the first thing that it could see. And unfortunately, I was the first thing that it saw. And so the shark is coming at me and I was whirling side-to-side trying to get away from it. And suddenly I feel this chomp and the nurse shark bit very hard into my rear end. The shark bite left a perfectly round scar that lasted for many years.

SEABROOK: Thanks to Susie Shane and Avner Ussan for their stories. On to next week's homework. We want to hear about the things you fight about at home, not the big questions but the little stuff. The everyday things. The ones you fight about all the time. Maybe it's how to properly load the dishwasher or what to set the thermostat to; that's the rub in my house. Whatever it is, tell us about it. Write to homework@npr.org or call the homework hotline at 202-408-5183. Again, that's homework@npr.org or the homework hotline at 202-408-5183. Make sure you leave us a number so we can get back to you.

LC 8: TEEN T-SHIRT ENTREPRENEUR WINS $ 10,000

	A	B	C	D
0	☐	☐	☒	☐
Q1	☐	☒	☐	☐
Q2	☐	☐	☐	☒
Q3	☐	☒	☐	☐
Q4	☐	☐	☐	☒
Q5	☒	☐	☐	☐
Q6	☒	☐	☐	☐
Q7	☐	☐	☒	☐

LC 8 – TRANSCRIPT: TEEN T-SHIRT ENTREPRENEUR WINS $10,000 (CD-TRACK 08)

SCOTT SIMON, host: This week, a young man named Kalief Rollins won a $10,000 grand prize at the 2009 National Youth Entrepreneurship Competition. He's 17 years old from Carson, California, which is in the L.A. metropolitan area, and won for his business that sells custom T-shirts with inspirational designs.

Mr. Rollins competed against 27 finalists and 24,000 initial high school entrants for an award given by the nonprofit Network for Teaching Entrepreneurship. Kalief Rollins joins us from New York. Thanks very much for being with us.

Mr. KALIEF ROLLINS (Winner, National Youth Entrepreneurship Competition): My pleasure.

SIMON: Inspirational designs for urban youths – like what?

Mr. ROLLINS: For example, we have several shirts. But for example, we have a shirt that says, Caution: Educated Black Male. We have shirts with, like, quotes from urban leaders like Martin Luther King and Malcolm X. For one, we have an Obama shirt as well. Just, you know, just shirts that have leadership themes and positive messages out there for people who want to support their urban leaders.

SIMON: Who designs them?

Mr. ROLLINS: My brother, Anthony Rollins.

SIMON: And how old is he?

Mr. ROLLINS: He's 22.

SIMON: And what's the name of your company?

Mr. ROLLINS: It's Phree Kountry Clothing, P-H-R-E-E K-O-U-N-T-R-Y.

SIMON: What's the best seller?

Mr. ROLLINS: Our best seller so far had to be the Obama shirt due to the campaign and everything. But as of now, like, since we made this new design, the one I told you about, the educated African-American male …

SIMON: Yeah.

Mr. ROLLINS: ... that seems like that's going to be the next best seller. Everyone seems to like that one as well.

SIMON: Ten thousand dollars – that's a nice prize.

Mr. ROLLINS: Yes, a very nice prize.

SIMON: Have any plans for it?

Mr. ROLLINS: Yeah, we're going to first get a silkscreen machine; that's a rank up from what we do now, heat press, just to make better quality shirts, and the rest of the money go back toward the business just to get all the equipment and more stuff that we need for the business just to keep moving forward.

SIMON: Are you permitted to take, I don't know, five dollars of that and treat yourself to a frappuccino or something?

Mr. ROLLINS: Yeah. Actually, we'll take a few, maybe 20 or $30 out of there and me and my brother will go celebrate at Roscoe's Chicken and Waffles.

SIMON: Ah, I've been to Roscoe's.

Mr. ROLLINS: Yeah. How do you like it?

SIMON: I liked it a lot. Famous place. I think it's nice that you and your brother own a business together.

Mr. ROLLINS: Yeah.

SIMON: Other family members?

Mr. ROLLINS: My mom. I hired my mom as my CFO.

(Soundbite of laughter)

SIMON: Well, mothers are CFOs whether you, you know, whether you hire them or not, aren't they?

Mr. ROLLINS: Right. She worked as an accountant, so she's good in that field of work. I pay a little money to her for the electricity I use for my equipment, but other than that she, you know, she just wants to see me do well, so she just says I could just do it and she's just proud of me. So she don't really ask for – for money.

SIMON: Well, I hope you and your chief financial officer maintain a good working relationship. It's important.

Mr. ROLLINS: We will.

SIMON: Mr. Rollins, thanks so much.

Mr. ROLLINS: Thank you.

SIMON: Kalief Rollins, 2009 winner of the National Youth Entrepreneurship Competition. To get a look at a few of his T-shirts, come to our Web site, NPR.org.

LC 9: USING MUSIC TO MENTOR VENEZUELA'S POOREST YOUTH

1.

conductor, tuxedo, abuse, maturity, adversity, desire

2.

Q0	classical music to kids
Q1	cost a fortune/is enormous/boasts a (shiny) (hardwood) floor
Q2	15 000
Q3	choose something different
Q4	are poor
Q5	a friend/a father
Q6	the program imposes
Q7	doesn't get frustrated
Q8	singing in the chorus
Q9	have experienced success

LC 9 – TRANSCRIPT: USING MUSIC TO MENTOR VENEZUELA'S POOREST YOUTH (CD TRACK 09)

GUY RAZ, host: There's a star-studded concert tonight at the Hollywood Bowl. Opening acts include Herbie Hancock, Taj Majal, Flea from the Red Hot Chili Peppers, David Hidalgo from Los Lobos. And the headliner: Gustavo Dudamel, making his official debut as music director of the Los Angeles Philharmonic Orchestra. The Venezuelan director is just 28 years old, the youngest conductor ever for the L.A. Phil, and may be the hottest name in classical music today. Dudamel is a product of El Sistema or The System. It's a Venezuelan program that teaches classical music to kids; many of them desperately poor.

Enrique Rivera visited the country's capital, Caracas, and spoke with a few of the quarter million young musicians who've come through El Sistema.

ENRIQUE RIVERA: This state-of-the-art concert hall is packed. You can tell the stage cost a fortune. It's enormous and boasts a shiny hardwood floor.

(Soundbite of music)

RIVERA: About 80 Venezuelan teenagers of all sizes and colors, between the ages of 16 and 18, are decked out in the most elegant dresses and crisp black tuxedos.

(Soundbite of music)

RIVERA: This building isn't merely a concert hall. It's a school where young people come to learn and practice playing classical music. The school has 84 classrooms and three concert halls. This one seats 400 people. There's another one that seats 800, and one outside that seats 15,000.
(Soundbite of music)
RIVERA: During the day, this mega-facility is flooded with thousands of young people eager to become better musicians, like 15-year-old Diana Tardes, who plays the contrabass, an instrument almost twice as big as she is.
Ms. DIANA TARDES (Contrabass Player): (Through Translator) This instrument caught my attention because it's an instrument that most skinny little girls like me don't normally choose. They usually choose the violin, but I wanted to choose something different.
RIVERA: A teenager wanting to do things differently isn't that uncommon, but one of the things that make El Sistema so unique is that 70 percent of those in the program are poor.
Unidentified Man: (Foreign language spoken)
(Soundbite of music)
RIVERA: Many of the young people come from Caracas' infamous slums, some of the most violent in the world. Being surrounded by poverty, drugs and murder is a lot of baggage for a young person to carry.
Ulysis Acano, a principal conductor in the program, helps them carry it.
Mr. ULYSIS ACANO (Principal Conductor): (Through Translator) People without a father, without a mother, with severe problems at home like abuse and the stuff like that. I am like a friend, like a father. You hear their problems and you can help find a place where they can seek help or you can help them yourself.
RIVERA: Kids in the program come here to practice every day after school from three to 7 p.m., and even on Saturdays. When you speak to some of them, you're immediately struck by the maturity they display. And it's largely due to the discipline, Acano says, the program imposes.
Mr. ACANO: (Through Translator) Music has a gigantic amount of mental, mathematic and physical training, and they've understood that message very well.
(Soundbite of music)
RIVERA: Learning to play a classical instrument can be extremely difficult, but Miguel Rodriguez, a 19-year-old clarinet player, says he doesn't get frustrated.
Mr. MIGUEL RODRIGUEZ (Clarinet Player): (Through Translator) I only get stuck, but then I reflect on what I'm doing wrong and I just continue. That's it.
RIVERA: It's an approach he applies to his day-to-day life. Most kids in El Sistema have learned how to overcome adversity well, since they've been doing it since kindergarten. Some were as young as 2 years old when they came to the program.
(Soundbite of music)
RIVERA: Most young people start out in El Sistema singing in the chorus. Then they work their way up: learning the instrument they choose, practicing and playing in the orchestras.
Susan Simon is the director of the Infant Academy in Caracas.
Ms. SUSAN SIMON (Director, Infant Academy): (Through Translator) We put them in contact with success at a very early age. The first thing they accomplish musically is applauded. So they start to learn that that's fun and recognized. They like to do it simply because they have experienced success.
RIVERA: They learn little by little, but the huge amount of musical knowledge these kids display is truly remarkable, like this orchestra of elementary school and junior high kids.
(Soundbite of music)
RIVERA: Most of these young people will become professional musicians when they grow up, but not all.
Maribel Cartellanos, a 25-year-old conductor in the program, says that's not the point.
Ms. MARIBEL CARTELLANOS (Conductor): (Through Translator) My sister also studied music, but she decided on another career. But this left her the discipline, the organization, the constant day-to-day desire to be better. That's why we are here.
RIVERA: They're here together as a clan, a family that is spread out to every city in Venezuela, now that each one has a youth orchestra.
From NPR News, I'm Enrique Rivera.

LC 10: A REAL-LIFE SCHOOL OF ROCK

1.

Q0	a Grammy
Q1	(an actual) college degree
Q2	Oklahoma City
Q3	a master class
Q4	a demo
Q5	guitar, bass, drums
Q6	(because) most are into it / kids like it
Q7	(about the) business / how industry works / music theory / general ed / oral skills
Q8	played the piano
Q9	(a great deal of) luck
Q10	requires actual skill / has different styles / different chords

2.
a. accredited   **b.** quit   **c.** scholarship   **d.** aspiring   **e.** degree, train hard   **f.** drop out   **g.** launch

3.
a. Members of The Flaming Lips are **teaching at** the new school of rock.
b. Students are going to earn a **college** degree at the new school of rock.
c. Steven Drozd is the band's **guitarist.**/**Scot Booker** is the band's manager.
d. **Steven Drozd** is going to teach a master class at the new academy.

4.
a. F   **b.** T   **c.** F   **d.** T   **e.** F   **f.** F   **g.** T   **h.** F

LÖSUNGEN ZU DEN BUCHSEITEN 22 UND 23

LC 10 – TRANSCRIPT: A REAL-LIFE SCHOOL OF ROCK (CD-TRACK 10)

DAVID GREENE, host: You know, if only I had gone to rock school, maybe my drumming would sound a little more like this.
(Soundbite of music)
GREENE: Yeah, I'm probably not going to win a Grammy any time soon, like The Flaming Lips, but the members of that band are hoping they can teach some aspiring musicians how to become full-fledged rock stars like they are.
(Soundbite of song, "Yoshimi Battles the Pink Robots")
Mr. WAYNE COYNE (Singer, The Flaming Lips): (Singing) Her name is Yoshimi, she's a black belt in karate.
GREENE: The band's manager has launched a new school of rock, and this is not a Jack Black joke. Students who start classes on Monday will be on their way to earning an actual college degree. And here to talk to us about this Academy of Contemporary Music are Steven Drozd and Scot Booker. Drozd plays guitar for the band The Flaming Lips, who we were hearing right there, and Booker manages the band, and they're joining us from Oklahoma City, where I understand the school's based. Welcome to both of you.
Mr. SCOT BOOKER (Manager, The Flaming Lips): Hello.
Mr. STEVEN DROZD (Guitarist, The Flaming Lips) Hello. Thanks for having us.
GREENE: Thank you. So what did you guys think of my drumming?
Mr. BOOKER: I thought that it sounded pretty good.
Mr. DROZD: Well, he would, but I would say you need to come to my school.
(Soundbite of laughter)
Mr. DROZD: Or learn how to program a drum machine, one of the two.
GREENE: Well, Steven, you're going to be teaching a master class at this new academy. Will you give me some tips, some basics?
Mr. DROZD: Go.
GREENE: Here I go, okay.
(Soundbite of drums)
Mr. DROZD: Wait, let me see if I can count you in. That's a start right there.
GREENE: Oh, count me in, yeah. Try counting me in. Show me how to do that.
Mr. DROZD: And if you can't, then we'll know strike one right there.
GREENE: Show me …
Mr. DROZD: One, two, three, four.
(Soundbite of drums)
Mr. DROZD: Um, showing promise with the funk, but a little herky jerky, so like a B, C. I would go with C.
GREENE: Okay.
Mr. DROZD: You keep working on that. Yeah.
GREENE: I'll try. Scot Booker, could I have gotten into this academy? I mean, what does it actually take? What are the admission standards?
Mr. BOOKER: Well, it depends. There's two paths and there will eventually be three. The first path is performance, and there's guitar, bass, drums and vocals.
GREENE: So you do actually send in some tapes or…
Mr. BOOKER: Exactly, you send in a demo. We hope it's you playing. I never considered that and one of the teachers the other day was like, what if it's not them playing…
GREENE: Terrifying. Make sure it's actually them.
Mr. BOOKER: Exactly. Well, we'll find out on Monday, I'm sure, you know. And on the production path, you send in something you've recorded, and that could have been on Garage Band or whatever. We just want to make sure you understand some fundamentals, so everyone's at a certain level right at the beginning.
GREENE: So you're looking for some sort of level playing field, but I mean different background, different interests, or is there a certain sort of mould you want in that classroom?
Mr. BOOKER: You know, the idea behind this program is really as much about business and the idea of learning how the industry works while you're learning to play better. We are leaning very much towards rock because the majority of the kids that are coming this first semester are into rock. So this first semester they'll be learning songs by The Who and The Flaming Lips and The Strokes and Spoon; we got the Eagles, so we have a little bit of country rock in there.
(Soundbite of song, "Take It Easy")
THE EAGLES: (Singing) Take It easy, take it easy, Don't let the sound of your own wheels drive you crazy.
Mr. BOOKER: And there's theory, I mean this is a degreed program, so not only are you taking general ed, but you're also taking oral skills and music theory and those things that anyone that's getting a music degree has to take.
GREENE: And is the program accredited? I mean it's actually part of a …
Mr. BOOKER: Absolutely, yeah, we're part of the University of Central Oklahoma, and I felt like this was important.
GREENE: Steven, you're sort of living the dream, you know, of many wannabe rockers. But it was a sort of a fantasy coming true. Did you have any real classroom training, and why – if not, why would you say it's necessary?
Mr. DROZD: Well, I think my big advantage was having a little bit of education, enough to, you know, I learned some piano and I based everything on that. I thought about going to school because I got a couple of scholarship offers through band and stuff, but then the idea of just straight college didn't appeal to me.
Mr. BOOKER: I've had several kids get their GEDs so they could quit high school early to come here, and their parents came to me and they're like, I was afraid that maybe he would have just dropped out of school.
GREENE: Have you had some scepticism? I mean are there parents out there who are saying, I'm not sending my kids to college to rock out?
Mr. BOOKER: Well, I think more the grandparents than the parents, to be honest.
(Soundbite of laughter)
Mr. BOOKER: But we've also been very clear that you're not coming here and we're promising you to become a rock star, because just like anything, there's a great deal of luck involved.
GREENE: Steven Drozd, you're a guitarist. Is there a song, you know, on your mind that you can point to and say you kind of need some training to do that? You know, you could learn about riffs or sort of the feel of music …
Mr. DROZD: Well, "Stairway to Heaven." You can start with "Stairway to Heaven" right there, so – I mean such an obvious choice, but that requires some actual real skill and it's got all kinds of different styles in it.
(Soundbite of song, "Stairway to Heaven")
Mr. DROZD: There's the, you know, the acoustic intro and then you – as you go through the song, it sort of slowly builds and you've got – there's different sorts of chords that are just quintessential classic rock chording, you know, which would be very helpful to learn. By the end you're doing the heavy sort of riff rock, and you've got that crazy guitar solo, which I think still is one of the best guitar solos of all time.

(Soundbite of song, "Stairway to Heaven")
GREENE: Before I let you go, I'm sitting, I'm sitting, as I said, at a drum set and, you know, dreaming myself about one day being a rock star. But I'll put you on the spot. Is there a Flaming Lips song that sort of is on your mind as it should be part of your school?
Mr. DROZD: Before I say anything, I'll bet Scot already has an agenda with that. What is it, Scot?
Mr. BOOKER: Well, my agenda is that since "Do You Realize" is the state rock song, it is definitely on the curriculum.
(Soundbite of song, "Do You Realize")
THE FLAMING LIPS (Rock Band): (Singing) Do you realise that you have the most beautiful face, do you realize …
(Soundbite of drums)
Mr. DROZD: David?
(Soundbite of percussion)
Mr. DROZD: David?
GREENE: Yes.
Mr. DROZD: Are you messing with me?
(Soundbite of laughter)
GREENE: I was just playing some more, you know. Steven Drozd is the guitarist for The Flaming Lips and he will be teaching a master class at the new Academy of Contemporary Music. And Scot Booker is the band's manager and also CEO of the school. Thank you guys both for joining us.
Mr. BOOKER: Thanks for having us.
Mr. DROZD: Thank you. Yeah.
(Soundbite of song, "Pinball Wizard")
GREENE: This is WEEKEND EDITION from NPR News. I'm David Greene. Scott Simon is back behind the drum set next week.

LC 11: NEW HAMPSHIRE SPLIT OVER HIGH SCHOOL CHEATING

1.

0	Q1	Q2	Q3	Q4	Q5
E	G	B	A	C	H

Extra sentences: D, F

2.
a. they stole a key
b. last year's finals
c. the principals
d. misdemeanour trespassing
e. pay only fines
f. prison
g. could get criminal records

3.
a. C   **b.** B   **c.** A   **d.** C   **e.** C

LC 11 – TRANSCRIPT: NEW HAMPSHIRE SPLIT OVER HIGH SCHOOL CHEATING SCANDAL (CD-TRACK 11)

ANDREA SEABROOK, host: Now to a small town in New Hampshire that is being ripped apart by a cheating scandal at its public high school. Nine students at Hanover High allegedly broke into school and stole advanced copies of exams.
They're now facing criminal charges. The incident has prompted deep soul-searching about how hard to come down on kids. And why some kids might think cheating is okay.
NPR's Tovia Smith reports.
TOVIA SMITH: It's easy to see why Hanover has been called one of the best places to live in America. It's an affluent, charming New England town centred around the prestigious Dartmouth College. And it's long cherished its golden reputation. That may explain why so many people here are so upset about this cheating scandal that's now attracting national reporters.
Unidentified Man: Whoa. So (unintelligible).
SMITH: In front of the high school where the so-called Notorious Nine, allegedly saw their final exams, some students tried to foil a reporter's interview by shrieking and throwing bottles.
(Soundbite of electric guitar)
SMITH: Other kids with an electric guitar and portable amp tried to thwart interviews by trailing a reporter like a heavy metal mariachi band.
(Soundbite of electric guitar)
SMITH: While most kids here wish they could make their story go away, they are divided about how to punish the nine students who allegedly used a stolen key to break into school and steal last year's finals.
Many like junior Mike Rotch says the kids do deserve to be punished by their principals, but not by a prosecutor.
Mr. MIKE ROTCH (Student, Hanover High School, New Hampshire): Yeah, I think they're really coming down pretty hard. I mean, cheating is bad, but it's not like this is unheard of, like, anywhere in America.
SMITH: As prosecutors see it, they went easy on the kids by charging them only with misdemeanour trespassing instead of burglary, which is a felony. The misdemeanour carries only fines, not prisons.

LÖSUNGEN ZU DEN BUCHSEITEN 25–27

But because New Hampshire treats 17-year-olds as adults, the students could end up with criminal records, a prospect freshman Ethan Forhour thinks is unfair.

Mr. ETHAN FORHOUR (Student, Hanover High School, New Hampshire) I mean, seriously, like, they are good kids and they made a mistake. And I think they know that they did make a mistake.

SMITH: But other students are less sympathetic.

Unidentified Woman #1: They are criminals.

Unidentified Man #1: Just because …

Unidentified Man #2: It's the same as if I walked into a convenience store and shoplifted, that's still the same thing. They stole.

SMITH: What's your name?

Unidentified Woman #2: We prefer to stay anonymous. We'd probably (…) kick the crap out of them.

SMITH: Other students, who didn't want their names used either, admitted they themselves would cheat because of all the pressure.

Jim Kenyon is a local newspaper columnist and the father of one of the nine students who've been charged. He says Hanover is a place where the college you go to is more of a status symbol than the car you drive, and parents put big-time pressure on kids.

Mr. JIM KENYON (Columnist, The Valley News): We've created a monster, and I'm as guilty as anyone, as a parent, because we want the best for our children. So we shouldn't be surprised when we have these kind of things happen.

SMITH: But Kenyon says treating kids like criminals does nothing to address the broader problem of cheating that he says is rampant.

Besides the nine accused of stealing the exams, he says, there are dozens of other kids who asked for copies and used them to cheat.

Mr. KENYON: It was working like a New York deli. I mean, kids were just calling up and putting in an order and that to me speaks of the culture of the school that needs to be addressed.

SMITH: As a parent, Kenyon says, he never really lectured his kids about academic integrity. He just never saw it as one of the biggies, like drugs and drunk driving.

Teachers also may be sending the kids the wrong message about cheating. Juniors Cory Burns and Dillon Gregory say kids know they won't get in trouble for things like sharing homework or finding out what's on a test from kids who've already taken it.

Ms. CORY BURNS (Student, Hanover High School, New Hampshire): Some teachers don't classify that as cheating, and some teachers…

Mr. DILLON GREGORY (Student, Hanover High School, New Hampshire): There are some who don't see it as such a serious issue.

SMITH: It may be part of the reason why cheating is on the rise in schools. Research suggests up to 75 percent of kids today cheat.

Ms. AINE DONOVAN (Executive Director, Ethics Institute, Dartmouth College): The millennial generation, kids born roughly after the year 1983, seem to have a different notion about honesty than previous generations did.

SMITH: Aine Donovan, head of Dartmouth's Ethics Institute, says kids today are more apt to rationalize their behavior as a means to an end, and they seemed to have invented their own particular code of right and wrong.

Ms. DONOVAN: When I ask my students, is there anything unethical about downloading music – absolutely not. They don't have a problem with it. And yet those same kids would never in a million years walk into a K-Mart and steal a CD. It's a different kind of orientation about morality.

SMITH: It's like the Hanover High sophomore who says kids couldn't really had stolen a teacher's keys if they just took the keys off the teacher's table right out in the open.

Tovia Smith, NPR News.

LC 12: SOME SPEND THOUSANDS TO SAVE PETS

1.

cancer, surgery, radiation, chemotherapy, treatment, organ transplant

2.

0	Q1	Q2	Q3	Q4	Q5	Q6	Q7	Q8	Q9
C	F	A	D	J	L	K	I	G	E

Extra sentences: B, H

LC 12 – TRANSCRIPT: SOME SPEND THOUSANDS TO SAVE PETS (CD-TRACK 12)

ROBERT SIEGEL, host: Our next story is about a man and his goose. It's really a story about the $20 billion a year that Americans spend on health care for their pets. But in this particular case, the pet is a goose named Boswell, 2 years old – that's young for a goose, we've learned, they can live well past 20. Boswell has had cancer twice, and he's had surgery, radiation, chemotherapy, treatment that costs thousands of dollars.

Writer Vicki Constantine Croke wrote about Boswell the goose and the many medical options now open to pet owners in a recent article for the Boston Globe Magazine. And she joins us now. Have you been able to calculate what the medical bill for Boswell totals?

Ms. VICKI CONSTANTINE CROKE (Writer): Even though his owner is squeamish about it, he has spent $20,000.

SIEGEL: Twenty thousand dollars. Tell us about the owner and the goose, for that manner.
Ms. CROKE: They are a team. You almost can't talk about one without the other. Mark Podlaseck is an IBM scientist. And his friend was getting a chicken, so he thought he would get geese at the same feed store. He spent $8 on Boswell, never imagining the bill that would come down the line for him.
SIEGEL: Now, the questions raised by a story like that of Boswell the goose and some of the other pets that you read about in the Boston Globe Magazine article. We love our pets – dogs, cats, birds, turtles, geese, whatever – but typically, the vet has been there for rabies shots or extracting some foreign object that the animal has ingested. But chemo, radiation, organ transplants?
Ms. CROKE: You know, the level of care has become so much more sophisticated today than it's ever been before. I met plenty of people who can afford these kinds of treatments. But not everybody can, and that's the really sad part of the story, is knowing that this animal, that you truly consider part of your family, can be saved, but you might not have enough money to do that.
SIEGEL: Apart from the ability to pay or not, did you come across people that just, as a point of principle, said, I could afford this, but this makes no sense to me. She's a cat, you know, this is not a member of my family?
Ms. CROKE: I heard people joke about it and say, you know, I could have three Irish Setters for the price of that cancer care. But no, Paul Gambardella, who used to be the head of Angell Animal Hospital here in Boston, said to me that people often get a cat or dog and they think, when I'm faced with an enormous bill for some horrible illness, I will just put the animal to sleep. But very often, 10 or 15 years of relationship has elapsed, and people feel very dedicated to saving their pets.
SIEGEL: Now, after reading your article in the Boston Globe Magazine, I saw that yesterday, the New York Times Sunday magazine has a big cover story on animal pharm, spelled P-H-A-R-M. In the various vignettes of the pet and the medical care, very often, we're talking about families that have a pet but don't have children, I found. Did you find a difference there between families with kids and without?
Ms. CROKE: As far as I know, there have not been any real surveys to try to delineate that. One study that I do know of was done at the Animal Medical Center in New York. And it found that the overwhelming majority of women in responding to the survey said that they were significantly closer to the pet in their life than any other human being. It is a really important point to make because one thing that we believed in our society, in our culture, is that our relationship with an animal is a substitute for something a human relationship that's missing in your life.
And the data seems to be indicating something different. One terrific study about this showed that in a stressful situation, your blood pressure obviously goes up. No one in your family can help you drop your blood pressure in that situation, not a spouse, not a child. But if your dog comes in the room, your blood pressure goes down. So, increasingly, we are beginning to think about the dynamic in a different way, that maybe a pet is not a replacement for a human, but is, in fact, its own thing, even though we don't have a name for it.
SIEGEL: But there's no human who'll ever be that happy to see you every day when you come back in the door from work.
Ms. CROKE: That's right. One of my favorite survey shows that something like three-quarters of married respondents say that they greet the pet in coming through the front door first before their spouse.
SIEGEL: Well, what's the update on Boswell the goose?
Ms. CROKE: Boswell is doing great. He's had a couple of chemo sessions. He's feeling better than ever. He's feeling so well, in fact, Robert, that he started his own blog called The Daily Honk.
(Soundbite of laughter)
SIEGEL: The Daily Honk. Well, Vicki Constantine Croke, thank you very much for talking with us today.
Ms. CROKE: Thank you, Robert.
SIEGEL: Vicki Constantine Croke's story about the billion-dollar industry of pet health care was published recently in the Boston Globe Magazine.

RC 1: HOW TO FIND OUT IF FOOD IS STILL GOOD TO EAT

Task 3

to bin: to throw away – to reduce: to limit – it was stated: it was mentioned/expressed/declared/said – to sniff: to smell – to reveal: to inform/tell/show – to work out: to find out – to buy: to purchase – to check: to test/probe/try out – to keep it: to store it – usually: normally/regularly – ill: sick – quickly: fast – durable: lasting/maintainable/non-perishable – firmness: tightness – immediately: at once – lettuce: salad – unopened: closed – to indicate: to show/reveal – disease: illness – tasty: tasteful – nasty: horrible – guidelines: laws/regulations – to ignore: forget about – to touch: to feel

Task 4

1d, 2b, 3d, 4c, 5d, 6c, 7a, 8b

Task 5

slimy surface, delicious food, brownish colour, nasty disease, durable potatoes, dangerous toxins, unopened tin, soft tomatoes, dull eyes, bad smell, important guidelines, clean fridge

RC 2: COUCH POTATOE LIFESTYLE VESUS SMOKING – WHICH IS WORSE?

Task 2

1 – F; 2 – D; 3 – H; 4 – A; 5 – E; 6 – C; not used: B, G

Task 3

1. The dangers of a poor diet are cancer, obesity, diabetes and cardiovascular diseases.
2. The campaign was started to inform people how to live a healthy life and to motivate them to exercise and train at least two times a week.
3. You should take care of a healthy diet, have an active lifestyle and a fulfilled life.
4. The problem is that parents start to outlive their obese children.

Task 4

survey, hardly, lazy, keen on, involves, additionally, lead to, harm

LÖSUNGEN ZU DEN BUCHSEITEN 34–41

RC 3: DOES E-MAIL DISTRACT?

Task 3
Writing e-mails is as popular as sending short messages from your mobile.
Spam mails might endanger your computer and can carry a virus.
Photos and other data can easily be sent via e-mail.
Writing and using e-mails has been popular for many years now.
Your computer should regularly be updated for new anti-virus-programs.
Your boss must not forbid you to check your e-mails regularly.
The number of people who don't have access to the Internet is very small.
Sometimes children are better at handling computers than adults.
These days it's popular to also send invitations via mail.
If you buy something online, you will get a confirmation via mail.
If your computer carries a virus, it might be advisable to set it up again.

Task 4
1 – false, They do so because …; 2 – true, The problem is that …; 3 – true, But in fact that …; 4 – true, Because it's proven that …; 5 – false; Some psychologists claim that …; 6 – false, If we receive work-related …; 7 – true, Ideally yes, it would …; 8 – false, Besides, in urgent cases …; 9 – false, Well, there are several …; 10 – true, That means that you …; 11 – false, A red flag, for …

Task 5
to explain – explanation – Erklärung, to distract – distraction – Ablenkung, to concentrate on – concentration – Konzentration, to interrupt – interruption – Unterbrechung, to receive – receipt – Erhalt, to decide – decision – Entscheidung, to remind – reminder – Erinnerung, to stimulate – stimulation – Stimulation, to reduce – reduction – Reduktion, Verminderung

RC 4: FOR A SHOPPER WHO HAS DRUNK ALCOHOL, A MOUSE CAN BE A DANGEROUS THING

Task 3
1 – H, 2 – D, 3 – A, 4 – F, 5 – E, 6 – C; not used: B, G

Task 4
With the development of new technologies, new problems come up. One of the most recent ones is called "sip and click". This means that once people have drunk too much, they are more likely to purchase goods online. The tricky aspect is that very often these people don't remember having bought the goods in question. They only realize their fault once the articles are delivered or they receive their credit card bill. Unfortunately, nothing can be done at that point. It is difficult how to handle a problem like that. A solution is to install a difficult password on your computer to stop yourself from buying unnecessary stuff.

Task 5
has become, doesn't, remember, stuff, push, had returned, was searching, must not

RC 5: HOW THE MOBILE PHONE IS CHANGING OUR LIVES

Task 3
to charge the battery of your mobile
to search your way via Google maps
to adjust the ringtone and volume
to download online aps
to put a colourful cover on your mobile

Task 4
B: take part in privacy/become part of privacy/we share private life
C: phone whenever and wherever/make us independent/give feeling of independence
D: fixed phone lines
E: give security/make us feel safe/people feel cared for
F: when you are controlled/control because of mobile
G: emit radio waves/emit radiation/possibly create cancer
H: not sure/divided opinions/no exact analysis/not clear

Task 5
1 – false (only 70%), 2 – false (it's 50%), 3 – true, 4 – false (China has more mobile phone users), 5 – false (it's about 20%), 6 – true, 7 – true, 8 – false (three times slower), 9 – false (it is an obligation)

Task 6
were not, possessed, had had, didn't understand, tried, was enjoying, didn't help, bought, became/have become, has, need, has, has become, will go on, are going to be invented

Task 7
fastest, most powerful, easier, best, less, most unexpected, more, most impressive

RC 6: YES, I'M AN INTERNET ADDICT

Task 2
addicted to, interested in, prepared for, suffer from, responsible for, bad at, good at (ACHTUNG: es ist immer good/bad at und NICHT in!), famous for, subscribe to, pay for, to get along with, to write back/in/to

Task 3
1 – D, 2 – H, 3 – A, 4 – G, 5 – B, 6 – F; not used: C, E

Task 4
interested, embarrassed, surprising, bored, annoyed, had done, could happen, have been working, haven't met, had started

Task 5
1d, 2b, 3d

RC 7: WHY IT'S SIMPLY FUN BEING RICH

Task 3
1 – false, Well, living a normal …; 2 – false, As you have already …; 3 – false, I attend a private …; 4 – true, Our driver takes me …; 5 – false, There is an oversized …; 6 – true, It's a four-storey …; 7 – true, If I ask Carmelita …; 8 – true, However, at the end …; 9 – true, He spends whole afternoons …; 10 – true, It's a wonderful four-poster …; 11 – true, You never know who …

Task 4
1. sporty, **2.** wealthy, **3.** nice, **4.** spoilt, **5.** friendly, **6.** intelligent, **7.** active, **8.** rich, **9.** young, **10.** polite

Task 5
1. If Jennifer weren't/wasn't rich, she would not have her own bathroom.
2. Sometimes Jennifer's mum is angry if Jennifer watches TV in her room instead of doing her homework.
   oder: Jennifer's mum is sometimes angry if … (Achtung: kein Beistrich!!)
3. If the family didn't have such a big flat TV, Jennifer's brother would not play PSP 3 games all the time.
4. Would Jennifer's life be better if her dad had even more money?
5. If Jennifer's dad hadn't worked hard when he was young, he would not have become rich.
6. If you enter the library through the living room, you will be amazed by the number of books. (Achtung: Beistrich!!)
7. Jennifer would not be spoilt if her parents were not rich and did not have a lot of money.

Task 6
1. Every day Jennifer is taken to school by the family's driver.
2. It is almost unbelievable that Jennifer has got a bathroom of her own.
3. It's often difficult for Jennifer to find out who her real and true friends are.
4. For Jennifer, being rich is great because she always gets the things she wants to have.
5. Wealthy people sometimes tend to be a little bit arrogant and snobbish.
6. Jennifer and her family live in a wonderful house that has got four large floors.
7. The 15-year-old girl absolutely enjoys living in a luxurious villa.

RC 8: ANIMAL EXPERIMENTS – ONE OF THE MOST CONTROVERSIAL ISSUES

Task 3
1 – D, 2 – A, 3 – G, 4 – B, 5 – E; not used: C, F

Task 4
Hilary Jones – B; Brian Jackobson – C; Julie Miller – C; Rob Johnson – B, Clair Welsh – A; Mike Tailor – C

Task 5
were found, have been used, was, describe, was first isolated, improved, was called, was born, was

RC 9: WHAT A DOG'S LIFE

Task 3
1 – E, 2 – A, 3 – H, 4 – C, 5 – F, 6 – D, not used: B, G

Task 4
responsibilities: duties you have to do, things that must be done
apartment: that's a flat, the place where you live
afternoon: the time between lunch and evening; usually from 1/2pm to 5/6pm
to be grateful: the be thankful for something
surprise: something you didn't know; you haven't thought about; you wouldn't have thought to become true
immediately: right way, at once
puppy: a baby dog
at least: at a minimum
undisturbed: without interruption, without being interrupted
cleanliness: tidiness, spruceness

Task 5

adverbs of frequency: always, usually, often
nouns: hobbies, midnight, afternoon, duties, destiny, walks, couple
verbs: split up, run, live, moved, enriched, take care, sympathised
adjectives: unfortunately, urgently, rational, definitely, enormous, grateful, immediately
reflexive pronouns: myself, yourself

Task 6

to sympathise – to immediately like somebody very much
to become a couple – to start a love relationship with someone
to sponge up something – to clean/hoover something
to gnaw on something – to bite on something (e.g. a bone)
uncountable – too many to count, numerous
to be desperate – to be frustrated
to enrich somebody's life – to influence another person's life positively

RC 10: TEENAGE PREGNANCIES: TOP OR FLOP?

Task 1

to be pregnant – schwanger sein
pregnancy – die Schwangerschaft
to have a baby – ein Baby bekommen / gebären
to raise a baby ein Baby großziehen / aufziehen
maternity leave – Mutterschaftsurlaub / Karenz
paternity leave – Vaterschaftsurlaub / Karenz
abortion – Abtreibung
contraceptive – Verhütungsmittel
toddler – das Kleinkind
paternity test – Vaterschaftstest

Task 3

B: three to five
C: headmaster, teacher, parents
D: teenagers believe pregnancy's easy
E: convey wrong message/present wrong picture/life's not like that
F: girls had a pact/girls had planned pregnancies/girls pregnant on purpose
G: campaign at school/distributed condoms/gave information
H: long winter/boring/nothing else to do/feeling bored

Task 4

1. they have been shocked, **2.** the question had come up, **3.** the boy is telling that, **4.** the headmaster is going to claim, **5.** people didn't have to, **6.** the result will be, **7.** Condoms have been distributed

Task 5

Number C best summarises the article

Task 6

1. Dear Auntie Mary Lou,
2. uncle George **has** already recovered
3. **alright** – nur mit einem "l"
4. and **tell** him (nicht "say him")
5. I've got **surprising** news for you
6. Yes, you **read/have read** correctly (aber keine *past perfect tense*)
7. herselfe – richtig: **herself**
8. At the beginning we **were really** shocked
9. … but then I **tried** to calm him down
10. … how she imagines her **life** to go on
11. She told us that she wanted to **have** the baby. (ACHTUNG: ein Baby bekommen heißt immer *to have a baby*!!)
12. … she **wants** to finish school later on.
13. … and **by** now …
14. We **have** already arranged the next appointments …
15. … your opinion **on/about** that topic

RC 11: HIGH SCHOOL PROM – THE BEST NIGHT OF YOUR LIFE

Task 1

To hire sth. – to pay money to borrow sth.; to date sb. – to meet sb. who you like very much; carnation – a small flower; a cocktail dress – a short evening dress which you wear at parties; a ball gown – a very elegant, usually long, dress for balls; a dressmaker – a tailor, person who produces clothes; a tuxedo – a formal dinner suit; wrist – part of your body where you usually wear a watch; a crown – a golden rim which is worn by a queen on her head

Task 3

1 – F; 2 – A; 3 – C; 4 – E; 5 – B; 6 – G; 7 – I; not used: D, H

LÖSUNGEN ZU DEN BUCHSEITEN 56–67

Task 4
Things you do: wear your date's carnation; be nice; wear a nice necklace; refresh your make-up; chat with your friends; amuse yourself
Things you don't do: drink too much alcohol; wear dirty shoes; wear short trousers; spill your drink on another girl's dress; flirt with another person's date; be angry because your date doesn't dance

Task 5
1 – true, A night they plan …; 2 – true, It is considered to …; 3 – true, The High School Prom …; 4 – false, Preparations and planning, however, …; 5 – false, Going to a High … (first sentence of the text); 6 – true, Needless to say that …; 7 – false, Fashions range from cocktail …; 8 – true, American teenagers must take …; 9 – true, As a rule, the …; 10 – false, In some cases two …

Task 6
American; February; April; location(s)/place(s); hotel; country club; cocktail dresses; ball gowns; tuxedos/suits; informal/dirty/shabby/ragged; date; party; pictures/photos; wrist; limousine; king; queen

RC 12: MAKING YOUR OWN MUSIC – CREATING YOUR OWN STYLE

Task 1
fantastic live performance; favourite band; meaningful lyrics; watch MTV; participate in a band contest; good voice; expensive concert ticket; listen to music; romantic love song; playing the drums; band leader; school band

Task 3
1. Tom is the singer, Tobi plays the guitar, Phil plays the drums and John organises gigs and plays the bass.
2. They met two to three times per week.
3. Phil split up with his girlfriend.
4. They participated in a locally-organised band contest and were discovered by the boss of a music label.

Task 4
1b, 2c, 3c, 4d, 5a, 6d

Task 5
1. The guys only rarely have bad performances.
2. Phil's mother was rather sceptical when he wanted to have drums.
3. John and Tobi hardly ever miss a rehearsal.
4. Tom is nearly perfect in writing lyrics on his own.

WRITING

Linking words (p. 62)
whereas/while, in the first place/firstly/first of all, but, however, for instance/for example, in contrast to, furthermore/in addition/what is more, all in all/to sum up/in conclusion/to summarise, nevertheless

INFORMAL (PERSONAL) LETTER

Complete the letter (p. 64)
Thanks a lot for/Thank you for, Anyway/However, so far/up to now/until now, reminds, another thing/there's something, but then/but in the end, Well/Anyway, a line, love/greetings

Mustertext: Task 3 (p. 65)
Dear Kerby,
How are things? Did you have a nice weekend or did you have to learn a lot for your nasty Maths test next Friday? My weekend was gorgeous, that's also the reason why I'm writing this letter.
I guess you still remember when I told you about Mary-Ann's invitation to her birthday party. The party was last Saturday and I can tell you it was definitely the best party I have ever been to. First of all, the people were great. They were very nice and extremely funny. Besides, Mary-Ann had organised a DJ and he really played good music throughout the whole evening. We danced a lot and enjoyed ourselves. We finally played some funny games and we had to laugh almost all the time.
By the way, would you like to meet next weekend? We could go shopping because I need a new skirt. Mum could take us to the mall. Think about it and tell me in time!
See you soon and all the best,
Cynthia

FORMAL LETTER

What is formal? (p. 65)
1a, 2a, 3a, 4b, 5a, 6a, 7b, 8b, 9b, 10b, 11a, 12b, 13b, 14a, 15b

Task 1 (p. 67)
am interested, am writing, Firstly/At first, appreciate/prefer/like/need/want, so kind, so/that is why/therefore, question, whether/if, ask, cost, would like, grateful/thankful, receiving

Task 2 (p. 68)

give/send/submit, are going to enjoy, make, (will) find, recommend/advise you, asked/inquired, included, offer, choose, paid, takes, takes/lasts, arrive, provide

Mustertext: Task 4 (p. 69)

Dear Sir/Madam,
On April 17th I ordered the new Apple Mac Book Pro via your homepage. As promised, the product was delivered within the next week. After having unpacked the laptop, I unfortunately realised that the display inside had a scratch. At first I carefully tried to remove it, but there was no chance to do so properly.
As I am not willing to keep the damaged Mac Book, I am going to send it back to the Apple headquarter and kindly ask you to replace the laptop or, at least, the damaged display and send it back to me as soon as possible.
As I would have needed the laptop urgently and great inconvenience has been caused to me, I ask you for an additional discount of 5% of the original price.
I hope to get a positive answer concerning this affair and look forward to receiving my laptop soon.
Yours faithfully,
Brian McMillan

E-MAIL

Task 1 (p. 70)

1 – E, 2 – B, 3 – A, 4 – D, 5 – C

Task 2 (p. 71)

1. Caroline organises a party to celebrate Hallowe'en; the party is going to be on the 31st of October because this is when Hallowe'en is celebrated.
2. Caroline has decided to dress up as a witch (her mum has already bought the costume) but Lydia doesn't know yet.
3. Lydia takes cranberry muffins to the party because they are usually delicious/tasty.
4. to annoy somebody, to go on somebody's nerves
5. *will-future*: spontane, ungeplante, unsichere Ereignisse in der Zukunft; *going-to-future*: geplante und sicher stattfindende Ereignisse.
6. If

Mustertext: Task 5 (p. 71)

Hi there,
I've just returned from my date with Max and here are the details: it was a complete … flop! Yes, you read correctly! We met at the cinema and he made me wait for 10 minutes. Incredible! Then he didn't invite me to the cinema and I had to pay for the ticket myself. An absolute no-go! Finally we went to Starbucks for a milk shake and he spilled most of his shake over my new blouse. A disaster! Worst of all was that he wasn't even really nice to me. Well, seems as if this was our first and last date!
Hope you had a better evening! See you tomorrow at school, sleep well.
Hugs'n'kisses, S.

STORY

Task 1 (p. 73)

was, left, went, had been, had told, didn't expect, enjoyed/was enjoying, happened, was lying, fell, started, stopped, dropped, ran, were standing, jumped, rescued, swam, pulled, had called, was taken (Achtung – hier brauchst du *passive voice* in der *past tense*!), felt, came, had rescued, were

Task 2 (p. 73)

rainy, warm; early, together; unhappy/sad, bored; worst, expected; open, slow; shallow/low, helpful; big, full of energy; silent/quiet, comfortable

Mustertext: Task 3 (p. 74)

When I woke up on that foggy November morning I was tired and exhausted and I would have never thought that a thing like that could happen. The moment I opened my eyes I remembered the nasty English test that I had to take that day. Glorious! As I was already late, I left out breakfast and rushed to the bus stop.

And that was the moment when my day started to become better. When I arrived at the bus stop I saw him standing there, that wonderful, handsome, cute guy. And then it happened: the sweet guy came over to me and asked me whether I wanted to go to the cinema with him the next weekend. Of course I wanted to and I couldn't believe my luck. I smiled brightly and we exchanged phone numbers. It didn't take long until he called me to fix the details for our date and it was a wonderful date.

Needless to say that the sweet guy and I have been a couple since that foggy November morning. I would have never thought that a day that had started out that terribly, could become so perfect.

ARTICLE

Task 1 (p. 75)

Michael Jackson – murder or natural death? – The king of pop – a legend – has died.
Obama's birthday parade – "Long live the president of the United States", these were the opening words of yesterday's celebrations.
Tourist drowned in lake – The holidays surprisingly stopped for a 45 year old man from Sweden.
The DNA and its discovery – Deoxyribonucleic acid is an acid that contains genetic instructions.

Sky-diving for beginners – Have you ever wondered what it would feel like to fall out of an aeroplane.
Teenagers and the www. – Are you interested in learning something about the "new Internet generation"? Well, here we go!

Task 2 (p. 76)

Just crazy about rock climbing!
You may be wondering why there are people **who** are crazy about something that can be quite **dangerous**.
Well … some time ago I was wondering about it, **too**. And **then** I gave it a try … Here is what it feels like to climb walls, fight your own fear and overcome your **personal** limits.
I can remember the day when I **decided** to go climbing for the first time. Of course I didn't know what to **expect** but I really felt **thrilled**. I went together with a friend of **mine**, a guy who **has been climbing** for almost all his **life**. He introduced the most important aspects to me, how to **handle** the rope and stuff like that. And then … off I went.
Surely, I did a bad job because I quickly found out that climbing is more difficult than I **had thought**. I started to sweat on my hands which made it hardly possible to grab the stone and **pull** my body upwards. But somehow I **succeeded** and I moved upwards a few meters. And that was the moment when I could feel the full sensation and the fascination.
I've been climbing now for two years and it simply didn't let me go again. In a way I got stuck with the kick you get out of it. Besides it really **keeps** you fit and you constantly meet new people with the same **interest** as you.
So, are you still wondering or do you already think about giving it a try yourself?

Task 3 (p. 76)

In the introduction the writer directly addresses the reader ("You may be wondering…"), later on there is an identification with the reader ("I was wondering, too"). Moreover, the writer describes personal experiences and what is so fascinating about rock climbing.
Reasonable arguments for rock climbing can be found in the fourth paragraph (keeps you fit, you meet people with the same interest)
The end brings back the reader to the beginning. The question whether the reader is wondering is repeated. Finally, there is also a call for action.

Mustertext: Task 6 (p. 77)

I've always wanted to spend a year abroad
Have you ever thought about leaving home, becoming independent and meeting new people? Sounds good, doesn't it? Well, that's what many students do in order to learn about other cultures and to enlarge their horizons. Just go on reading and find out yourself about the many advantages of leaving your old life behind for some time.
Deciding to spend a year abroad is always a big business as it means leaving your friends and family behind. It's a step towards the unknown because you mostly don't know a lot about your host family, the school you are going to attend and the people you are definitely going to meet and befriend.
But once you have decided to take this step, you will be rewarded as you are going to make incredible new experiences. Exchange students usually enjoy the freedom to decide for themselves and it's one of their most important lessons to find out that they can manage their lives on their own.
Going to another country as an exchange student, discovering other cultures and people and, above all, learning a lot about yourself is definitely worth doing it! So just go for it!

REPORTS

Task 1 (p. 79)

adjective	comparative	superlative	opposite
healthy	healthier	the healthiest	unhealthy
negative	more negative	the most negative	positive
expensive	more expensive	the most expensive	cheap/inexpensive
happy	happier	the happiest	unhappy/sad
new	newer	the newest	old
difficult	more difficult	the most difficult	easy
successful	more successful	the most successful	unsuccessful
reasonable	more reasonable	the most reasonable	unreasonable

Mustertext: Task 3 (p. 79)

The aim of this report is to make suggestions for the stay of Portuguese exchange students. They are going to arrive on Sunday, January 12th and their stay will last for one week.
The idea is to start the programme on Monday morning with a sightseeing tour through Vienna. The city's most important and most impressive sights should be covered (for example Vienna's Town Hall, important museums like the museum of history and science, Saint Stephan's Cathedral, Vienna's Giant Ferry Wheel, the Prater, and many more). It might also be a good idea to go skiing for one day. The *Hochkar* in Lower Austria would be a suitable destination. One could also think about making a tour through the *Weinviertel* and visiting some nice castles. Last but not least Vienna's nightlife might also be presented to the students from Portugal, as entertainment should also be part of their stay in Austria.
Summarising it is to say that there are many different options of what to do. In the end it will probably also depend on the weather.

ARGUMENTATIVE ESSAY

Task 1 (p. 80)

A: additionally, what is more, as well as, furthermore, moreover, last but not least, apart from that, let's not forget that, it must also be mentioned that, besides
B: in contrast to, by contrast, nevertheless, compared to
C: all in all, to put it in a nutshell, summarizing it can be said that, in conclusion, on the whole, to sum up, in short, finally

Task 2 (p. 81)

hate, positive, excluded, poor, afford, save, related, disadvantages, possibilities, difficult, impression, express

Mustertext: Task 5 (p. 81)

No matter how different students are, there's one thing they all agree on: home-exercises are nasty, time-consuming and, most important, absolutely useless. Nevertheless the following question comes up: is that really the case or does it make sense to set home-exercises?

On the one hand setting a home-exercise does make sense as it gives students the chance to practise something they learned at school. It's a way to repeat new facts and newly gained knowledge. If the teacher corrects the homework, he/she gives the student the chance to learn out of his/her own mistakes. It goes without saying that this is very valuable and could help the student a lot.

On the other hand, the value of home-exercises also depends on the exercise itself. Does it make sense or is it just useless repetition or filling in of something? In that case the student is only little or not motivated at all and is definitely not going to learn anything from it.

To put it in a nutshell, teachers have always set home-exercises and will go on doing that, no matter if students consider it important or not. In the end it probably depends on one's personal motivation how much one learns through the given tasks or if a home-exercise is only done for the teacher.

OPINION ESSAY

Task 1 (p. 83)

Only ONE side is presented, there are no arguments against school uniforms, only the ones in favour of it. Personal opinion and experience is expressed throughout the whole essay.

Task 2 (p. 83)

aim – purpose, attitude – opinion, check – look through, just – only, like to wear – fancy wearing, whether – if, expensive – costly, think – believe, fit to – go together with, advantages – positive aspects

Mustertext: Task 4 (p. 83)

Do you also belong to those people who can't imagine living without the Internet any longer? Me too, because I would not want to miss all the chances for information, entertainment and knowledge it offers. But would the world – especially for teenagers – be a better place without the www?

Well, that's a rather difficult question to answer. To begin with, I personally believe that the Internet is extremely important and a very valuable source for getting information and finding amusement and distraction. Just think about how many teenagers use the Internet to find additional and useful material for their home-exercises. This can sometimes be really helpful. If a student copies the whole homework from the Internet (as this might be the case for a literary essay, for example) the sense and usefulness of the Internet might, of course, be questioned. So using the Internet in a sensible way to obtain information is, from my point of view, good and also important. Furthermore, the Internet is a perfect way to communicate with your friends. This can either be done via e-mail, Skype or in a chat room. But here again, one has to be careful not to misuse these media.

In conclusion, I believe that the Internet is a blessing because the chances and possibilities it offers, simply outrun the disadvantages.

VOCABULARY

HOUSING AND ACCOMODATION

Exercise 1

6a, 5b, 8c, 7d, 3e

Exercise 2

master bedroom, utility room, cellar, restroom, roof terrace, front garden, dining room, balcony

Exercise 3

individuelle Lösungen

Exercise 4

When a suitable lot of land **is found/is chosen/is purchased/is bought** by the future owner of the premises, a ground-plan **is drawn/is made** by an architect. Then, the foundation **is laid** by a building firm. Brick by brick, the walls **are erected** and then the shell of the building **is plastered**. When the exterior of the house **is finished**, the owners can start working on the interior design. The walls **are painted** or they **are wallpapered**. Then the floors **are carpeted, tiled or inlaid**. In the bathroom and the kitchen, the electrical equipment, such as the fridge, the oven or the washing machine **is connected**. Very often, professionals **are employed/ are called** for these little jobs because they can get quite tricky. Then, the cupboards, wardrobes and other pieces of furniture **are assembled**, which sometimes turns out to be rather difficult. Most of the times, there is one important thing missing, like a bolt or a screw. When the rooms **are furnished** with all the furniture, they can **be decorated** with rugs, curtains, pillows and plants. In order to add a little bit of colour pictures **are fixed** on the walls and flowers **are arranged** in vases. In the garden the lawn **is sowed** (**sown**), flowers **are planted** and, perhaps, a swing **is erected**. Finally, the house-warming party **is celebrated** with the family and friends.

Exercise 5

Father **wears** his Sunday best.
Mother's tired she needs a **rest**.
The kids are playing up **downstairs**.
Sister's sighing in her sleep.
Brother's got a date to keep, he can't hang around.

Our house, in the middle of our **street**.
Our house, in the middle of our ...
Our house, it has a **crowd**.
There's always something happening.
And it's usually quite loud.
Our mum, she's so **house-proud**.
Nothing ever slows her down, and a **mess** is not allowed.

Our house, in the middle of our street.
Our house, in the middle of our ...
Our house, in the middle of our street.
(Something tells you that you've got to **get away** from it).
Our house, in the middle of our ...

Father **gets up** late for work.
Mother has to **iron** his shirt.
Then she sends the kids to school.
Sees them off with a small **kiss**.
She's the one they're going to miss in lots of ways.

Our house, in the middle of our street.
Our house, in the middle of our ...
I remember way back then when everything was true.
And when we would have such a very **good** time, such a **fine** time,
such a **happy** time.
And I remember how we'd play simply **waste** the day away.
Then we'd say nothing would come between us
two **dreamers**.

Father **wears** his Sunday best.
Mother's tired she needs a **rest**.
The kids are playing up **downstairs**.
Sister's sighing in her sleep.
Brother's got a date to keep, he can't hang around.

Our house, in the middle of our street (3x)
Our house, in the middle of our...
Our house, was our **castle** and our keep.
Our house, in the middle of our street.
Our house, that was where we used to sleep.
Our house, in the middle of our street. (2x)
Our house ...

Quelle: Madness, *Our house*

Exercise 6

1. mow/cut
2. wash
3. cook/prepare/serve
4. clean
5. do
6. take
7. load/unload/empty
8. do/wash
9. do
10. feed/walk

MUSIC

Exercise 1

9a 4b 6c 3d 8e
2f 5g 1h 10i 7j

Exercise 2

1. catchy 2. soft 3. provocative 4. tremendous 5. sweet
6. meaningful 7. jarring 8. insistent 9. vocal

Exercise 3

1. performance, 2. lyrics, 3. beat, 4. voice, 5. melody, 6. entry, 7. lead singer, 8. impact

Exercise 4

1. I 2. A 3. B 4. K 5. L 6. J 7. C 8. F 9. G 10. H 11. D 12. E

Exercise 5

I've just bought the **latest** CD by Mando Diao "Give me Fire". At first, the CD did not **meet** my expectations, but after listening to it for a few times some songs really **grew** on me. I remember that two years ago, the **last** album was an immediate **success**. It **went** into the charts in the first week of its **release** and it very quickly **climbed** the charts. Also the new album **hit** the charts on place 10, I think, and I am sure it will **go** platinum soon. Some of the **singles** have already entered the charts like "Gloria". What I really like **about** Mando Diao is that they have got a blend of stirring **rhythms** and **thoughtful** lyrics. It's also that blend of relaxing and arousing **tunes** that is quite impressive and that really makes you sing along. One might not call this album **easy listening** as the style is sometimes quite demanding, but if you give it a **try** you will surely appreciate it.

ANIMALS

Exercise 1

1. tomcat
2. school
3. mare
4. flock
5. kitten
6. jack(ass)
7. hen
8. piglet
9. litter
10. lioness
11. swarm, cloud
12. bunny
13. sow
14. pack
15. fawn
16. fry, fingerling
17. brood
18. calf
19. litter
20. stag
21. buck
22. drone

Exercise 2

1. H 2. K 3. A 4. M 5. O 6. L 7. B 8. D 9. C 10. J 11. E 12. F 13. G 14. I 15. N

Exercise 3
individuelle Lösungen

Exercise 4

CATS		DOGS	
+	−	+	−
4. are independent	13. do what they want	18. make you do more exercise	1. annoy neighbours because they are loud
3. are silent and calm	6. bring home dead mice or birds	5. are true friends	11. can't leave them alone
7. can be kept in a flat	12. difficult with children	21. can guard the house	16. have to take them for a walk
2. are clean	8. can climb everywhere and damage things	22. you can teach them tricks	24. you have to train them
20. purring makes you feel comfortable	23. you find hair everywhere (even in hidden places)	10. you can take them nearly everywhere	9. can get quite dirty
14. don't need a lot of space, just some entertainment	15. you have to clean the toilet	17. like children (in general)	19. need a lot of space to move about in (garden)

Exercise 5
1. take responsibility
2. muzzle, put, lead
3. looks after
4. fed
5. walk
6. romping around
7. taught
8. abandon
9. worrying about, take
10. give, treat
11. trim

Exercise 6
1. E: tickle
2. C: chuck
3. H: run
4. G: cuddle (A, B, D)
5: F: hug (A, D, G)
6. B: scratch (A, D)
7. I: carry
8. D: stroke
9. A: pat

Exercise 7

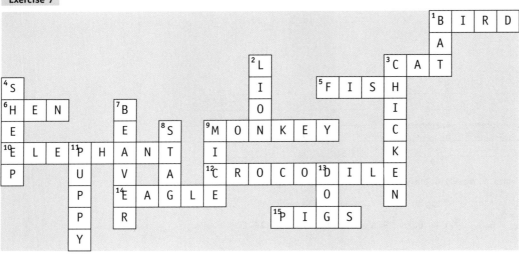

FOOD

Exercise 1

tree fruit		berries	citrus fruit	1 year fruit
apple	nectarine	bilberry	grapefruit	aubergine
apricot	papaya	blackberry	kumquat	cucumber
avocado	passion fruit	black currant	lemon	melon
cherry	peach	blueberry	lime	squash
date	pear	gooseberry	mandarin	sweet corn
fig	plum	grapes	orange	sweet pepper
guava	quince	raspberry	tangerine	tomato
lychee		red currant		water melon
mango		strawberry		zucchini

kiwis and pineapples are exceptions

Exercise 2

garlic, spinach, leek, carrot, broccoli, pea, lettuce, cauliflower, cabbage, rice, onion, potato, kidney bean

Exercise 3

sugar/fat/oil	proteins				carbohydrates
	meat	fish	seafood	dairy products	
chocolate	beef	carp	clam	butter	boiled potatoes
biscuits	chicken	cod	crab	buttermilk	bread
cake	game	haddock	lobster	cheese	cereal
crisps	lamb	mullet	mussels	cream	chips/fries
ice-cream	mutton	salmon	oysters	cottage cheese	corn on the cob
marmalade	pork	sardine	prawns	milk	mashed potatoes
olive oil	poultry	snapper	scallop	skimmed milk	pasta
pie	sausage	sole	scampi	whipped cream	potato wedges
pumpkinseed oil	turkey	trout	shrimps	whole milk	rice
sunflower oil	veal	tuna	squid	yoghurt	toast

Exercise 4

artificial – natural
cold – hot
delicious – disgusting
mild – spicy/hot
frozen – boiling/deep fried
fizzy – stale
fresh – rancid
creamy – crispy, crunchy
tasty – tasteless
sweet – sour/bitter
soft – hard
cooked – raw

Exercise 5

1. artificial 2. pungent 3. rancid 4. refreshing 5. soothing 6. thick 7. Yummy 8. flavoured with 9. topped 10. leathery

Exercise 6

1. e. 2. h. 3. f. 4. i. 6. a. 7. j. 9. c. 10. g. 11. d. 12. b.

MOBILE PHONES

Exercise 1

on	TV	by	sign language	in	Morse	by	drum signals
by	e-mail	on	the radio		verbal	by	texting
	non-verbal		face to face	on	a mobile phone		online
in	gestures	by	fire signals	on	a telephone	by	fax

Exercise 2

1. to text(-message) sb.
2. to pick up
3. to make a voice call
4. to ring up/ to call sb.
5. to log on
6. to hang up/to ring off
7. to turn off/ to switch off
8. to navigate via GPS
9. to pimp
10. to charge

Exercise 3

2. h. 3. f. 4. a. 5. e. 6. b. 7. c. 8. d. 10. g.

Exercise 4

I was **sitting** on the fence –
And I thought that I would kiss you –
I never thought I would've **missed** you –
But you never let me fall –
Push my **back** against the wall –
Every time you **call** –
You get so emotional –
Oh, I'm freakin' out.
Ring ring
Is that you **on** the **phone**?
You think you're clever –
But you're never **saying** nothing at all.
Hey hey
The way you **spin** me around –
You make me **dizzy** when you play me
Like a kid with a crown.
You got a dangerous **obsession** –

Won't somebody **save** me –
From you now?
Ring **ring**
Is that you **on** the **phone** –
You think you're clever –
But you're never **saying** nothing at all.
Hey hey
The way you **spin** me around –
You make me **dizzy** when you play me –
Like a kid with a crown.
It's **all** I wanted –
Until you lost it –
Why won't you **leave** me alone?
Hang up the phone –
Just let me go.
Ring **ring**
Is that you **on** the **phone**

You got a dangerous **obsession** – Now I'm in need of some protection – That was never my **intention** – Used to love me – now you **hate** me – See I drove you crazy – Well if I **did** – You **made** me –	Is that you **on** the **phone** You think you're clever – But you're never **saying** nothing at all. Hey hey The way you **spin** me around – You make me **dizzy** when you play me Like a kid with a crown. (2x)

Quelle: Mika, *Ring, Ring*

Exercise 5

The very first thing I do in the morning? That's, of course, having a look at my mobile phone. You know, I have to **turn/switch** off the alarm- and **check** my messages. Who knows? Perhaps someone has **texted** me? I always have to be in the loop. Of course I know that having your phone turned on at night is unhealthy. I have heard that the phone **emits** harmful radiation, so I always try to keep it off my head. People say that those rays can affect our health and even **cause** cancer. This definitely makes me think about it, but on the other hand, what's life without a mobile phone? I don't want to say that I **am addicted** to my phone, but a day without it? No way. I need my phone to **stay** in touch with my friends, to plan my day, to take pictures of the beautiful things I do every day, to listen to music, to **log on** the Internet. You see, there are so many functions and features, I can't stop telling you about them. Phones **are getting** more and more versatile and the individual features **improve** constantly. Take for example texting. It's so easy and quick – especially with all these abbreviations. Do you know what that means: RU OK? Don't you think that the mobile is a very effective timer-saver? My favourite feature, is, however the camera. **Taking** a pic and sending it to your friends is such a convenient way of **keeping** them **up-to-date!** Another advantage is, of course, that you are always **available**. Some people might consider this as a negative aspect. It's definitely quite annoying when the guy sitting next to you on the tube **picks** up his phone to discuss his shopping list with his wife. But in other situations the mobile can come in handy. When my mum starts worrying about me, she just has to **give** me a call. And when I am alone I **feel** safe because I can call for help in case of an emergency. There are of course people who claim that having a phone can also be dangerous. At some schools, attacks on pupils with mobile phones have increased as some of the brand-new, expensive mobiles are targets for thieves. Anyway, this wouldn't keep me from having a mobile. I can't imagine how people managed to **stay/keep** in touch with their friends before mobile phones. Of course, I don't want to say that my mobile kills face-to-face communication. I still love meeting my friends in a café, but there are times when this is not possible. And that's when my mobile comes in. When I feel lonely, I just grab my phone and call Jenny or Mark and then we **chat/talk/gab** for hours. This leads me to one of the major drawbacks of mobile phones: the costs. One really has to **keep** track of the speaking time, which can be quite annoying. Anyway, I have a 15 € line rental plus 1000 mins and unlimited texts. I think that this contract is quite fair. So, as a conclusion, I want to stress one more time that my mobile phone has become an integral part of my everyday life which, however, will never **replace** having a face-to-face chat with my pals.

INTERNET

Exercise 1

printer, scanner, palm top, keyboard, tower, floppy disk, mouse, hard drive, laptop, speakers, memory stick, notebook, monitor, desktop

Exercise 2

motherboard, modem, disk drive, adapter, battery, USB flash drive, CPU, RAM disk

Exercise 3

1. H	4. O, B	7. B	10. E	13. F
2. K	5. A	8. M (O)	11. C, D	14. G
3. N	6. L	9. C	12. J	15. I

Exercise 4

happy	:-) :) =) :]	tongue out	:P :-P =P	annoyed	:-/ :-\
sad	:-(:(=(:[	love (playful)	>3 S2 :3	confused	:S
wink	;-) ;) ;] ;>	shocked	:o :([	yelling	:-()
large grin	:D =D :))	bored	:l	kissing	:x

Exercise 5

1. AML — all my love
2. A/S/L — age/sex/location
3. WWW — world wide web
4. LOL — laugh out loud
5. CUL — see you later
6. DYK — do you know?
7. FAQ — frequently asked questions
8. GFU — good for you
9. H&K — hug and kiss

Exercise 6

4a 6b 8c 10d 5e 1f 3g 2h

SCHOOL

Exercise 1

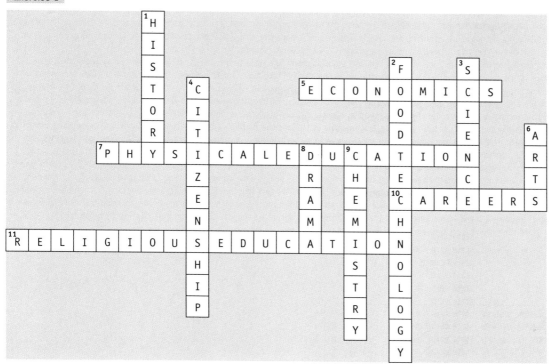

Exercise 2

to admonish – to reprimand
to assign homework – to set homework
to teach – to instruct, to educate
to encourage – to motivate
to put right – to correct
to test – to assess, to examine
to compliment – to praise
to plan – to organise
to favour – to prefer
to pay attention – to listen

Exercise 3

a. 1, 6, 12 **b.** 2, 10 **c.** 11 **d.** 9 **e.** 3 **f.** 4 **g.** 8 **h.** 5 **i.** 7

Exercise 4

The school **education** system in Britain is divided into three stages:
primary education – up to age eleven: compulsory
secondary education – up to age sixteen: compulsory
undergraduate (tertiary) education – for those over the age of sixteen: **voluntary**
'School education': refers to the **compulsory** phases of education which the law requires children to **attend** primary and secondary. These are 11 years of **mandatory** education, comprising children from the age of 5 to the age of 16. In other words, pupils in Britain have to attend school from year 1 to year 11.
Primary schools (5–11-year-olds): In the UK, the first level of education is known as primary education.
Secondary schools (11–16-year-olds): Secondary schools provide compulsory education for children between the ages of **eleven** and **sixteen**. Children may stay on at school until the age of **eighteen** in order to pursue further studies, however this is not compulsory.
From the ages of fourteen to sixteen, pupils study for the General Certificate of Secondary Education (**GCSE**).
Pupils who stay on at school from the ages of sixteen to eighteen in England, may take the **Advanced** (A) level examination, which traditionally is required for entry into higher education.

LÖSUNGEN ZU DEN BUCHSEITEN 108–111

Exercise 5
1. K 2. O 3. I 4. M 5. A 6. B 7. H 8. N 9. C 10. E 11. G 12. D 13. F
14. J 15. L

Exercise 6
1. sit 2. hand in 3. pass 4. fail 5. retake 6. achieve 7. revise

Exercise 7
individuelle Lösungen

GRAMMAR

PRESENT SIMPLE

Exercise 1
1. goes
2. do Gill and Pat live; live
3. watches
4. do not play *or* don't play
5. are; are
6. cries; does not want *or* doesn't want
7. does Gina do; plays
8. is; does not like *or* doesn't like
9. catches; puts
10. does your father get up
11. are not *or* aren't
12. plays *(remember: Wenn du nach dem Subjekt fragst, entfällt das „do" oder „does"!)*

Exercise 2
The present simple tense is used for **b. general statements and regular events.**

Exercises 3 and 4
1. D: opinion — state verb
2. E: general statement — state verb
3. A: regular activity — activity verb
4. E: general statement — state verb
5. E: general statement — state verb
6. E: general statement — state verb
7. B and C: present state and present feeling — state verb
8. B and C: present state and present feeling — state verb
9. B: present state: present state — state verb
10. E: general statement — state verb
11. E: general statement — state verb
12. B and C: present state and feeling — state verb
13. B: present state — state verb
14. A: regular activity — activity verb
15. B: present state — state verb
16. D: opinion — state verb
17. B: present state — state verb

Exercise 5
1. ☑ 2. ☑ 3. ☐ 4. ☑

Exercise 6
A: <u>never</u>: 2: modal verb (can)
C: <u>often</u>: 1: full verb (eat)
E: <u>often</u>: 3: two-part verb (have got)
B: <u>usually</u>: 3: two-part verb (doesn't smoke: negation)
D: <u>usually</u>: 2: modal verb (is)
F: <u>never</u>: 2: modal verb (might)

PRESENT PROGRESSIVE / PRESENT CONTINUOUS

Exercise 1
1. is not sitting/is flying
2. are you doing/am doing
3. are dying
4. is the alarm clock beeping
5. are not travelling *or* aren't travelling
6. is rising
7. is getting
8. Are you having
9. is not riding *or* isn't riding
10. Are Max and Fran dancing
11. is having
12. Is your father writing

Exercise 2
2. Currently we are living in a small apartment.
1., 2. Mo tells Pia, "I'm reading a great book at the moment." *(Both solutions possible)*
1. Susan? She is checking her e-mails in her room.
1. Oh no! Ruff is running after a squirrel!
2. I am doing a Pilates course this semester.

Exercise 3

1. b **2.** b **3.** b **4.** b

Exercise 4

2. a: are preferring
   b: prefer

3. a: are you tasting *or* are you smelling
   b: tastes *or* smells

4. a: look
   b: is she looking

5. a: enjoys
   b: are enjoying

6. a: loves
   b: is loving

7. a: are having
   b: has

PRESENT SIMPLE OR PRESENT PROGRESSIVE?

Exercise 1

1. are **2.** am having **3.** is looking **4.** doesn't like; hates **5.** Does; has **6.** do/play **7.** looks; is **8.** do/do/relax

Exercise 2

1. ☑
2. I **think** that this is a very cute dress. (state verb)
3. What **is** he **doing**? (activity: at the moment)
4. Where **does** Alan **play** tennis?
5. Why **are** you **tasting** the soup so carefully? (activity: at the moment)
6. The teacher **is looking** at me angrily. (activity: at the moment)
7. They **are having** a meeting. (activity: now)
8. Stephen doesn't **like** swimming in cold water.

Exercise 3

2a: A **2b:** B **3a:** B **3b:** A **4a:** A **4b:** B

Exercise 4

Julie: Hi Terry. Could you help me with my homework please? I **am trying** to do this exercise, but I **do not have** *or* **don't have** a clue how to start.
Terry: No problem. What **are you doing**?
Julie: I **am struggling** with today's Maths homework. Normally, I always **find** the answers immediately, but this exercise **is** too hard for me, I'm afraid.
Terry: I see. You **are doing** (*begrenzte Zeitspanne*) Maths with Mr. Jenkins this semester, right? **Do you like** his course?
Julie: It **is** okay. Which courses **are you attending** this semester?
Terry: English III, French II and Trigonometry II. You know, I **prefer** languages to science. Julie, tell me, do you know the girl that **is sitting** over there?
Julie: Sure. That's Mona. She **is not** *or* **isn't** in any of my courses this semester, but I **know** (have known also possible) her from last semester's volleyball. Mona **adores** languages too.
Terry: Great. You see – I **am thinking** of asking her for a date, but I simply **do not dare** *or* **don't dare** asking her out of the blue...What **do you think**? Could you help me?
Julie: Okay, okay. I will ask her for you ... if you don't mind helping me. I **guess** that this should be okay for you?
Terry: 'Course. So, let's see ...

Exercise 5

1. My father usually cooks dinner on Sunday.
2. Tina never minds helping her brother with the homework.
3. Jonathan is taking part in a Salsa course this year. This year, Jonathan is taking part in a Salsa course.
4. I am thinking of buying a cat.

PRESENT PERFECT SIMPLE

Exercise 1

1. have been; have not been *or* haven't been
2. has lost
3. Have you ever gone
4. have Doug and Carrie had
5. has forgotten
6. have not lived *or* haven't lived
7. have always wanted
8. Have you painted
9. have hit
10. have stumbled

Exercise 2

4. Don't worry. I have just sent you an e-mail.
1. I am tired because I haven't slept well.
2. Jenna has already been to Singapore and Manila.
3. Pamela has had her turtle for three years now.
1. Mum is angry because I have broken her favourite vase.
4. It has just stopped raining. We can go now.
2. This year, my team has already won seven matches.
3. I have been to Ferro High School for seven years now.
2. Have you ever seen a more gorgeous man?

PRESENT PERFECT PROGRESSIVE

Exercise 1

1. have you been doing
2. have been waiting
3. have been living

4. has been getting
5. has Hugh been working

PRESENT PERFECT SIMPLE OR PRESENT PERFECT PROGRESSIVE?

Exercise 1

	We use the present perfect tense when there is a connection between an action in the past and the present!
	Present perfect simple
A, B	We use the present perfect simple tense to emphasize the **result** a past action has on the present.
D	When we talk about **repeated actions** and mention the number of times the action was repeated, we use present perfect simple.
C	When we talk about a **changing situation** over a period of time up to now, we use the present perfect simple.
	Present perfect progressive
E	We use the present perfect progressive to emphasize the **action** itself, rather than the result.
F	We use the present perfect progressive to emphasize the **durational** aspect of the action.
H	When we talk about **repeated actions** from the past up to now without mentioning the number of times the action was repeated, we prefer the present perfect progressive.
G	When we talk about a **changing situation** without mentioning specific facts, we prefer the present perfect progressive.

Exercise 2

1a: has been looking
 b: Have you already looked for
2a: has run
 b: has been running
3a: has disappeared
 b: have been disappearing
4a: has visited
 b: have been visiting
5a: has been seeing (a concerned father might say this sentence)
 b: have not seen her *or* haven't seen her

PRESENT PERFECT OR PRESENT SIMPLE?

Exercise 1

1. We use the **present simple** to talk about general statements and regular activities.
2. We use the **present progressive** to talk about activities happening now, at the moment.
3. We use the **present perfect simple** to talk about past events having a connection to now.
4. We use the **present perfect progressive** to stress the duration or repetition of events up to now.

Exercise 2

1. We have had our dog for three years. (You do not stress the durational aspect, but simply stress the fact)
2. Jill often goes dancing with her friends.
3. How often has Yves already been to Scotland?
4. Edward has had his car for two years.
5. Mary has not fed her mouse yet.
6. How long have you already lived *or* been living in New York?

PAST SIMPLE

Exercise 1

1. Kate didn't **win** the first price in the Maths competition.
2. Who **played** tennis with you? (Remember: Wenn du nach dem Subjekt fragst, entfällt das „did"!)
3. **Were** you at the club last weekend?
4. I **bought** this dress last week in a new boutique in town.
5. Yesterday Jane didn't **write** an e-mail to her friend Sienna.
6. When **did you go** to the dentist's?
7. I **wasn't** at the cinema with Michael.
8. Jonathan didn't **do** his French homework.

Exercise 2

1. caught/went
2. did not fly *or* didn't fly; did not have *or* didn't have
3. did not do *or* didn't do; tried
4. did Steve leave; wanted
5. Was Caroline; did not see *or* didn't see
6. rose; did it set
7. was not *or* wasn't

8. was not *or* wasn't; felt
9. drove; did you do

PAST PROGRESSIVE / PAST CONTINUOUS

Exercise 1
1. was shining; were singing
2. was cooking; was watching
3. were you doing; was having
4. Was Sue having
5. was getting
6. was playing
7. was staying; was living
8. was not waiting *or* wasn't waiting

Exercise 2
A: 4, 8   B: 3, 6, 8, 4   C: 2, 7   D: 1, 5

Exercise 3
1. What **were you doing** last Friday at ten o'clock?
2. Who **was** Jody waiting for when you met her yesterday?
3. **Was** the sun **shining** when you went into the mountains?
4. I **was watching** TV when suddenly the doorbell rang.
5. Phil wasn't **doing** the washing-up when his mum called him.
6. P.J. **was entering** the room when suddenly her cat **jumped** out.

PAST SIMPLE OR PAST PROGRESSIVE?

Exercise 1

	Past simple		Past progressive
4	finished actions in the past single events happening in the past	5	unfinished actions in the past that were in the middle of taking place
1	one event happening after the other	2	comparing parallel actions
		6	actions happening around a certain time
		3	background information

Exercise 2
B: She was in the middle of making breakfast.
A: She started making breakfast when she saw me.

Exercise 3
1. were you doing; wanted (state verb!)
2. saw; was looking for
3. did Peter think (state verb!)
4. stole; was not looking *or* wasn't looking
5. Did I disturb; called; wasn't doing
6. heard; was trying; did not know *or* didn't know (state verb!)
7. met; was going; did not have *or* didn't have (hier: have: state verb); were waiting; were having (hier: have: activity verb!)
8. did Jake want (state verb!)
9. was driving; happened
10. drove; did not have *or* didn't have

PAST SIMPLE OR PRESENT PERFECT?

Exercise 1

Past simple	Present perfect
Last year we travelled to San Francisco.	I have **never** been to San Francisco.
I saw *Dr. House* **yesterday** evening.	Have you **ever** seen *Dr. House*?
Columbus discovered America **in 1492**.	Has Rory discovered her present **yet**?
I tried to call you **an hour ago**.	My boyfriend hasn't called me **yet**.
Stephanie Mayer wrote *New Moon* **in 2006**.	We have **already** read *New Moon*.
Last week was the best week in my life.	**This week** has been the best week ever.
William Shakespeare wrote many plays.	J.K. Rowling has written seven books **so far**.
We moved into this house in 2001.	We have lived here **since** 2001.
We lived here for ten years, but then we moved to a bigger house.	We have lived here **for** eight years and we are still very happy.

! 'seit': for or since: 'for': Zeitspanne (a year, a week, a long time, …)
'since': Zeitpunkt (last year, 1999, last Christmas, …)

Exercise 2

The **past simple** is a **past** tense. It refers to actions that are **finished** from today's perspective. They **do not have any** connection to the present.
The **present perfect** is a **present** tense. It refers to actions that **have** a connection to the present. Either, the action is **unfinished** or it has a **result** in the present.

Exercise 3

1. has been; went; studied; did not start *or* didn't start
2. Did you see; have just called
3. did not feel *or* didn't feel; has recovered; has already been

PAST PERFECT SIMPLE

Exercise 1

present perfect	past perfect
Why are you tired? Because I haven't slept well.	I was tired yesterday because I hadn't slept well.
Your boyfriend is looking angrily at you. What have you said to him?	Yesterday at the party, your boyfriend was looking angrily at you. What had you said to him?
The school bell is ringing. Have you all finished?	I had finished my paper just before the bell rang.
Ausgangszeit: **present tense**	Ausgangszeit: **past tense**
This tense is used for events happening before the **present.**	This tense is used for events happening before the **past.**

Exercise 2

1. had forgotten
2. came; had not turned off *or* hadn't turned off; was
3. were having; rang; had called
4. started; had thought; was cutting; had not bought
5. had eaten
6. had heard; started

PAST PERFECT PROGRESSIVE / PAST PERFECT CONTINUOUS

Exercise 1

1. had been snowing
2. had Jody been practicing
3. had been working
4. had been listening
5. had been raining
6. had your father been asking
7. had not been shining

PRESENT PERFECT PROGRESSIVE OR PAST PERFECT PROGRESSIVE?

Exercise 1

Present perfect progressive	Past perfect progressive
Time basis: Present	Time basis: **Past**
The present perfect progressive is used to stress the duration of actions taking place from the past up to **now.**	The past perfect progressive is used to stress the duration of actions taking place before the **past.**

Exercise 2

1. has been sitting
2. had been discussing
3. have you been sitting
4. had been working
5. had been going on
6. have been occupying
7. has been singing and dancing

PAST PERFECT SIMPLE OR PAST PERFECT PROGRESSIVE?

Exercise 1
1. had broken; had been trying
2. had been asking
3. had been thinking of; had made
4. had closed
5. had just seen; had been talking
6. had stolen

FUTURE TENSES

Exercise 1
1. Will you close
2. will stay
3. will help
4. will join
5. will not be able to *or* won't be able to
6. will call

Exercise 2

Offering to do something. Spontaneous decision out of the moment.	3
Agreeing to do something. Spontaneous decision out of the moment.	3, 4
Promising to do something. Spontaneous decision out of the moment.	3, 4
Asking somebody to do something. Spontaneous decision out of the moment.	1
Predicting events that are not sure to happen. (probably, I expect, I'm not sure, I (don't) think)	2, 5, 6

Going-to-future

Exercise 1
1. am going to visit
2. is going to marry
3. is going to hail

Exercise 2

Personal decisions that have already been planned.	1
Future predictions based on present observations.	3
Something is sure to happen.	2

Exercise 3
1. will call (spontaneous decision)
2. am going to see (personal plan)
3. is going to break (present observation)
4. is going to meet (personal plan)
5. will not have *or* won't have

Present progressive and present simple with future meaning

We use the **present progressive** for future activities that are already arranged. These are personal arrangements with fixed dates.
We use the **present simple** for official future activities. They may be fixed on timetables or programmes. (e.g.: public transport, cinema, invitations)

Exercise 1

Robin: What **are you going to do** (personal plan) this weekend? Have you already made any plans?
Spence: I'm not sure. I think I **will spend** (not sure) some time with Mona. Why?
Robin: 'cause Jake and I **are having** (fixed arrangement) a great party Friday night. If you change your mind, you can come, of course.
Spence: Good idea. I **will ask** (spontaneous decision) Mona. Where **is the party taking place/ does the party take place?** (fixed arrangement)
Robin: At *Paddy's*. I'm sure that there **are going to be** loads of people.
Spence: Sounds great. If we come, we **will take** some crisps with us. Is that okay?
Robin: Sure! We **are serving** (fixed arrangement) sandwiches, chips and brownies. Crisps would be great.
Spence: Fine. So I **am going to ask** Mona, but I am quite optimistic that she **is going to say/ will say** yes. Bye Robin.
Robin: Bye.

MODAL VERBS

Exercise 1
1. Our cat is able to climb trees faster than squirrels.
2. We are allowed to go to the cinema.
3. We are not supposed to eat the cake.
4. I couldn't fix the blender.
5. You must not leave now.
6. Sue doesn't have to worry about it.
7. I won't be able to see you tomorrow.
8. Paul could forget about it.

Exercise 2

1. should visit/ought to visit
2. was not allowed to go shopping
3. Will the mechanic be able to repair
4. should study
5. should buy
6. doesn't have to do; might
7. didn't have to look after; was allowed to go out
8. have not been able to read
9. must not wear/are not allowed to wear
10. Do you have to ask

Exercise 3

1. Joey **doesn't have** to do much homework today.
2. In Austria, children **don't have** to go to school on Sunday. (must not = nicht dürfen)
3. Mary **wasn't able** to do her homework.
4. We didn't **have** to help in the garden yesterday.
5. Jake **is** not allowed to stay up late on schooldays.
6. Chris **didn't have** to help is father in the garden last weekend.

Exercise 4

1. Peter is not allowed to call his girlfriend after ten.
2. We won't be able to come to your concert tomorrow.
3. May we borrow you car to drive to the mall? Are we allowed to borrow ...
4. I have never had to do such a stupid exercise in my whole life.
5. Last Sunday, we were not able to reach the summit because the weather was bad.

Perfect modal verbs

Exercise 1

Perfect modal verbs express modalities happening in the **past.**
They are built with **modal verb + have + third form of the verb**

Exercise 2

1. should have asked/should ask
2. might have helped
3. can't have broken
4. could have bought
5. must have studied
6. may have invited
7. shouldn't touch
8. had to buy
9. won't be able to do
10. must have spent
11. must have slept
12. could have helped

Mixed tenses

Nina: Hi Sue! Nice to see you! How **are** you? I **haven't seen** you for quite a while.
Sue: Hello Nina! I'm okay, but I **am** a bit stressed at the moment.
Nina: Really? Why?
Sue: Well, yesterday we **had to** write a Maths test and the day before our English teacher **(had) wanted** us to hand in our book reports.
Nina: Oh, poor you! That **doesn't sound** good! But I'm sure that you **are going to get** an A or a B on your Maths test.
Sue: Well I hope so. Because if I **don't pass** it, I **won't be allowed** to go to the cinema at the weekend. And I really **want** to go because Jason, this cute guy from class 5B, **has asked** me to go out with him.
Nina: Wow! That's great! Tell me all about it. How **did that happen?**
Sue: Well, last Friday after we **had come** back from the Physics lesson, Jason **was waiting** in front of our classroom. I **was wondering/ wondered** what he **was doing** there but I would have never thought that it **was** because of me.
Nina: I can imagine. Because if you **had known** that he was waiting for you, you **would have been** excited, I guess.
Sue: That's absolutely true! Let me go on! I **went** into the classroom and he **followed** me. At first I **didn't see** that he **was standing** behind me, but suddenly he **called** my name and so I **turned** around.
Nina: **Did he look** good?
Sue: Oh yes, he did! He **was wearing** his blue polo short, the one that perfectly **matches** his eyes.
Nina: Gorgeous! But hang on for a minute because my mobile phone **is ringing**. ... (on the phone) "Hello Peter! ... Well I **can't** talk to you right now because I **am chatting** with Sue at the moment. ... Alright – I **will call** you in the evening, I promise. Bye ..."
Sue: **Was** that Peter?
Nina: Yes. He just **wanted/wants** to know if I **had already done/have already done** my German homework. But never mind. Just go on telling me about Jason and you!
Sue: Well ... there isn't much more to say. He **asked** me if I **wanted** to see the new James Bond film on Friday and I **said** yes. So if I **pass** that stupid Maths test, Jason and I **will have** a date at the weekend.
Nina: That's so romantic! When do you think **will you get** back the test? Before the weekend?
Sue: Yes I'm sure that Mrs Jackson **is going to give back** the tests by Thursday because she **is travelling** to Ireland with class 6C on Friday.
Nina: I cross my fingers for you and Jason! Call me as soon as you **know** the result and **give** my love to your sister!
Sue: I will! Oh by the way – **have you heard** about Eric and Meredith?
Nina: No! What **are you talking** about?
Sue: I'm not sure, but some people **say** that they **have split up**. It's not sure, but I **saw** Meredith with another guy in yesterday's dancing class.
Nina: That **can't** be true! Eric and Meredith **started** dating three years ago and from that moment on they **have spent** every single minute together, as far as I know.
Sue: Sure. I know what you mean. Before Meredith **met** Eric we **had been** best friends. But then she **stopped** seeing me. I **felt** quite unhappy back then, you know.
Nina: Yeah – I can imagine. Do you think this **will change**, now that Meredith and Eric **have split up?**
Sue: I **doubt** it. You see – we **haven't had** much contact in the last years. So, our interests **may have changed** a lot. I **must admit** that I **don't know** much about Meredith.
Nina: I see. Sorry Sue, but my bus **is leaving/leaves** in a minute and I **mustn't** miss it. See you tomorrow?
Sue: Sure! See you!

LANGUAGE IN USE

Task 1

0	1	2	3	4	5	6	7	8	9	10
B	A	D	A	D	C	B	D	A	C	B

Task 2

0	1	2	3	4	5	6	7	8	9	10	11	12	13
N	P	B	M	K	D	J	C	I	E	O	G	A	L

Not used: F, H

Task 3

3 all
4 always
5 OK
6 OK
7 strictly
8 OK
9 the
10 as
11 more
12 OK
13 OK
14 about
15 OK
16 OK
17 OK
18 up
19 a
20 OK
21 of
22 such
23 an
24 as
25 OK
26 OK
27 OK
28 all
29 no
30 so
31 OK

Task 4

1 development 2 easily 3 explained 4 disappear
5 developments 6 known 7 precision 8 difference
9 changing 10 protect 11 destroy 12 achieve

Task 5

0	1	2	3	4	5	6	7	8	9	10
C	D	A	D	C	A	D	C	B	C	B

Task 6

0	1	2	3	4	5	6	7	8	9	10	11	12	13
G	J	N	A	K	H	B	E	M	C	O	I	P	D

Not used: F, L

Task 7

3 OK
4 OK
5 more
6 there

7 least
8 deep
9 sometimes
10 OK
11 less
12 OK
13 so
14 OK
15 not
16 partly
17 OK
18 at
19 OK
20 OK
21 all
22 the
23 OK
24 more
25 OK
26 OK
27 OK
28 who
29 the
30 of (because ~~of~~)
31 OK
32 less

Task 8

1 exhaustion	2 appearance	3 treated
4 observe	5 described	6 necessity
7 deny	8 important	9 possibility
10 understandable	11 emptiness	12 relax

TESTING SECTION

TEST 1

Reading comprehension

1 – G; 2 – A; 3 – E; 4 – D; 5 – B; 6 – F; not used: C, H

Language in Use

0	1	2	3	4	5	6	7	8	9	10
C	B	D	A	A	B	C	D	A	B	D

Tenses

Karen: Hi Donna! Why **are** you so late? I **have been sitting** here for an hour and I even **called** you half an hour ago, but you **did not answer/ didn't answer** your phone. You seem to be quite upset. **Has anything happened** to you or your family?

Donna: Sorry, Karen. I **know** that I'm too late, but you **can't** imagine the hell I **have had to** go through this afternoon. This **has been** the most horrible day in my life.

Karen: Oh no, Donna! Tell me all about it.

Donna: Okay. When I **came** home from school today, my parents **were waiting** for me at the kitchen table. After I **had taken** off my shoes I **sat** down next to my mother. I **could** see that there **were** tears in her eyes. So I **asked** her what **had happened**.

Karen: Oh my dear – what **did she tell** you?

Donna: She **grabbed** my hand and I **realized** that she was very upset. Then she **pointed** at Cinnamon's basket …

Karen: Your dog's basket?

Donna: Yeah. Cinnamon **wasn't** in it. That **was** strange because my dog **usually sleeps** in his basket in the afternoon.

Karen: That moment must **have been** horrible for you. I know how much Cinnamon **means** to you. **Have you got** a clue what might **have happened** to your dog?

Donna: That's the problem. I **don't have** any idea. According to my mum, Cinnamon **was playing** in the garden all morning long. At eleven, mum **wanted** to call him in, but Cinnamon **didn't come**. We **spent/have spent** all afternoon looking for him, without success.

Karen: Oh Donna. I **am** so sorry for you.

Donna: Thanks, Karen. Oh – wait a second, please. My mum **is calling** me on my mobile. *(Two minutes later.)* Oh Karen! I **must/have to** leave you now. Cinnamon **is waiting** for me at our neighbour's place. They **have just found** him in their garden.

Karen: Oh, great! Tell me when you have found out what exactly **has happened**.

Listening comprehension

1. A	2. A	3. K	4. B	5. K	6. K	7. K	8. K
9. B	10. C	11. C	12. K	13. G	14. K	15. K	

LÖSUNGEN ZU DEN BUCHSEITEN 147–151

LC: Seattle Program claims to treat Internet addiction (CD-Track 15)
From NPR News, it's ALL THINGS CONSIDERED. I'm Noah Adams. And it's time now for All Tech Considered.
(Soundbite of music)
ADAMS: You can waste a lot of time on the Internet. That's not a surprise. But can you get addicted to it the same way people get addicted to heroin or alcohol or even gambling? Well, some psychologists say yes, and they started what they say is the country's first Internet detox program. It's just outside Seattle. We asked NPR's Martin Kaste to pay them a visit and here's his report.
MARTIN KASTE: Ben Alexander(ph) says he's an addict.
Mr. BEN ALEXANDER: Hi, I'm Ben and I'm a gamer.
KASTE: He's a soft-spoken 19-year-old, still kind of teenagey, wearing a high school drama T-shirt. He says around the time he went off to college, he got involved in an online game called World of Warcraft.
Mr. ALEXANDER: It fairly quickly got out of hand to where I was missing classes and spending entire days just playing and not doing anything else.
KASTE: About to flunk out, he asked his folks for help. His family is now spending $300 a day to keep Alexander away from the Internet. He's the first client at a startup detox program called reSTART. It operates out of a massage therapist's country home in the woods outside Seattle – a place with goats, doves, and chickens.
(Soundbite of chicken)
KASTE: Alexander helped to build the new chicken coop.
Mr. ALEXANDER: Construction is really new to me. I've never done anything like it before.
KASTE: He says outdoor activities help to suppress his urge to go online. Alexander also gets counselling from Hilarie Cash, a psychologist from suburban Seattle who co-founded this program. Cash has made a career treating what she calls Internet and technology addiction.
Dr. HILARIE CASH (Psychologist; reSTART Co-founder): We know that people tend to get hooked by things that are rewarding, but unpredictably so. And the Internet is just built around that principle.
KASTE: The Internet can be habit-forming, she says, just like booze or gambling.
Dr. CASH: If you do it compulsively, and in spite of the negative consequences, then we'd say that's an addiction.
KASTE: It's a pretty broad definition of addiction – too broad for some people. Psychologist John Grohol is founder of the mental health Web site PsychCentral.
Dr. JOHN GROHOL (Psychologist; Founder, PsychCentral): It becomes this catch-all label for anything that people find themselves spending a lot of time doing and find it very enjoyable to do so. And that's not really what an addiction is, traditionally.
KASTE: Grohol is more inclined to see excessive Internet use as a symptom, not a disease – a symptom of, say, depression or anxiety. But back at reSTART, Hilarie Cash is confident that recognition of Internet addiction will grow, and she is busy recruiting more clients. She's lost track of how many media calls she's had or how many reporters have already interviewed the program's young first patient. He doesn't seem to mind. It's something else to fill the hours, now that he's not online.
Martin Kaste, NPR News, Seattle.

TEST 2

Reading comprehension
1 – false, When I started to …; 2 – false, This means that on …; 3 – true, Of course my parents …; 4 – false, About one year ago …; 5 – true, At first I completely …; 6 – true, Therefore I decided to …; 7 – true, He's great and he …; 8 – false, Well, most people say …

Language in Use

0	1	2	3	4	5	6	7	8	9	10	11	12	13
C	P	A	O	H	E	K	B	J	F	I	G	N	L

Not used: D, M

Tenses
Lauren: Hi Jake! You **look** tired. What **have you been doing** all afternoon long?
Jake: Oh, hi Lauren. I'm sorry for **looking** so horrible, but I **have been working** in the garden for five hours. My mum **had already asked** me weeks ago to help her, so I **had to** go through with it, you see?
Lauren: Yeah, I know what you mean. By the way, Sophie **called** me half an hour ago. You should **have been** at her place about an hour ago, she said. **Did you forget** to tell her that you were busy?
Jake: Of course not! I **left** a message on her mobile as soon as I **was** sure that I would not **be able to** see her today.
Lauren: That's too bad. She must **have missed** your message.
Jake: Seems so. I **will call** her now because I **don't want** her to be too angry with me. (Two minutes later.) She **couldn't talk** to me because she **was stirring** some soup in the kitchen. I **will have to** apologize later, I'm afraid.
Lauren: Good idea. Sounds like she **hasn't forgiven you yet**. Anyway, what **are you going to do/are you doing** at the weekend?
Jake: I'm not sure. Perhaps, I **will stay** at home and relax.
Lauren: I **have got** a better idea. I **am going** to this great party at Monika's place. Why **don't you come/won't you come** with me? Sophie can join us too.
Jake: I'm not sure. Sophie **doesn't like** parties too much.
Lauren: That's a pity. Ah, what I wanted to ask: What **were you doing** yesterday evening at ten? I **tried** to phone you, but you **didn't answer**. **Were you allowed to** go to the cinema with Jim? I thought that your mum **didn't want** you to see Jim yesterday.
Jake: You are right. I **wasn't** at the cinema. I **was writing** my paper for German all evening long. I **was working** really hard and I **had turned off** my phone before I started.
Lauren: I see. No problem. It was great to talk to you. See you tomorrow!

Listening comprehension
a. C   b. D   c. D   d. C   e. B   f. B   g. A

LÖSUNGEN ZU DEN BUCHSEITEN 151–153

LC: Airline going to the dogs ... and cats too (CD Track 16)

There is a new airline starting this summer which will offer passengers free meals and no baggage fees, though there actually probably won't be that much baggage to check because the passengers are dogs and cats. Pet Airways will start flying its four-legged customers between five cities – L.A., New York, Washington, Chicago and Denver. Fares start at $149, less than what it would normally cost to send your dog or cat the old fashioned way. The airline's co-founder is Alysa Binder.

Ms. ALYSA BINDER (Co-founder, Pet Airways): Pet Airways is the first pet-only airline where pets fly in the main cabin, not in cargo.

MONTAGNE: Right. That's the key here. Up to now, pretty much a dog or cat you have to put them in the cargo.

Ms. BINDER: If they're about 15 pounds and you can take them in the cabin, then you should. But if they're bigger than 15 pounds and they can't fit in the cabin under the seat, then they're relegated to cargo or luggage.

So we're a completely different service. And we call our pets pawsengers as well.

(Soundbite of laughter)

MONTAGNE: Okay.

Ms. BINDER: Well, they're our pawsengers. And they're always with a pet attendant who will monitor them at all times. So once a pet parent leaves their pet with us, or our pawsenger, they're always taken care of and always monitored by a pet attendant.

MONTAGNE: Give me a scenario. Let's make it a dog, for argument's sake. What happens?

Ms. BINDER: Let's use Oscar, a dog, right? You bring Oscar into one of our pet lounges, walk right in. Once you drop Oscar off, we feed, walk, give him water, and then put him on the plane. We fly Beechcraft 1900 planes, 19 person, or 19 passenger planes. We take out all the human fittings and we reconfigure it with pet carriers, and then we are working on a specialized strapping system so that they won't move during turbulence or what have you. Again, a pet attendant on board at all times, watching them in a climate-controlled, well lit, fresh air circulating at all times, as a passenger would have the same experience.

MONTAGNE: Now, so they are in little pet carriers, so, I mean if the dogs start barking they can't fight or anything like that.

BINDER: No, they cannot fight. And we're doing everything, again, about the pets. So, we are using special essences that are calming for pets.

MONTAGNE: Now, do you, per chance, have any plans for a first class cabin?

BINDER: We don't discriminate. So right now everybody is one class.

MONTAGNE: That's Alysa Binder, co-founder of Pet Airways. Flights are scheduled to start July 14th. Right now only cats and dogs can get on board, though the airline is considering in the future allowing birds to fly.

TEST 3

Reading comprehension

A: higher food & energy prices/food & energy more expensive/increased living costs/life more expensive/higher interest rates
B: go on living comfortably/still have enough money/enough money left/still live comfortable life
C: mother housewife – children school/only father has job
D: they compare bargains/can talk about bargains/look for special offers/compare special offers/talk about special offers
E: they don't keep well/difficult to store/they go off soon
F: repay house in 9 years/pay back credit fast/credit for only 9 years

Language in Use

3 all
4 were
5 grown
6 OK
7 of
8 a
9 most
10 global
11 for
12 been
13 OK
14 who
15 which
16 in
17 OK
18 OK
19 few
20 that
21 did
22 OK
23 some
24 the
25 is
26 OK
27 OK
28 a
29 OK
30 all
31 OK

LÖSUNGEN ZU DEN BUCHSEITEN 154 UND 155

Tenses

Tristan: Hey Luke! **I haven't seen** you for ages! **Did you enjoy** your skiing holiday last week?
Luke: Yeah, Tristan, I really **did**. Before we **arrived** it **had snowed** a lot. So the snow **was** perfect. You know that I **adore** skiing. I **was** really looking forward to racing down the slopes. Of course, I **wanted** to be early, but it **took** Tony ages to get started.
Tristan: I see. When **did you get** to the gondola, then?
Luke: At eleven! When we **arrived** a big crowd **was waiting** to be taken to the mountain top. We **had to** queue up for forty-five minutes.
Tristan: That must **have been** hard for you!
Luke: Sure it was. But then we **were finally able to** put on our skis and to enjoy the perfect weather and the great snow.
Tristan: Oh, that **sounds** fantastic.
Luke: Absolutely. On the third day, however, something unexpected happened. We **were sitting** on a chair lift, laughing and joking, when it suddenly **came** to a halt. We **didn't bother** much because we **had got** stuck on that lift before. After fifteen minutes, however, Joey **started** panicking. It **had begun** to snow shortly before the lift stopped and it **was getting** worse from minute to minute. We **couldn't/weren't able to** see much, but we **guessed** that we **were** the only people on the lift! Then Mike **had** an idea. He **took** his mobile phone and phoned Mike and Tessa, who **were waiting** for us at the bottom of the mountain. Five minutes later, the lift went on. Imagine! The lift staff **had turned off** the lift as they thought that it was empty because of the bad weather.
Tristan: That's horrible. However, you can't say that your holiday was boring. So, **are you going to do** that trip again next year?
Luke: I'm not sure. Perhaps, **I will go** somewhere warm next year.
Tristan: I see. So, tell me about Mike and Tessa…

Listening

a. 1. Twilight, 2. Southern Vampires
b. takes her without remorse
c. they reflect culture
d. frightening, sexy, forbidden
e. romantic, chivalrous
f. others object to crush
g. protect her from danger
h. his restraints; he restrains his instincts
i. Bella and Edward
j. refuses to bite people (to feed off people)
k. you have a choice
l. saved women from narrowness
m. kind of boring
n. having a wonderful time

LC: The modern vampire: Bloodthirsty, but chivalrous (CD-Track 17)

Finally this hour, time for a dispatch on the mixed-up lives of vampires. They are best known for sucking their victims' blood. But somehow, vampires manage to be eerily attractive – at least in pop culture. Two series are dominating bestseller lists – the "Twilight" books and the "Southern Vampire" books, which are the basis of HBO's latest hit, "True Blood." Both have vampire heroes who practice remarkable restraint, as NPR's Lynn Neary reports.
Mr. BELA LUGOSI (Actor): (As Count Dracula) I am Dracula. I bid you welcome.
LYNN NEARY: You don't see much blood or fangs for that matter in the 1931 film, "Dracula." But when Bela Lugosi leans over his victims, he is one creepy guy. And when this vampire wants a pretty woman, he takes her with no remorse. Vampires or something like them have been part of culture since ancient times, says my colleague Eric Nuzum, who has written about the creatures in his book, "The Dead Travel Fast." And while vampires cannot see their own reflection in the mirror, Nuzum says, they are a perfect reflection of the culture which creates them.
Mr. ERIC NUZUM (Author, "The Dead Travel Fast"): You look at vampires from any given era and you see what they thought was frightening. You see what they thought was sexy, and what they thought was forbidden.
NEARY: The latest craze, Nuzum says, is the romantic, even chivalrous vampire. Take "True Blood" for example. The HBO's series is set in a time when vampires prowl openly through small-town America and even campaign for their civil rights. Sookie Stackhouse, a young, pretty waitress, falls for a vampire named Bill. And like any young woman, her interest only intensifies when others object to her new crush.
(Soundbite of TV series "True Blood")
Ms. ANNA PAQUIN: (As Sookie Stackhouse) He's not like that.
Unidentified Woman: OK, OK. You spoke to him for like a minute. You don't know how many people he sucked the blood out over the last – many centuries he's been alive.
Ms. PAQUIN: (As Sookie Stackhouse) But he's so not scary.
Unidentified Woman: Sweet Jesus in heaven. Sookie, he is a vampire.
NEARY: "True Blood" is based on the "Southern Vampires" book series written by Charlaine Harris. She inhabits her fictional world with both good and bad vampires. But in Bill, she creates as a genteel vampire who protects Sookie from the worst of his kind – even as he tries to reign in his own baser instincts. And of course, says Harris, his restraint makes him all the more alluring.
Ms. CHARLAINE HARRIS (Author, "Southern Vampire"): Yes, definitely. Gosh. I could rip you limb from limb, but because I think you're so great, I'm going to be very, very careful. That's got to be kind of intoxicating.
NEARY: But the gentleman vampire, who has stolen the heart of teenage girls everywhere, is Edward, the hero of Stephenie Meyer's "Twilight" series, soon to be released as a movie. Edward's fans live vicariously through his romance with high school sweetheart, Bella.
(Soundbite of movie "Twilight")
Ms. STEWART: (As Bella Swan) You're what you are. Your skin is hell white and ice cool. You don't go out into the sunlight.
Mr. ROBERT PATTINSON: (As Edward Cullen) Say it out loud. Say it.
Ms. STEWART: (As Bella Swan) Vampire.
Mr. PATTINSON: (As Edward Cullen) Are you afraid?
Ms. STEWART: (As Bella Swan) No.
NEARY: Edward and his clan refuse to feed off humans, and it is that choice, says Meyer, that makes him so popular.
Ms. STEPHENIE MEYER (Author, "Twilight"): These are vampires who should be these creatures who exist to hunt humans. I mean, they are evil and they choose something different. They find another way. And I think that kids respond to the idea that it doesn't matter where I am in life. I always have a choice.
Ms. NINA AUERBACH (Author, "Our Vampires, Ourselves"): Vampires aren't supposed to be restrained. They're all our hungers. That's why they're vampires.
NEARY: Nina Auerbach, author of "Our Vampires, Ourselves," believes every age gets the vampire it wants. In the 1960s and '70s, she says, vampires took young women away from their narrow lives and transformed them. It's understandable, she says, that with the advent of AIDS, uninhibited bloodsucking may have lost some of its appeal. Still, she finds this latest crop of vampires kind of boring.
Ms. AUERBACH: And these are very abstinent vampires. The implication being, if he truly loves you, he will not do it to you. And I'm old and I thought if he truly loves you, you would have a wonderful time together.
NEARY: Whether they terrify, entrance or court their victims, vampires are always on the prowl. Waiting for that moment when the moon comes out, and the cultural spotlight shines on them again. Lynn Neary, NPR News Washington.

LÖSUNGEN ZU DEN BUCHSEITEN 156–159

TEST 4

Reading comprehension
1d, 2c, 3a, 4d

Language in Use:

Portuguese	significant	entertainment	doing	exposed	wooden
sold	tiring	produce	financially	survive	means

Tenses

Claire: Danny, listen! I **have just won** four tickets for the *Green Day* concert next March. **Will you come** with me?
Danny: Sure! But tell me when and how you **got** the tickets?
Claire: Last week, there **was** a quiz show on Radio W. I **called** them, I was put through, and then I **had to** answer some questions about *Green Day*. Of course, I **was able** to give all the correct answers. And then they called me back today, telling me that I had won.
Danny: Cool! But you **have won** four tickets. What **are you going to do (will you do)** with the other ones?
Claire: I think that I **will ask** Julie and Tim to join us.
Danny: So you **haven't heard** the news? Julie **is staying** in Canada for a semester. You **will have to** ask someone else, I'm afraid.
Claire: Wow, thank you for telling me. I **was looking** forward to going to the concert with you, Julie and Tim. **Do you remember** the last time we **went** to a *Green Day* concert?
Danny: Definitely. We **were waiting** for Julie and Tim at the back of the concert hall when the backstage door **opened**.
Claire: Yeah, you and I **were** in the middle of a discussion about our favourite songs, when –BANG- Billy Joe **appeared**. I **couldn't** believe my eyes and ears. He **invited** us in and **gave** us a backstage tour!
Danny: We **were talking** to the rest of the band when we **remembered** Julie and Tim!
Claire: As far as I remember, they **were** quite angry. When we **called,** Tim even **shouted** at me, "What's the matter with you? Julie and I **have been standing** here in the cold for half an hour. "
Danny: They sure **were** upset, but when they **heard** what **had happened**, they **got** excited. And when they **were allowed** to come backstage too, they **didn't blame** us anymore.
Claire: Oh, I **will never forget** that day …

Listening

1.
a. F   b. F   c. F   d. T   e. T   f. T   g. F   h. T   i. F   j. F

2.
a. water molecules
b. six
c. three or twelve
d. five or eight
e. wrong picture in "Nature"
f. melt away faux (wrong) flakes/campaign against wrong snowflakes
g. true beauty of science
h. printed version of "Nature"

LC: What's wrong with this snowflake? (CD-Track 18)
MICHELE NORRIS, host:
This is ALL THINGS CONSIDERED from NPR News. I'm Michele Norris.
ROBERT SIEGEL, host:
And I'm Robert Siegel.
During the holiday season, we see a lot of images that cannot be found in nature: flying reindeer, sugarplum fairies and geometrically incorrect snowflakes. Well, one scientist has gotten tired of the snowflake problem.
NPR's Jon Hamilton talked with him about his efforts to correct the record.
JON HAMILTON: Thomas Koop is a chemist who thinks ice crystals are masterpieces of natural beauty. Unfortunately, he says …
Professor THOMAS KOOP (Bielefeld University, Germany): This beauty is sometimes corrupted.
HAMILTON: By artists, especially at this time of year, when a blizzard of snowflake images sweeps through advertisements and store displays and greeting cards. Koop, who is a professor at Bielefeld University in Germany, says the problem is that many of these images show ice crystals with five sides or eight sides. In other words, he says, they are scientific abominations.
Prof. KOOP: Since I'm a chemist, I know what the crystal structure of ice typically is. And therefore, I know that there's no way of having pentagonal or octagonal ice crystals. And therefore, such snow crystals shouldn't exist in nature – and they don't.
HAMILTON: Koop says snowflakes can assemble ice crystals into all kinds of complex shapes, but the crystals themselves will usually have six sides.
Prof. KOOP: The reason is because the molecular building blocks are water molecules. So there's only a certain way they can fit together. And what comes out is that they are always in a six-cornered shape, even at the tiniest molecular scale.
HAMILTON: Actually, water molecules occasionally form ice crystals with three or 12 sides, either half or double the usual number, but never five or eight. Koop says he'd been pretty much ignoring this season's predictable onslaught of fake snowflakes until he saw a wintry ad for the online version of the scientific journal Nature.
Prof. KOOP: And that was entitled: For Anyone Who Loves Science. But all the snow crystals depicted in the advert were octagonal.
HAMILTON: Koop responded with a letter that offers a sort of snowflake manifesto. It calls for a campaign to melt away faux flakes. And ist asks people to spend part of their holidays discussing the true beauty of science preferably over a mug of hot punch. Koop's letter appears in the printed version of the journal Nature. Jan Hamilton, NPR News.